# Disney Stories

Krystina Madej • Newton Lee

# Disney Stories

## Getting to Digital

2nd ed. 2020

"An affectionate portrait of how 'the mouse' learned to use the mouse."

–Dr. Alan Kay

 Springer

Krystina Madej
School of Literature, Media and
Communication
Georgia Institute of Technology
Atlanta, GA, USA

Newton Lee
Institute for Education, Research, and
Scholarships
Los Angeles, CA, USA

Vincennes University
Vincennes, IN, USA

ISBN 978-3-030-42740-5          ISBN 978-3-030-42738-2    (eBook)
https://doi.org/10.1007/978-3-030-42738-2

This Springer imprint is published by the registered company Springer Nature Switzerland AG
The registered company address is: Gewerbestrasse 11, 6330 Cham, Switzerland

*Dedicated to all the children and adults in the world who enjoy "the happiest place on earth" physically and digitally.*

*Newton Lee*

*Dedicated to Nicola, Michael, and Daniel Budd, my enthusiastic companions in many Disney story moments.*

*Krystina Madej*

# About the Book

As I continued to use Disney Stories to bring Disney's history of storytelling across media to university students, it became increasingly important to write a second edition. The original book had been intended as a brief introduction that showed how story and technology evolved hand-in-hand to make for audience-engaging entertainment. I'd written about Disney animations through the 1920s and 1930s until the first feature, *Snow White*, before moving on to the Disney Master Narrative, and then video games and online sites. The book leaped expediently from *Snow White* to *Mickey's Game and Watch*; the class discussions, however, included films from the 1940s to the 1990s, the new approaches used for live action hybrid animation, and CGI and CAPS. I was intimately familiar with most of the Disney repertoire from that time as I had been a steadfast viewer of the Sunday night television program *Walt Disney Presents* in the 1960s and was also a collector of classic Disney films, a hobby that was facilitated by the studio's policy of releasing their classics every seven years, and encouraged by my three children's devotion to watching every film at least a dozen times. The Eagle Marahute's dramatic dive towards the river in *Rescuer's Down Under* is still etched in my memory. It was not difficult then to add three new chapters which discussed how these films reflected the evolution of story and technology in Disney's movie history.

Since the research completed for the first edition ten years ago, the web has exploded with blogs, you tube videos, and discussion forums on Disney's extensive world. These are a boon to a researcher prepared to winnow to find the nuggets. In one lucky foray into YouTube searching for the film *Looker*, I came across a comment from Richard Taylor, the film's creative supervisor. He had not seen the film in years: finding it online brought back a forgotten experience and allowed him to see its place in the history of computer graphics.

The primary purpose of this edition is to provide key moments in the development of animated films as they evolved to embrace digital technology. It is, however, still about stories-across-media. One of the most exciting recent events has been Disney's acquisition of the well-loved story property *Star Wars* when it purchased Lusasfilm in 2012, and bringing that story to real life. Our story concludes with *Galaxy's Edge*, the latest in Disney's theme park lands, and the engagement audiences enjoy with the animatronic character Hondo Ohnaka on their way to see the Millennium Falcon in an across-media digital experience.

Newton Lee teaches Disney in his game design courses and I want to thank him for his suggestion to include *Star Wars* and for the review of *Kingdom Hearts* he provided for this edition, it is an exciting game that warrants a place in Disney game history.

Dr. Krystina Madej
December 2019

## From the first edition:

Disney stories are, more than ever, present across all media. This book provides readers with a brief and accessible look at how Disney has used technological innovation to create characters and stories that engage audiences in many different media, from early film to today's video games and online environments.

Drawing on Disney films from the 1920s until they became digital, and on the extensive collection of writings both in print and on the Web by Disney historians of all ilks, the book presents how innovation in film and animation techniques worked to evolve ideas about character and content to produce stories that very successfully engaged audiences. The evolution of the genre took animation from gags to full-length animated films in theatres, then across media into people's homes through merchandising, television, and into a virtual world through theme parks, all the while creating a Disney Master Narrative. This historical sketch provides the back-story for considering Disney stories move into the virtual *digital* world in the 1990s and the online communities of the 2000s. When Disney reached out to its audience with *The Lion King Animated Storybook* in 1994, it was following a well-established tradition of using leading-edge technology to remediate its stories and engage its audience in new ways, in this case, through the interactivity potential of digital environments. With the subsequent move into online MMORPGs such as *Toontown Online*, the community that had developed around Disney stories could now communicate and share the experience, one to one, across continents.

Dr. Alan Kay, president of Viewpoints Research Institute and former Disney Fellow, describes the book as "an affectionate portrait of how 'the mouse' learned to use the mouse."

Newton Lee
Krystina Madej

# Acknowledgements

I would like to thank the authors of the many books which tell the story of the Walt Disney Company and that have been an invaluable resource in writing this edition. Some had access to Walt himself, a few to colleagues and employees who they were able to interview, and others to the extensive material in the Disney archives. They include Michael Barrier, Andreas Deja, Christopher Finch, Neal Gabler, Christian Morran, David Price, Jason Surrell, Bob Thomas, Jay Telotte, and Steven Watts, among others. I am an armchair researcher, who now has at hand the formidable resources of the World Wide Web. If I think about it, I must thank Tim Berners Lee for inventing the WWW, ensuring it was free, and promoting it for general interest. The result is an expanse of information that would probably not have been available to me otherwise. The interest in Disney, in Pixar, and in CGI by researchers and Disney fans has created a motherlode of docushorts, interviews, articles, original films, and original documents from past eras. Thank you to Disney for sharing so many of its resources online, to Pixar for the extensive number of videos they have made available on the process behind the films (to Disney for this as well), to newspapers and periodicals across the country whose archives have been made freely available, and to those who had original materials and shared them. During one search into Pixar, the original proposal written at Graphics Group for the Disney CAPS project showed up; it was a treasure of information about the development process the Pixar team had planned for the project. Particularly helpful for clarifying the many company moves CGI researchers made was Mike Seymour's interview with Alvy Ray Smith, for insight into CAPS was Barbara Robertson's article for Computer Graphics World (the first reveal about the system), and for their explanation of the work on the early CGI test short *Where the Wild Things Are* was John Lasseter and Glen Keane's discussion in Disney Newsreel. I had seen the test previously and Amid Amidi's posting of the Disney newsletter helped fill out the story. Thank you too for all the docushorts posted on the development of *Toy Story*. Listening to Ed Catmull, John Lasseter, and others who worked on the film discuss the process brought forward their perspective on a complex story. This documentation follows in Walt's footsteps; the studio archived all its meeting from its beginning—even early gag notes are available to researchers. Searching for history, however, only goes so far. Then the work to filter it begins: but that is the joy of research, finding the kernels. In this I am inspired and encouraged by Dr. Jay Telotte, a Disney scholar, and my teaching colleague at Georgia Tech, Richard Utz, who freed me from many academic responsibilities so I had time to work on writing, and to Jan Stasienko at the University of Lower Silesia in Wroclaw, Poland, who has trusted his Erasmus students to my Disney enthusiasms. I want to say thank you in particular to my children, Nicola, Michael, and Daniel, who were always prepared to watch one more Disney film with me, one more time; they are now grown and will soon be inculcating a new generation of Disney fans, and to my spouse, Jim Budd, for his ongoing support.

Krystina Madej

We would like to posthumously thank Mark Mandelbaum, our agent for the original edition of Disney Stories. Mark was a digital publishing enthusiast and Director of Publications at ACM for 30 years. He had a very positive approach to helping people and promoting new ideas.

Krystina Madej<br>Newton Lee

# Contents

# About the Authors

**Newton Lee** He is an author, educator, and futurist. He was the founder of Disney Online Technology Forum, creator of AT&T Bell Labs' first-ever commercial artificial intelligence tool, inventor of the world's first annotated multimedia OPAC for the U.S. National Agricultural Library, and longest serving editor-in-chief in the history of the Association for Computing Machinery for its publication Computers in Entertainment (2003–2018). Lee is the chairman of the California Transhumanist Party, education and media advisor to the United States Transhumanist Party, and president of the 501(c)(3) nonprofit Institute for Education, Research, and Scholarships. He graduated Summa Cum Laude from Virginia Tech with a B.S. and M.S. degree in Computer Science (specializing in artificial intelligence), and he earned a perfect GPA from Vincennes University with an A.S. degree in Electrical Engineering and an honorary doctorate in Computer Science. He has lectured at Massachusetts Institute of Technology, University of Southern California, Vincennes University, and Woodbury University. He has been honored with a Michigan Leading Edge Technologies Award, two community development awards from the California Junior Chamber of Commerce, and four volunteer project leadership awards from The Walt Disney Company.

**Krystina Madej** She is an author, speaker, and professor of the Practice at Georgia Tech, Atlanta. At Tech since 2011, she teaches about and researches how humans have adapted their narratives to changing media throughout the centuries, physical play, and children's interaction with digital games that are based in narrative, and in Disney's approach to stories across media since the 1920s. Adjunct Professor with the School for Interactive Art and Technology (SIAT) at Simon Fraser University, Vancouver, for 10 years, she taught as Visiting Professor for the *Center for Digital Media's* Master's degree program. She is research faculty at the University of Lower Silesia, Wroclaw, Poland, where as Visiting Professor she teaches Disney History and Children's Game Design for the Erasmus Program and Design Thinking and

History of Social Media for the *Big Data, Digital Media, and Trendwatching* Master's Program. Prior to returning to academia in 1999, she was the principal of a communications and design firm for 15 years, where, as design strategist, she planned and created successful branding programs and exhibits for government, business, industry, and museums.

# Chapter 1
# Introduction: Stories Across Media

*I honestly feel that the heart of our organization is the Story Department.*

Walt Disney

## 1.1 From There to Here: The Beginning of Interactive Stories

The early 1990s was a heady time for interactive digital stories. Just a few years earlier, in 1987, Amanda Goodenough had used the newly-released HyperCard to write the first interactive digital story, *Inigo Gets Out.*[1] Her motivation? To capture the traditional storytelling atmosphere her grandmother had created for her when she was a young child: a vital interactive environment in which her grandmother would say, "what do you think happens next?" and in which the lines were never the same. The stories her grandmother told became Amanda's as she helped shape them with her own interpretations and brought them into her everyday reality. In Amanda's *interactive story*, children make Inigo's actions their own. "Children know intuitively where to click," and how to make the story happen. It is no longer a "print" story, with words and pictures on a page, but a virtual story environment with which to interact and in which things can be made to happen.

---

Online photos and graphics provide extra detail and are identified by urls the reader can refer to. This additional reference information will be particularly beneficial as an enhancement for the online version of this book. URLs are current at time of printing.

---

[1] *Inigo Gets Out* is the first interactive digital story created in 1987 by Amanda Goodenough using the HyperCard program. Archive: *Inigo Gets Out:* https://archive.org/details/hypercard_inigo_gets_out.

© Springer Nature Switzerland AG 2020
K. Madej, N. Lee, *Disney Stories*, https://doi.org/10.1007/978-3-030-42738-2_1

*Inigo* was closely followed in 1988 by one of the first edutainment video games, *Mixed-Up Mother Goose*.[2] Sierra On-Line's Roberta Williams, who had created the first graphic adventure game *Mystery House* in 1979, wanted to develop a game for her children that was more than entertainment, that also had an educational component. She chose to work with popular nursery rhymes and in *Mixed-Up Mother Goose* created an interactive story in which children travel to a land where the rhymes are real and have gotten themselves all mixed up. The children help each of the characters put their rhyme back in order by bringing back objects, people, or animals that belong to the rhyme but have been lost. Companies such as Voyageur, Broderbund, Simon and Schuster Interactive, Discis, and numerous smaller publishers, soon began publishing stories in CD-ROM format for children to engage with. Kids clicked their way through adventures with *Peter Rabbit, Lil Critter, Brother and Sister Bear*, and animated characters created just for the genre such as *Slater and Charlie*. They listened, sang, made things happen, played games, and even did so in the language of their choice—English, French, or Spanish.

Disney has been a part of this video game landscape since 1981. The Nintendo *Game and Watch* video game *Mickey Mouse* has Mickey, in typical arcade game action, juggling eggs (Madej, Children's Games from Turtle to Squirtle, 2018). It wasn't until 1994 that the company gave one of its stories, *The Lion King*, an interactive story life in CD-ROM format as *Disney's Animated Storybook: The Lion King*. 1994 was also the year that brought Netscape Navigator to the Internet and made it user-friendly for the general public. Disney, never shy about being either the first or among the first to take advantage of new media opportunities to bring its characters and stories to the public, continued its move into interactive media and set up Disney Online. Today, sites such as *Pirates of the Caribbean* offer players an environment where they interact with their friends to create stories for themselves.

Disney has entrenched its stories in online media since the mid-1990s; in doing so it has continued to add to the transmedia mix that is a distinctive characteristic of the way it brings its story products to a diverse audience. Disney stories are like a Ferris wheel, the story is the hub from which media radiate as a spoke: different activities are the cab at the end of a spoke and engage parents, kids, and all manner of folks as they get on and off. Disney taps into humankind's innate interest in communicating stories as it uses media this way.

## 1.2  Stories and Communicating

Through historical time—and even among our aboriginal forefathers—all the races of man have been dramatizing these eternal quests and conquests of mind and heart; in arenas, around tribal fires, in temples and theaters. The modes of entertainment have changed through the centuries; the content of public shows, very little. (Walt Disney)

---

[2] *Mixed-up Mother Goose* was first released by Sierra On-Line in 1988. Designed as an adventure game for toddlers, it brought them into a fantasy world of nursery rhymes. Great gameplay and engaging graphics (for the time) made it a very popular story game. *Mixed-Up Mother Goose*: http://www.mobygames.com/game/amiga/mixed-up-mother-goose.

People's drive to share stories has been with us since time immemorial. In the days when our ancestors gathered around a fire to keep warm, the desire to bring stories to an audience through a media other than speech resulted in such dynamic scenes as those depicted in the wall paintings in the Chauvet Caves (France). In these caves there are over 416 picture stories—paintings of "bold lions, leaping horses, pensive owls and charging rhinoceroses" that are 32,000 years old, the oldest such paintings known and "a veritable Louvre of Paleolithic art" (*Time Magazine*).[3]

Why do we make this effort to share stories? Because stories are an integral part of who we are as human beings. Psychologist Donald Polkinghorne says of narrative that it is "a primary form by which humans experience meaning." He tells us that narrative is ubiquitous to humans and a fundamental component of how they shape their worldview (Polkinghorne). Stories are the way we link our daily activities into a whole and provide for their significance within the entity that is our life. Literary critic Gerald Prince tells us "[narrative] does not simply record events; it constitutes and interprets them as meaningful parts of meaningful wholes..." (Prince 129). Stories are important to us because they connect new knowledge that we come in contact with, with past experience; this gives it context and makes it more understandable and more memorable. Stories are not only a way we make sense of the world however. They are also the fundamental way in which we communicate with each other: the way we tell each other what we've done, who we are, and what we believe in.

We hear stories, we participate in stories, and then, we pass stories on. It is human nature to tell stories—they have been used as a way to share experience and pass on learning to others since time immemorial. As the Chauvet Caves show us, 32,000 years ago stories were shared through paintings on cave walls. These paintings were not just images of static figures. The artists endeavored to show action, movement, a sequence of events; they created images that showed their ideas clearly because the provided a *story* about their experience.

Over the many centuries our need to communicate through stories has encouraged the creative use of media available at any particular period in time to do so. Stories have been carved into stone, embellished on pottery, laid in mosaics; they have been told orally by bards, sung by choruses, and acted out by theatre groups; they have been printed on pages, transported over telephone lines, and sent by radio waves; they have been carried on celluloid film, captured by cathode ray tubes for television, and built with wood, bricks, and mortar for museums and entertainment parks. Today they are brought to us in virtual online worlds courtesy of computers and gaming systems. Stories are ubiquitous in the world and, more than ever imaginable, stories are common to us all. Thanks to global online environments, not only is the generic idea of story common to us all, but stories once specific and available only to a culture, are common to us all.

---

[3] "What those first artists invented was a language of signs for which there will never be a Rosetta stone; perspective, a technique that was not rediscovered until the Athenian Golden Age; and a bestiary of such vitality and finesse that, by the flicker of torchlight the animals seem to surge from the walls, and move across them like figures in a magic lantern show (in that sense, the artists invented animation)."—Judith Thurman. https://www.newyorker.com/magazine/2008/06/23/first-impressions

## 1.3  Our Story

Walt Disney was passionate about cartoons and animation; early on in his career his animated shorts were more about presenting gags then about telling stories. It was his nature, however, to take things first as he found them and then to find a way to make them better and in that way transform them into something completely different.[4] Over the years, his affinity for creating personalities, his inclination to develop storylines, and his drive for innovation in use of technology and new media became distinctive features of the approach he took to creating stories that so engaged and entertained audiences. Our story is, in part, an exploration of the marriage between technology and story, for in his quest to make the best of animation, Walt pushed the one to attain the best in the other. The following chapters of this book describe Walt's approach and show the changes wrought through his exploration. Some history is provided to give the reader context for the discussion, but there are many books that offer historical details about Walt Disney, the films he made, and how he conducted his business, and that is not the intent of this book. Rather the intent is to present an overview of what changed in the way a story was presented as new media were explored and new technologies developed.

The first third of the book describes Walt's approach to developing his animations and provides a frame of reference for the next two parts. During the *Alice* and *Oswald* years Walt moved the content of animated shorts from a series of often unrelated gags, to a storyline consisting of gags that were contextual and based in personality. With the move from silent to sound in *Steamboat Willie* and subsequent talkies, Walt designed sound effects that helped establish characters' personalities, added complexity to the story environment, and also added to the shorts' comedy. Color, when it finally came to Disney animations in *Flowers and Trees*, added nuances to each character's persona, heightened the underlying emotions of the story, and intensified its impact on the audience. The 33rd *Silly Symphony, The Three Little Pigs* brought "true personality" to the characters of the three pigs and their nemesis the wolf, and "depth and feeling" to a story the audience could empathize with.

Walt believed animation as worthy of being a full length feature as any live action film of the time and in 1934 chose the fairy tale *Snow White and the Seven Dwarfs* to make the studio's first. The leap from a 7-min short to an 83 min feature required major technical problems be tackled and gagmen to "develop into men who will be capable of carrying a story through to completion" (Thomas 133). The multiplane camera added visual depth, a more realistic approach to drawing human figures made Snow White and her friends more believable, gags were created to be consistent with the different personalities, songs were woven contextually into the story, and the integrity of the storyline took precedence over any "piece of business," no matter how funny, lovingly rendered, or costly. Engaging the audience became a

---

[4] Walt worked for the Kansas City Slide Company for two years from 1920 until 1922 learning the animation trade. https://waltinkc.weebly.com/the-kansas-city-years.html

matter of analyzing each scene and presenting ideas with maturity and subtlety, not crudeness and overemphasis—a tactic used in many animated shorts.

With *Snow White* a success, the studio went on to tackle challenging new stories, *Fantasia, Pinocchio,* and *Bambi*, that introduced new methods of storytelling but proved challenging and financially ruinous. Package films, more entertainment than feature, and hybrids, gave opportunities for experimenting with the combination of live action and animation that proved itself in the success of *Mary Poppins.* With Disney's next hybrid, *TRON,* CGI entered the production scene and helped create exceptional graphics in the film but distracted from the story. Disney was inspired to look to computers to help with the time consuming work of production, worked with Pixar to develop CAPS, and adopted the paint system for all of its features from 1990 on. The Pixar connection grew and the studios worked together on the first all-CGI film *Toy Story,* a breakthrough in the industry as both a great story and an exceptional achievement in technological innovation. Disney's first all CGI feature was *Chicken Little* in 2005, but not until *Frozen* did they achieve grandeur with story, and not until *Big Hero 6* did they distinguish themselves with technology. One innovative step the studio is taking in telling stories today that engage the audience emotionally in digital space is Virtual Reality, tested in the short, *Cycles*. The part concludes on the much larger stage: well-loved classic animations are being re-envisioned as live action CGI hybrids.

Part II presents Walt's overarching vision for his characters and his business; his comprehensive approach forged a Master Narrative for his star Mickey and for "Walt Disney." Walt made Mickey into a universally loved character not only through the weekly animated shorts but also through merchandising products, establishing *Mickey Mouse Clubs*, and performing vaudeville reviews. Such cross media appearances of Mickey and friends substantiated and added to the Disney Master Narrative. Walt's interest in using all media to bring Mickey and his stories to a wide audience sent Mickey journeying into comics, books, radio, television, and eventually Disneyland. Taking Mickey's stories across media gave the character different ways to express his personality and to reach out to and engage the audience. A live Mickey jumping through the screen to land on stage gave a three dimensional life to what had been a two-dimensional figure. A Mickey storybook read to a child in the comfort of the family living room made Mickey's stories personal in a way Saturday afternoon features could not.

Part III shows how Disney stories moved into a digital world and continued the pattern of innovation in both technology and story development that Walt had set in his quest to develop personable characters and create stories in which every aspect is carefully designed to engage as it entertains. The first Disney games were entertainment products that used classic Disney characters in traditional arcade style games; similar to other such games, the action had little to do with stories. The first full-length Disney film that was made into an adventure game was *The Black Cauldron.* The interactive digital environment required that the story be adapted to accommodate interaction and new storylines were created to give players opportunities to be involved. The interaction was also designed specifically with children in mind. The graphics in the game, although crude, were more realistic than other games of the time. It wasn't until almost 10 years later in *Disney's Animated Storybook: The Lion King* that Disney achieved stunning visual quality in an interactive digital story on par with that in the animated films. Newly developed software allowed game developers to use graphics from the award winning film and create an environment in which children could become a part of *The Lion King's* story and interact with all their favorite characters like Simba, Pumbaa, and Timon. At the same time *The Lion King* animated storybook was being created, Disney established an online presence with *Disney.com* and then launched an ambitious entertainment site for children, *Disney's Daily Blast*. For the first time, an online site brought stories, comics, arcade games, and educational games to children through a site that was designed specifically as a safe environment for them, was available in their home, and gave them a range of ways to play in one easy-to-access environment. The next digital technological innovation Disney tackled was Massive Multiplayer Online Role-Playing Games (MMORPGs). Taking what was perceived until then as an adult medium, Disney game producers developed *Toontown Online*, a safe and engaging interactive entertainment environment for children. Here children could choose their own avatar *Toons* to represent themselves as they entered different lands, engaged with classic cartoon characters, challenged themselves with different task, and had the opportunity to interact with other players online. With the development of the MMORPG *Pirates of the Caribbean* Disney brought one of the last themed rides Walt had personally helped design for Disneyland into an online environment. *Pirates of the Caribbean* is an example of the comprehensive reach across media that Disney stories attain and how they change in the process. Following Walt's original precepts about bringing stories to audiences through a range of communication media, *Pirates* became more than a ride, a movie, and a virtual world. It became a merchandising opportunity that both extended the Disney Master Narrative and crossed into other storytelling media including video games, books for young readers and Lego, both traditional blocks and online.

In conclusion, Part III looks at how Disney has taken a story property it has purchased rather than developed in-house, Lucasfilm's *Star Wars*,[5] and integrated it completely into the Disney Master Narrative through its films and theme park presence. *Galaxy's Edge* brings a new level of cross-media reach in its detailed representation of the *Star Wars* universe, the animatronic representations of its characters, the guest apps capability to make things happen in Batuu, and the simulated Millenium Falcon mission.

We end the book with two addendums: One, an interview with Roy E Disney in which he concludes that "Everything we've done since *Beauty and the Beast*, at Disney, has passed through the computer, so you could probably say that everything we've done for the last 12 or 14 years is, in a sense, computer graphics." And two, Newton Lee's memoire of his 10 years at Disney which provides an excellent overview of Disney's moves in and out of games and online worlds.

---

[5] Disney purchased Lucasfilm and with it the *Star Wars* franchise in October 2012.

## 1.4 Disney Stories

Since the beginning of mankind, the fable-tellers have not only given us entertainment but a kind of wisdom, humor, and understanding that, like all true art, remains imperishable through the ages. (Walt Disney)

Disney stories cross all cultures and are present in all strata of society. They are without peer in being represented in every media available. How is it that *Disney* stories above others have endured for decades and woven their enchantment over each new generation?

When one of the creative directors at Disney/Pixar spoke to a group of students about his creative team's process, he used as an example developing sketches of characters and scenes for the film *Ratatouille*. He spoke about the hows and whys of making decisions about the characters' personalities and the storyline, and provided insight into the philosophy that is part of the company's, not just the team's, creative process. The phrases he used—"believability through authenticity," "studying reality in order to caricature it," "getting to the heart of the matter,"—have been used consistently to describe Disney's approach to the development of its animated stories since the 1930s. Disney stories engage because of compelling and believable characters.

The stories endure because they are *intended* to endure, because the characters and stories are developed as signifiers that tap into archetypes we inherently understand, relate to, and connect with. The personalities are believable and their actions elicit empathy. Walt's goal was to engage and entertain the general public with his stories. That he did so successfully was a result of his "great sensitivity to people in the mass. He knew instinctively, how to reach Mr. and Mrs. America; he's a great entertainer" (Jackson 2005, p. 87). How did Walt acquire this sense of stories people wanted to hear? Where did this sensitivity come from?

# Part I
# From Gags to Stories

[Disney] has always taken things as
he found them, and then found a way
of making them better; and by so
doing has transformed them into
things entirely different. He saw the
animated cartoon [not] only as it
then existed, but with a strange,
unaccountable insight he knew that
the limitations imposed upon it were
self-imposed and could be broken down
if only one had the courage of one's
convictions.

Robert D. Feild

# Chapter 2
# Early Animation: Gags and Situations

*The way to get started is to quit talking and begin doing.*
Walt Disney

## 2.1 Life Experience, Joy of Entertainment, Love of Drawing

Three things become apparent when we look at Walt's early life. It was filled with experiences that gave him a familiarity with people from all walks of life in innumerable situations. It was filled with merriment as Walt delighted in entertainment of all kinds. It was directed by Walt's love of drawing and cartoons.

By the time Walt was eighteen he had lived through more types of experiences than have many people in their entire lives. He had been part of a farming community, lived and worked in a medium-sized mid-western town, and worked in a large city by the time he was fifteen. Although born in Chicago, his parents moved to the community of Marceline when he was just four; there he enjoyed the freedom of life on the farm. His familiarity with the cycle of seasons on the farm and his earthy, often farm-animal related humor stem from his early experiences participating in daily farm life, herding pigs, leading horses, and helping with harvesting. With three older brothers to carry the burden of the work he had the freedom to watch the rabbits, foxes, and squirrels in the local woods and the many birds that nested in the trees. He could cool himself off at a nearby creek or forage the woods for wild nuts, grapes, persimmons, and chokeberries. When his two oldest brothers left to start life on their own, his father could no longer manage the farm and moved the family to Kansas City where he purchased a newspaper distribution route. Here, for 6 years until he was fourteen, Walt together with his brother Roy, delivered papers from 3:30 in the morning through all weather conditions. Walt's father did not pay him to deliver

---

Online photos and graphics provide extra detail and are identified by urls the reader can refer to. This additional reference information will be particularly beneficial as an enhancement for the online version of this book. URLs are current at time of printing.

© Springer Nature Switzerland AG 2020
K. Madej, N. Lee, *Disney Stories*, https://doi.org/10.1007/978-3-030-42738-2_2

papers, although he did give him a small allowance—his room and board were his pay. To make pocket money, Walt worked at a pharmacy delivering prescriptions; he got a hot noon meal by sweeping out the candy store across from his school. The distribution business was not a success and the family moved back to Chicago. Walt stayed in Kansas City for the summer to work for the Santa Fe Railroad as a news butcher hawking fruit, candy, and soda pop across half a dozen states.

When he got to Chicago, Walt began attending McKinley High School. Work was a constant, however, and he took a job as a handyman at his dad's jelly factory, even serving as watchman outfitted with 0.38 caliber revolver at his side for a night. He tried his hand as a guard and gateman for the elevated railway line, and worked at the post office, sorting mail, delivering it in a White truck, and picking it up in a horse-drawn mail wagon. The tide for the War in Europe had turned for the Allies and with Roy in the Navy and Ray in the Army, Walt didn't want to be considered "a slacker" and also wanted to serve. There were few opportunities for a 16 year old, but when the American Ambulance Corps of the Red Cross began to look for volunteers, he changed his birth date to 1900 and signed up. He arrived at Le Havre in war-torn France in December 1918 and spent his 17th birthday celebrating in a local cafe in St. Cyr. When he returned to Chicago a year later, he was more mature and more confident about what he wanted to do. After his experiences in France he did not feel he could return to high school, and he had no calling to work in his father's jelly factory. At 18 Walt took the train to Kansas City to find a job among his old contacts—he intended to be an artist.

For all the hardship and work in his life, from an early age Walt loved entertainment. He would play tricks on his parents, in particular his mother, who appreciated his jokes and added a sense of "gaiety" to their home. He organized events such a circus parade with his sister and his friends. He enjoyed the warmth of friendly neighbors, the Pfeiffers, joining them for evenings of song, piano playing, and joke telling. He went to vaudeville shows and copied acts to perform at his school. He learned how to put a gag or a story across to entertain.

> His most popular performance was "Fun in the Photograph Gallery." Walt portrayed an antic photographer, posing his fellow students, then dousing them with a jet of water from the camera. The audience was delighted when Walt produced the "photograph"—his own caricature of the student who had been squirted. (Thomas, Walt Disney, An American Original, 1976)

He (with Walter Pfeiffer) entered amateur night at a local theatre as "Charlie Chaplin and the Count" and won fourth prize. He even performed at the neighborhood vaudeville house as the topmost boy in a balancing act.

Above all, Walt loved to draw and developed a facility for cartooning and caricature. While in school he was constantly drawing: in his textbooks, on the blackboard, on the neighborhood clubhouse walls. When he was nine and his sister Ruth was sick, he drew pictures and made his first animation—a flipbook—to entertain her. He drew a caricature a week for a local barber who had seen and admired his drawings. In exchange, he received free haircuts. When he graduated from the seventh grade, he received a seven-dollar prize from one of his teachers for a comic character he had drawn. He took children's art classes at the Kansas City Art Institute and later he took art lessons at the Chicago Art Academy. While at McKinley High School he joined the staff of the school magazine as a cartoonist and photographer. He went to burlesque houses (when these still offered family entertainment) and copied gags, compiled a "gag file," and tried the gags out on his father. While he was in France and working for the American Ambulance Corps he drew caricatures for his fellow soldiers, illustrated advertising posters for hot chocolate and baths, and decorated his canvas-topped truck with cartoons. He sent cartoons to *Life* and *Judge*, popular humor magazines of the time (none accepted!). He used his artistic skills at every opportunity and could turn them to any direction.

Walt made use of all that he saw and did in his work. His wealth of life experience and his abiding interest in entertainment serendipitously dovetailed with his love of drawing and cartooning and gave him an advantage over others in the animation field. Walt believed:

> Nothing in a lifetime of picture making has been more exciting and personally satisfactory than delving into the wonders, the mysteries, the magnificent commonplaces of life around us and passing them on via the screen. (Smith 2015)

## 2.2   Becoming an Animator

By the time Walt arrived in Kansas City from Chicago in 1919 he was already accustomed to hard work, to taking chances, to looking to new ideas, whether to expand his repertoire of jokes and gags or to find new avenues for his drawings. Through a friend of his brother Roy, he learned Pesmen-Rubin Commercial Art Studio was looking for an apprentice. He got his first job at this two-man commercial art shop. Six weeks later, the holiday rush was over and so was his job. His next job was a quick dip—2 months—into a partnership with Ub Iwerks (aka Ubbe Ert Iwwerks), a fellow-worker at Pesmen-Rubin. Moderately successful during its very brief existence, the partnership was nevertheless a wavering enterprise. Walt, keen on making it as a cartoonist, applied for a position that came up at the Kansas City Film Ad Company, a studio that made promotional slides shown in movie theatres, and work there for 2 years. There he was introduced to the technology of animated pictures and was soon "intoxicated with animation"—"The trick of making things move is what got me" (Gabler 2006, p. 50). Even before he turned twenty, Walt's goal was to have an animation studio that would turn out new films each week.

## 2.3   Getting into the Business of Animation

Walt Disney officially incorporated *Laugh-O-Gram Films* on May 18, 1922 while he was still working for the Kansas City Film Ad Company. His job had brought him into the world of animation but his tremendous curiosity and interest led him to experiment on his own time and eventually to make his own films.

The ad animations Walt worked on were made entirely of figures cut out of paper. Joints were riveted so figures could be manipulated and changed for each frame of film shot. Animated cartoons on the other hand, a staple at theatres by 1915, consisted of drawings. The first animations entranced audiences with their "magic" quality: moving drawings were novel and audiences loved them no matter what the quality or content. In 1914, Winsor McCay, of *Little Nemo* fame, brought a realistic personality to animation with *Gertie the Dinosaur*. McCay depicted a style of movement that endeared Gertie to the audience. In the film, Gertie comes lumbering out of a cave by the side of a lake and proceeds to eat an entire tree. McCay asks Gertie to do some tricks but when she doesn't raise her left foot as he has asked, he scolds her and she cries. She gets over it quickly and subsequent action includes her meeting an elephant and tossing it into the lake, lying down for a nap, scratching her head, her nose, and her chin with her tail in a charming fashion, drinking the lake dry, and finally, giving McCay a ride out of the picture. In creating a personality for Gertie, George McManus laid the road for animation as a new film genre based in characters not in magic.[1]

Such animation intrigued Walt. He had come to Kansas City Film Ad Company as a commercial artist and a cartoonist without any experience in animation, a typical trajectory at the time. Most animators (and there were few of them) were "eager young print cartoonists... who had no training in animating figures... (Gabler 2006, p. 54)." Like many others, he took on the task of educating himself and was lucky in finding at the local lending library a new release by E.G. Lutz on how to make animations: *Animated Cartoons—How they are made, their origin and development*.[2] The book not only gave rudimentary lessons on how to animate but also advocated what were, at the time, advanced techniques, such as using drawings on celluloid sheets to reduce the number of drawings required.

At the time, animators also relied on the work of Eadweard Muybridge to get a better understanding of the steps of an action. In the late 1800s Muybridge had made hundreds of thousands of photographs of people and animals to study their movement. He published a number of popular books that showed particular sequences, such as a man walking down the stairs, or in one of the most often reproduced, a horse galloping.[3] These sequences provided a resource of realistic movements for animators that helped them with their drawings.

---

[1] Newspaper cartoonist George McManus bet Winsor McCay that a dinosaur could not be brought to life. To win, McCay made Gertie, the world's first animated dinosaur. McCay's cartoon: https://www.youtube.com/watch?v=TGXC8gXOPoU

[2] "The first attempt at giving to a screen image the effect of life was by means of a progressive series of drawings. When photographs came later, drawings were forgotten and only when the cinematographic art had reached its great development and universality, were drawings again brought into use to be synthesized on the screen. To describe how these drawings are made, their use and application to the making of animated cartoons, is the purpose of this book" (Lutz 1998): http://openlibrary.org/books/OL6622808M/Animated_cartoons

[3] *The Horse in Motion*: http://100photos.time.com/photos/eadweard-muybridge-horse-in-motion

Such new ideas provided Disney with fodder for his interest to experiment and to bring new techniques to his ad work. Verne Cauger, Film Ad's owner, was not against Walt's ideas to improve the ads, at least incrementally. But the management at Film Ad balked at too much innovation and would not consider using animation techniques such as drawings. Walt not only made suggestions that led to the animated images being clearer and the action smoother, but he also made suggestions about copy. He was interested in expressing *ideas* visually—the editorial cartoons he did for his high school paper and those he sent to magazines when he was in France demonstrated this. He brought this interest into the advertising world where he became adept at coming up with the clever idea and suggesting quips that caught the imagination. In one advertisement for a company that reconditioned old cars he wrote: "Hi, old top, new car?" "No, new top, old car?" (Gabler 2006, p. 51).

Walt eventually persuaded the company to let him shoot his own films, because, "I would plan things with my drawings and I couldn't get those guys [the regular camera operators] to do it... . The cameramen weren't doing half of what you prepared" (Barrier 2007, p. 57). Walt thought through a scenario, wrote it down, and expected it to be followed. It was at this time that he developed the habit of paying close attention to every detail and personally following up every bit of action, a habit which became a dominant feature of his working style for not only his later animated films but for all of his projects.

Walt needed a studio and when his father built a modest garage addition to their home to rent out for some needed income, Walt rented it. He spent his evenings and weekends drawing, filming, and experimenting with techniques. Walt's entrepreneurial spirit came to the fore and he made a funny editorial cartoon about the "slow" Kansas City streetcar service as a speculative business venture with fellow-worker, Hugh Harman. This reel had Louis Pesman (of Walt's earlier Pesman-Rubin experience) laughing "loud and hard" (Gabler 2006, p. 57). Pesman suggested Walt try to sell this sample reel to the Newman Theatre, one of Kansas City's grandest movie houses. Walt gave it the title *Newman Laugh-O-Grams* to make it more appealing. Milton Feld, who ran the theatre, purchased the short reel, and first showed it on March 20, 1921.[4]

Walt and Hugh could only send him new cartoons irregularly over the next few months, as they were both working full time. Walt advertised for apprentices and co-workers and soon found a high school student, Rudy Ising, who would work "for experience" with him in the family garage. The Newman *Laugh-O-Grams* often used the "lightning sketches" technique that showed an artist's hand drawing the cartoon. The artist used a light blue pencil that would not show on the film to draw the images; the lines would then be inked in increments and filmed. When the film was run continuously it looked like the hand was drawing the image amazingly quickly. The short animations commented on current fashions, lampooned political issues and scandals in Kansas City, and also provided information about coming

---

[4]Walt became acquainted with the Newman Theatre chain while at the Kansas City Film Ad Company. https://disney.fandom.com/wiki/Newman_Laugh-O-Grams

theatre attractions and protocol. They proved to be popular and Walt continued providing Field with one-minute shorts, including *Cleaning Up!!?,* and *Kansas City's Spring Cleanup.*

By February 1922 Walt had saved enough money from his job at Kansas City Film Ad Company (he made no profit on selling his films) to buy a Universal camera and tripod. Cauger had let him rent a shop where he could experiment on films in the evenings after working at the advertising studio all day. Walt enjoyed some small measure of fame because of the films and Cauger showed the films as what the company was capable of, even though in their own ads he would not use drawings.

## 2.4   Laugh-O-Grams

Walt officially started his new business on June 17, 1922, while he was still an employee at Kansas City Film Ad Company. *Motion Picture News* announced the start up of *Laugh-O-Grams* (Gabler 2006, p. 64):

> They will produce Laugh-O-Gram animated cartoon comedies which will be cartooned by Walter E. Disney.

One of the last projects Walt worked on was a new series of animations based on fairytales. He was heavily influenced by the work of Paul Terry, a leading New York animator who in 1921 had released a send-up of *Aesop's Fables* that was an instant success with audiences. Terry produced one fable every week for 8 years until 1928. Walt felt he needed a similar hook for his animations. He decided to use well-known fairy tales, put them into a contemporary context, and give them a modern twist. *Little Red Riding Hood*[5] was the first fairy tale that Walt produced in this series. *The Four Musicians of Bremen,* a second tale, was also completed while he worked at Film Ad. These were released in July and August respectively of that year.

Walt had raised some $ 2500 from friends and the young associates who were working with him to run *Laugh-O-Grams.* The remainder of the money (the company was capitalized at $ 15,000 with around $ 5000 in assets) was difficult to raise (Barrier 2007). With *Little Red Riding Hood* and a reel of *Lafflets*, an experimental short that consisted of jokes and commentaries, Walt went out to sell his new company. He had success with investors such as John Cowles, a Kansas City doctor, who was also a speculator and interested in new investments. Walt quickly rented space, took out ads, and hired staff; but there was a weak market for animated shorts at the time, and selling the idea was more difficult than he anticipated. He sent his sales manager to New York; after a stay that cost the company more money than they had in the bank, he finally concluded a deal in September for six animations with *Pictorial Clubs, Inc. Laugh-O-Grams* was to receive $ 100 down and the remainder, $ 11,000, was to be paid January 1924, almost 18 months later (Burnes

---

[5] *"Laugh-O-Grams"* were based on traditional fairy tales and given a contemporary twist. https://www.youtube.com/watch?v=Hz31ZQOASno

2002; Thomas, Walt Disney, An American Original 1976). This was a highly impractical payment plan as it gave the company no money during the production of the animations, but *Laugh-O-Grams* had few other offers; the animators set to work immediately.

Under situations which were "never less than dire" financially, and while often deferring salaries and borrowing from family, friends, and employees to keep afloat, the company completed *Jack and the Beanstalk,* and *Cinderella* between 1922 and 1923. Walt and the staff he had hired, which included Rudy Ising and Ub Iwerks who had left Kansas City Film Ad and joined them in November as animators, "arrived at the office at nine each morning and stayed until midnight" doing work that for them was "more fun than pay" (Gabler 2006, p. 67). Despite the constant worry about money, they continued to be upbeat and had "many belly laughs" while discussing the stories or wild gags they could incorporate into their material.

## 2.5 Production and Story Techniques

*Laugh-O-Grams* was a young company with staff that was inexperienced. No one knew very much about animation and their drawings were crude in comparison to the animations coming out of New York. The cartoonists studied the latest *Aesop's Fables* and *Krazy Kat* cartoons for technique, trying new things, making improvements, and learning as they went along.[6]

Occasionally their experimentation led them to an improvement in technique over the New York studios. Placement pegs for the drawings were placed at the top of the drawing board; Walt's artists started putting them at the bottom of the board instead. This new technique allowed the artist to flip through the action more easily when creating a scene. Another invention was the "biff-sniff" (Barrier 2007, p. 35). Ub Iwerks constructed an addition to the projector that let the artists project their animation drawings in different sizes; this allowed for greater consistency for the characters and the backgrounds and better speed in completion. These were the first of a long line of innovations to come.

The animation technique of inked lines on paper with just the occasional use of cels (celluloid sheets) used for *Little Red Riding Hood* was a very time intensive technique. With only Walt and Rudy Ising doing the work, very simplistic line drawings of the characters and the backgrounds with many repetitions of the same action were necessary. For the remainder of the *Laugh-O-Grams*, cels on which characters were painted and were then photographed over a background drawing were used (at least for the most part). This was a newer approach to making animations and provided artists with flexibility to draw more complex and detailed backgrounds. It was

---

[6]Walt admired Paul Terry's *Aesop's Fables* and wanted to emulate their success. *Aesop's Fables:* https://www.youtube.com/watch?v=L-KyOgEVn7U&list=PLoDXjsS-wI0z901x_P-AYzk 28Q584fvBm

also a more expensive technique as celluloid sheets needed to be cut down to size and then punched with peg holes.

Walt was ambitious and wanted to create animations as good as Terry's. There is progressive improvement in the animation technique from the first fairytale *Little Red Riding Hood*, with its primitive drawing, to a later one such as *Puss in Boots,* which is well-drawn for the time. In *Puss in Boots*, besides the main characters, there are extras that make up a large crowd leaving a movie theatre, and then there are more crowds in the stands at the bullfight. Though there are "cycles," or repetitions of the same action in the animation, new gags are introduced and there is less of the type of repetition that was used extensively in *Red Riding Hood*. The many characters are drawn with attention to detail, the backgrounds are painted with shading, and the landscape is drawn with perspective. This is the longest of the shorts at over 9 minutes, but the action moves more quickly than does *Red Riding Hood*, which is repetitious during the first 2 minutes.

The same type of learning and progress can be seen in how the story is presented. In their early history, cartoon animations were all about gags. They were based primarily on the comic strips that appeared in daily papers and consisted of quick laughs, funny situations, and jokes that were often crudely constructed and strung-together; to make the animation longer, more gags were added. In line with the need for good gags, one of the new staff Walt hired was a "scenario editor" whose main job it was to scour the newspapers for jokes. It was not difficult to entertain an audience with novelty gags for a minute or two, particularly in a new medium that itself was a novelty. But to maintain that interest and keep the audience laughing for 6 or 7 minutes required not only good gags but also a good idea and the ability to get the idea across fluently. As the novelty of the medium wore off and audiences were no longer entertained just by seeing the action of animation, animators had to move on and ask themselves questions about engagement: could the audience understand the characters and their actions? Was the sequence of events of sufficient interest to keep them watching? Did the timing help keep the audience engaged and entertained?

One story technique Walt used was a trickster figure that provided a number of the gags and helped move the story forward. The cat first introduced in *Little Red Riding Hood* acts as a trickster in subsequent shorts. In *Puss in Boots* it plays a double role, both as the trickster figure and as the protagonist.[7]

Although Walt loved gags, the area in which he would challenge his New York competitors' work, and in which he would later shine, was in developing the idea for the animation and arriving at a story that would convey it. To the belly laughs of good gags and funny situations he and his staff came up with, he added a story that provided for continuity. Based on the production experience he had gained from making film ads, Walt wrote out scenarios with extensive details in much the same way live action film scripts are written and used for directing action. Within this tighter format, the sequence of actions for the gags and situations held together as a story (at least it had potential to do so). In his biography of Walt Disney, Neal

---

[7] *Puss in Boots*: https://www.youtube.com/watch?v=H9n4Jb1kFns

Gabler provides an example of the directions for a scene in the *Laugh-O-Gram Cinderella* (Gabler 2006, p. 67)[8]:

> FLASH TO CLOSE-UP OF ONE FAT LADY IN HAMMOCK reading 'Eat and Grow Thin'—another girl very skinny sitting in chair—they are eating out of it—slim girl puts down book—she is cross-eyed—she begins talking to fat girl—fat girl answers back.

In the margins of these instructions, in blue pencil, were the initials of the animators for each scene. In a field that was ruled by the style of the individual artist, Walt wanted, even at this early stage in his career, to control the production of the animations. This may be partly because his skills did not lie so much in drawing, but rather in managing and producing the story, a skill that he would further develop with time. In Walt's earliest animated fairy tales, however, it is still often difficult to figure out the story as the shorts consist predominantly of a string of gags that often have no relation to either each other or the story, the events barely follow the original fairy tale, and, to add to the lack of continuity, the setting is contemporary. Of all the *Laugh-O-Grams*, *Little Red Riding Hood* suffers from these problems the most. In addition it has both the crudest drawings and the greatest number of cycles, the technique the animators used most regularly to save drawing time.[9]

The cartoon begins with Red Riding Hood's mother making the dough for donuts. Her cat is shooting holes in the dough as she tosses it into a pot; an old man in a picture on the wall looks on and laughs. This gag is typical of the *gags for gags sake* approach that set the scope for animation at the time. It is cycled relentlessly and the scene runs for almost 2 minutes. The little story that follows begins when the mother goes out on the porch and gives Red Riding Hood a basket of donuts to give to her grandmother. Red Riding Hood takes her flivver out of the garage, and dangling a sausage from a fishing rod at the front of it as a teaser, has her dog pull the car. The animators make some minor attempts to connect gags: in one scene a tire bursts and Red Riding Hood replaces it with a donut she has blown up to the right size. However, most gags are arbitrary and not contextual to the story.

The wolf in this contemporary take of the old fairytale is a dirty old man, driving in the opposite direction, whom Red meets, and with whom she has a quick chat. As they go their separate ways, the conniving wolf manages to get to Grandma's first. When Red Riding Hood arrives, a tussle ensues. We do not see the struggle directly, only the house bouncing around with "help" popping out of it. The dog runs for help to a nearby pilot who uses his plane to make a dramatic rescue: the pilot lowers a hook from his plane and drags the house into the air revealing Red and the wolf to the audience. The wolf runs off to his car; Red Riding Hood grabs the hook at the plane's second pass over, and is pulled up into the plane. Once there, she kisses her rescuer. The fade out screen reads "And they lived happily ever after???" as two hearts appear.

---

[8] *Cinderella*: https://www.youtube.com/watch?v=pn5YWSP1O5M

[9] *Little Red Riding Hood*—the first *Laugh-O-Gram*—was roughly drawn and consisted of many cycled and unrelated gags.

The story in each of *The Four Musicians of Bremen* and *Puss in Boots* is closer to the original fairy tale than is the story in *Little Red Riding Hood*. Of the four tales that remain today (*Jack and the Beanstalk and Goldilocks* are lost) *Cinderella*, which was the last short made, keeps closest to the original fairytale. In doing so however, it is also less adventurous and has fewer interesting gags and funny situations. This lack of creativity may have been more a result of the stress the studio was suffering from a worsening financial situation than because the fairy tale was adhered to.

## 2.6  Cracking the Market

*Pictorial Clubs, Inc.* went bankrupt only months into the Studio's work of production on the six contracted shorts. The parent company in New York refused to pay creditors so there was no payment to look forward to at the end of the lengthy and hard work it took the animators to make the cartoons. It was many years before the parent company settled their obligations—and not in time to save *Laugh-O-Grams* from bankruptcy.

After attempting to sell a number of different ideas for series, one of which combined animations with spicy jokes, Walt tried one more series that he thought might save the company by "cracking the market." He created *Alice's Wonderland* to be different from the very popular animations of the time in which cartoon characters came into the real world. *Alice,* played by Virginia Davis, a Mary Pickford look-alike, was a real girl who hopped *into* the cartoon world.[10] Walt felt this twist on the original idea would give the audience a new experience, one in which they could see and empathize with a real person in a cartoon world. "We have just discovered something new and clever in animated cartoons!" Walt wrote to distributor Margaret Winkler in May 1923 in an attempt to sell her the idea (Thomas, Walt Disney, An American Original 1976, p. 65).

This was bravado in the face of a ruinous financial situation. There was barely enough money to complete the animation: filming took place in different locations as the company was evicted from one space after another for non-payment of rent, and because most of the staff had left—they had been paid, at best, only fitfully— Walt ended up completing the animation himself.

Credit ran out for *Laugh-O-Grams* and without staff or money to pay even Walt's own rent and food, the company succumbed to financial failure. Walt declared bankruptcy. Cadaverous-looking from living on scraps of food, he looked to leaving failure behind and made plans to move on. Through a contact he managed to get a contract to make a live action film, a *Song-O-Reel* with lyrics written on title cards, called *Martha: Just a Plain Old-Fashioned Name*. He made just enough money to

---

[10]Virginia Davis, a Mary Pickford, look alike and an audience pleaser, in *Alice's Wonderland*. Photo of opening screen in *Alice's Wonderland*: http://www.bcdb.com/cartoon/3947-Alices_ Wonderland.html. Photo of Virginia Davis: http://www.thestar.com/entertainment/article/682302.

pay for his trip to Hollywood where his brother Roy was recuperating from TB and where his uncle lived. Walt still continued to hope something would turn up, and before he left, he sent out dozens of letters to distributors promoting *Alice's Wonderland*. Though *Alice* was no longer his (he had mortgaged it along with all the company assets when raising money to run *Laugh-O-Grams*) he brought a reel with him to Hollywood and continued to promote it, promising "new ideas in animation" for audiences to enjoy.

During these very early years of his career, Walt absorbed the information he needed to create successful "gag" shorts. In taking on all tasks involved in production from doing the drawings to filming, he learned about current techniques and experimented with new ones. To his new skill of developing gags he added the understanding of how situations evolve into stories and the knowledge of what entertained that he had gained as a youngster. The result: the *Laugh-O-Grams* progressed from being a primitively drawn series of barely-related gags to a series of events that had a basic storyline to carry them forward and gags that were, at least occasionally, related to the character and the story. When he made the cat in *Little Red Riding Hood* a character in some of the other shorts, he took his first opportunity to create a recognizable recurring comic figure. With the idea of a series based on a single character, *Alice*, Walt took another step in his progress towards developing animated characters with personalities that the audience could empathize and engage with.

# Chapter 3
# From Gags to Characters

> *Until a character becomes a personality, it can't be believed,
> and you have to believe these animated stories. Without
> personality, the character may do funny or interesting
> things, but unless people are able to identify themselves
> with the character, its actions will seem unreal. And without
> personality, a story cannot ring true to an audience.*
>
> Walt Disney

## 3.1   A New Animated Experience for the Audience

Margaret Winkler, a New York distributor, had received the promotional letter Walt
had sent out in May, 1923. She was having problems with two of the series she
represented and was eager to find a new cartoon series with which to replace them.
Without seeing *Alice's Wonderland* she had written back immediately. Walt, dis-
couraged with the financial problems of *Laugh-O-Grams*, had already left for
Hollywood in early August 1923 and had "put my drawing board away. What I
wanted to do was get a job in a studio—any studio, doing anything" (Gabler 2006,
p. 77). He visited them all, looking for ways to get introductions and find work in
the film industry, but he made little headway. Walt wrote Winkler back from Los
Angeles in August saying he was starting a new venture and was intent on working
at one of the film studios so that he could "better study technical detail and comedy
situations and combine them with [his] cartoons" (Thomas, Walt Disney, An
American Original 1976). Winkler was persistent in wanting to see the reel and Walt
finally got a copy to her in October. She immediately offered him US$ 1500 each
for the first six films and US$ 1800 each for the next six. Even more important for
a fledgling business, she offered to pay for each of the animations as they were
completed and wanted to have the first one delivered by January 2. As part of the

---

Online photos and graphics provide extra detail and are identified by urls the reader can refer to.
This additional reference information will be particularly beneficial as an enhancement for the
online version of this book. URLs are current at time of printing.

© Springer Nature Switzerland AG 2020                                                     23
K. Madej, N. Lee, *Disney Stories*, https://doi.org/10.1007/978-3-030-42738-2_3

contract she sent out to Walt, she included an option for 24 more shorts (two series of twelve) to be produced in 1925 and 1926. This was an offer that had some potential to provide the type of financial security required to build an animation studio.

While Walt could rely on his staff at *Laugh-O-Grams*, however dwindling, to produce *Alice's Wonderland*, when he was first getting started in Los Angeles, he was little equipped to deliver on his promise of even one animated short. Relying on Roy as a partner, he hustled to set up a studio. The two brothers borrowed money from relatives and friends, bought a new camera, and set up shop in a small office on Kingswell Street. They named their new studio Disney Bros. Cartoon Studio.

Walt had conceived *Alice's Wonderland* as a new take on an animation schema popular at the time. Cartoon characters had been popping in and out of the real world in Max Fleischer's *Out of the Inkwell* cartoon series since 1919. Fleischer's character, *Koko the Clown*, flowed out of his pen, and moved back and forth between worlds, as part of his adventures in the *Inkwell* shorts. In *Alice*, Walt offers the audience a different approach, one that gives them a real person to identify with in a cartoon world. Viewers could identify with Alice as a human being and join her in an adventure wonderland where anything could happen. Walt used the frame story format (a story within a story) in which the live action is used as a framing device for the cartoon action. The framing scene shows Alice being introduced to animated cartoons in Walt's studio. This is followed by a dream sequence in which Alice enters the cartoon world.[1]

The story: Little Alice visits Walt at his studio and says, "I would like to watch you draw some funnies" (Burnes 2002, p. 6). He takes Alice to his drawing board where a drawing of a doghouse comes alive and a puppy jumps out of it. Alice is enchanted and a smiling Walt brings her further into the studio and shows her a series of gags the artists are creating. He points out two cartoon cats dancing to a trio of cat musicians on one of the drawing tables. On another drawing board a cartoon mouse thrusts a sword at a rather lethargic fluffy white cat. Walt's fellow artists are working in the background. Ub Iwerks calls them over to his art board to watch two cats in a fight ring, duking it out.[2] When one cat is kayoed the cartoon ends and it is time for Alice to leave. Alice goes home and excitedly tells her mother about the wonderful things she has seen.[3] When she goes to sleep she dreams she is part of the *cartoon* world and finds herself on a train that takes her to Cartoonland. Here she is welcomed by a reception committee of animals and participates in a big parade. She entertains the animals by doing a dance but while she is dancing the lions escape from their cage and chase her. In typical gag fashion, one of the lions, in anticipation of a fine meal, takes out his teeth and sharpens them. Alice escapes by jumping over

---

[1] In a new twist in animation, Alice, a real person visits Cartoonland where a parade is thrown in her honor. *Alice's Wonderland*: http://www.youtube.com/watch?v=H58meqbp5Ps.

[2] Alice gets to see a cartoon cat fight as the animators look on. *Alice'sWonderland*: http://www.youtube.com/watch?v=H58meqbp5Ps

[3] As she is put to bed Alice tells her mother about her exciting day. *Alice's Wonderland*: http://www.youtube.com/watch?v=H58meqbp5Ps

a cliff and we see her falling down, down, down, and the film ends without any concluding scenes. It seems that bankruptcy got in the way of it being finished.

The action is lively but there is little story structure. While the framing scene provides an effective transition to the cartoon world, once Alice enters this world, the only action is a parade and a series of gags. The events do not constitute a story and the gags are of the gags-for-gags sake variety; although they are entertaining, they do not move the events forward.

The credits for *Alice's Wonderland* tell us that Walt was responsible for "Scenario and Direction," Ub Iwerks and Rudy Ising for the "Photography," and Hugh Harman and Carman Maxwell for the "Technical Direction." These were the employees at *Laugh-O-Grams* who had worked on the short at the time the company closed down. When Walt and Roy started anew in Hollywood, they had no employees; Walt did the animation on the first six *Alice* shorts by himself.

In *Alice's Day at Sea*, the first in the *Alice in Cartoonland* series he contracted with Winkler, Walt continued with the frame story dream sequence format he used for *Alice's Wonderland*.[4] Beginning with live action, the cartoon begins with a cute gag that shows Alice's dog being woken up by an alarm clock that won't stop ringing. Annoyed, the dog picks up the alarm clock and tosses it into the trash. The dog wakes up Alice and then runs off only to return driving a child-sized Model-T. Acting as chauffeur, the dog drives Alice to the seaside. There she meets a fisherman who spins her a yarn about a giant octopus. Tired, Alice falls asleep in a dinghy drawn up on the beach. She wakes to find herself in a cartoon world. The first scenes are dramatic white-on-black line drawings of a storm at sea with much buffeting and tossing. Her ship sinks to the bottom of the sea and there she encounters all manner of sea life including singing and dancing fish. She is chased and swallowed by a very large fish, saved by a swordfish, and then captured again by an octopus. As she struggles in the octopus's arms she wakes to find herself entangled in a real fish net. The dog goes for help and the fisherman whom she first met comes to rescue her. The end has everyone in smiles.

This short is similar to *Alice's Wonderland* in that it uses the same type of frame structure and dream sequence transition, and the cartoon scenes consist mainly of unrelated gags. But there is more attempt at presenting a cohesive story that begins with the fisherman spinning a yarn about an octopus, links the cartoon underwater scenes to the live scene with the octopus gag, and ends with the fisherman rescuing Alice from the "octopus".

Walt delivered the short early, on December 26. But it was, according to Winkler, only "satisfactory." She wrote asking that they include more "gags and comical situations" in the next productions (Gabler 2006, p. 84), a request that became a nagging refrain and reinforced the continuation of the animated cartoon as a gag-fest rather than a story. Because Disney Bros. first few shorts were animated solely by Walt with the live-camera work being shot by Roy, the quality of the production and

---

[4]The first animated scenes in *Alice's Day at Sea* are stark and dramatic. *Alice's Day at Sea*: http://www.youtube.com/watch?v=YE1F1UMJ0m0

the gags and story was not comparable to the final *Laugh-O-Grams* animated shorts. When Walt completed *Alice Hunting in Africa*, the next cartoon which he also created and drew himself, Winkler rejected it as unreleasable: there was not enough comedy and the production standards "must be much higher." This short was reworked by Walt and released later in November. Although stymied by lack of talented animators such as Ub Iwerks, Walt was nevertheless sincere in that he wanted to make better animations. He wanted to be "a little different from the usual run of slap stick" and his next attempt, *Alice's Spooky Adventure*, which he shipped to Winkler February 22, was improved such that Winkler wrote it was "the best you have turned out" (p. 85). Initially the company could only afford to hire one inker and this happened to be Lillian Bounds, who Walt married a couple of years later. With financial resources coming in from the first animation they could afford to hire two more women to help with inking and a couple of men to help with the camera and assist generally. In February they took on their first animator, Rollin "Ham" Hamilton, and Walt was no longer doing all the drawing himself.

## 3.2  Renewed Focus on Animation

The earliest *Alice's* were more live action than animation and were this way for a number of reasons. It was important to get the films out quickly. Animated sequences were very time-consuming to produce and even when Hamilton joined him Walt needed to use every short cut available to complete the animations on schedule. It simply took less time and it was less expensive to shoot live action than to draw animations. Walt knew he needed drawing talent and had contacted Ub Iwerks to join him in California. After much persuasion Iwerks arrived in June of that year. Iwerks had become a skilled animator capable of producing drawings quickly and Walt now had the opportunity to return the focus in the shorts from live action to animation.

The last short made before Iwerks joined Disney Bros., *Alice and the Dogcatcher*, was predominantly live action in the manner of the popular *Our Gang* comedies that featured neighborhood kids in funny adventures. The animation scenes are incidentally dropped into the short; they appear with no transitional event such as Alice going to sleep or being hit on the head, and there seems to be no particular reason for them being in the short. In contrast the next (and subsequent) cartoons included more animation sequences and by the end of 1924 with the release of *Alice and the Three Bears*, the live action framing scenes were no longer used and the cartoons opened with Alice as just another character in Cartoonland. Over time Alice's role became limited to introductory sequences and generic actions such as clapping and jumping up and down that could be inserted almost anywhere into the cartoon.

Iwerks added more to the studio than excellent drawing skills and an eye for a gag. He had an abiding interest in improving the technology required to make animations and, as when he had developed the "biff-sniff" at *Laugh-O-Grams*, his ideas helped the animators with daily production issues. Before he arrived at the studio, the animators hand-cranked the camera when they were shooting the individual frames for the animation. Ub made a motor-drive for moving the film forward that was operated by pressing a telegraph key—a simple device that saved labor and time. He also worked with Walt to improve the appearance of the live action animation. Alice was normally filmed against a white background. The film was then run in the studio and, frame by frame, Walt would animate cartoons in the white spaces around Alice. He would then shoot the animations and combine the two films in the development process so Alice and her cartoon friends appeared in the same place. Ub and Walt worked on a system in which a matte, or cutout of the areas where the cartoons were to appear, was placed on the camera lens to make Alice "stand out plain and distinct when she is acting with the cartoons" (Gabler 2006, p. 86). Walt continued to make improvements in the equipment they used by purchasing such items as a new tripod to keep the camera steady and a motor drive for the animation camera to sharpen the image of the cartoons.

Even though Walt wanted his animations to "be a little different from the usual run of slap stick and hold them more to a dignified line of comedy," (Thomas, Walt Disney, An American Original 1976) Winkler instructed him to "inject as much humor as you possibly can" (p. 84). The potential for Walt to build character and improve story gave way to broad gags in the face of this instruction. Walt says at a later date, "In the very early days of making pictures it was a fight to survive.... I used to throw gags and things in because I was desperate" (Barrier 2007, p. 42). Making an animation every 2 weeks meant that there was little time to develop even good jokes—the artists drew them as fast as they thought of them, and borrowed heavily from other cartoons they saw. One character that began to take the lead in the action was the cat Julius.[5] Winkler had suggested that the cat that appeared in *Alice's Spooky Adventure* be included as a recurring character. As the live action was reduced in the shorts and the cartoon action increased, the cat did appear more often and eventually morphed into Julius, who, like the cat in the *Laugh-O-Grams* fairy tales, increasingly instigates and is the hero of the action. His character, although thinly developed, is shown to be resourceful and often ingenious in the inspired ideas he has for helping out in situations. Julius's personality was also a function of his look and movement. Ub Iwerks method of drawing animations was more fluid than that of other animators who would draw key poses with "inbetweeners" filling in the movements between the main action. Iwerks preferred to draw all of the poses himself. This method created a fluid motion from one action to the next that, in these early cartoons, was noticeable. Julius and the other characters drawn by Iwerks had a full range of motion that was smooth and not jerky. Because this way of creating an animated figure occupied a senior animator with what Walt considered less important work, it became a point of dissension between Ub and Walt in the future.

---

[5] Ub Iwerks made Julius the cat resourceful and inventive. Julius the cat: https://disney.fandom.com/wiki/Julius_the_Cat

As the number of cartoons Disney Bros. was required to deliver increased to one every 3 weeks, and then under their contract for 1925, one every 2 weeks, the animation got sketchier and the jokes and gags more repetitious. Some of the cartoons were not as well thought out or drawn as some of the *Laugh-O-Grams* such as *Puss in Boots.* The grind of business took a toll on the quality and the type of improvement Walt had expressed he would like to see in his animations, both in the technique and in the story.

To keep up, Walt hired more staff, including some from the *Laugh-O-Grams* days. Developing the cartoon ideas was a group effort. Walt would get everyone together and toss out an idea about what could happen to Alice in the next episode, then, they'd all brainstorm gags. Walt would take the gags and work out a cause and effect sequence that had a semblance of story. In most animations of the time gags simply piled up without any story sequence; in many *Alice's* this was also the case. Some shorts, however, such as *Alice the Jail Bird*, are not only packed with gags, but have a recognizable story as well.

The gags in *Alice the Jail Bird* are some of the most innovative in the series. From the first gag that sets the story in motion, the gags are mostly contextual and move the action forward. Alice and Julius, as they are riding along on the back of a turtle, see a pie in the window of a three-story tenement building. The turtle obligingly stretches his neck up to the window for them and they steal the pie. This is followed by an elaborate chase sequence before they end up in jail. The gags come fast and furious.

To escape from the jail yard Julius uses his tail as a crane to lift his prison ball.[6] He then convinces an ostrich to peck off the chain and give him a lift up over the wall on its extended neck. The guards shoot madly; Julius grabs a smoke ring from one of the gunshots and uses it to float down to the ground. He meets a prickly cactus on the way down and keeps himself from harm by flapping his arms and flying. In a brilliant thought, he extends his tail into a ladder and picks up Alice to successfully break her out of jail as well. The cause and effect of the story are carried from the beginning, in which the scene is set for future action, through to an action-packed series of gags, and conclude with a satisfying ending.

The animation credits show that by the sixth cartoon, released in August 1924, Walt had stopped doing animation drawings. He had moved into the role he would keep from then on: he directed the animation done by others and "devoted" more time to the story. Walt's concern for having detailed scenarios and his interest in directing the filming of the animation closely came from his Film Ad days and was fostered throughout the *Laugh-O-Grams* years. He would write out a scenario that he had typed up and would provide a visual guide for the animators by making rough sketches of key positions of the live action and animated characters. The animated characters were often reproduced in three sizes to help provide consistency. While each animator would write below his drawings how often to repeat a cycle,

---

[6] Julius makes his tail into a ladder for Alice to use in her escape from jail. *Alice the Jail Bird:* http://www.youtube.com/watch?v=GfVcjDfkdTY.

whoever was doing the filming might decide that a scene looked better with a different number of repetitions. Walt began to make these decisions and provided exposure sheets to the camera operator with explicit instructions on how each animation was to be shot. He would time the action then make suggestions for the number of repetitions.

The quality of the animation for the *Alice* series varied and did not reach the more realistic movement achieved by competing animators such as Max Fleischer in his animation of *Koko*. Fleischer was using a Rotoscope technique in which he traced over live action footage as the base for his drawings, something Disney animators did not do extensively until *Snow White and the Seven Dwarfs* in the late 1930s. Ub Iwerks talent and animation approach had helped improve both the quality of the drawings and the gags and as the studio's animators became more experienced and skilled, Walt's cartoons became successful enough to command some attention. *Motion Picture World* would say, "Each one of these Walt Disney cartoons... appears to be more imaginative and clever than the preceding [one]" (Thomas, Walt Disney, An American Original 1976).

The drawing, the animation, and the character development and storyline all improved over time. While there were both successes and failures (*Jail Bird* being a success and *Hunting in Africa* a failure), Walt felt that the series was "in a rut in regard to the [style] and general construction of our plots and gags" (Gabler 2006, p. 101). Through the process he had discovered that the stories with complicated plots were less successful than those that were gag heavy, but that a storyline was necessary to keep the action moving and the audience interested. Even with some new ideas for revitalizing the series, *Alice* began to suffer from ennui and started to "lose steam." Work on the last cartoon of the series, *Alice in the Big League*, began in March and was previewed in Los Angeles on July 16, 1927.

## 3.3   Creating a Character with Personality

Long before the final *Alice*, a change to a new character and new series was instigated by the series' distributor Charles Mintz, Winkler's husband. Mintz had been approached by Universal Studios to produce a new animated cartoon with a rabbit as the main character. The first iteration of *Oswald the Lucky Rabbit* by Disney's animators was unacceptable to Universal: they wanted an elegant rabbit not one that was "elongated with a heavy torso, short legs and oversized feet." They also asked for a real story not a string of gags.

Walt took advantage of Universal's directive as he had always leaned towards stories while Winkler and Mintz had always pushed him for more gags. When defending the first Oswald being gag heavy, he explained to Universal that it was difficult to integrate a story with the continuous need for gags to keep the laughs coming; the cartoons they had produced which were most poorly received were the ones with the most traditional story structures. They had yet to successfully achieve both continuous laughs and a real story.

With Oswald, Walt wanted to create a distinctive personality.[7] He felt that an animated character's personality should be recognizable and that gags should grow out of that personality rather than just be pasted on him, "(Thomas, Walt Disney, the art of Animation, The story of the Disney Studio contribution to a new art., 1958). With Universal's directive, Walt had the opportunity to create a character with personality. To help achieve this, Oswald was drawn with more attention to reflecting what he was feeling in a situation. The animation was sufficiently reflective of expression that the trade publications commented on the improvements Walt had made in animating a character that could "simulate the gestures and expressions of human beings."

Oswald was also drawn to have more flexibility as a cartoon figure. Whereas Julius was a flat black shape that occasionally inventively used his body, as with the tail-into-ladder transformation noted earlier, Oswald was more pliable and his body could be stretched and contorted by the animators to create a whole new range of gags. Oswald became the "industry standard" for many of the animators of the day. To improve the story Walt wrote more detailed scenarios for *Oswald* than he had for *Alice* and often attached sketches that showed the main action. These are forbearers of the storyboards that he would use later to work out scenes and story sequences. Walt had a talent for using gags to help the story along with more than laughs: he would give the gags some context in the situation and make them a part of the story sequence.

In *Oh What a Knight*, the twenty-first of the animations, Oswald is a knight who goes to rescue his maiden fair from a tower in which her father, a formidable knight clad in armor, is keeping her.[8] Oswald takes on the swashbuckling characteristics of Douglas Fairbanks in the film *Robin Hood* and prevails against the evil knight. In the fight scene the background replicates the cinematic technique of casting dramatic shadows on the castle walls used in the film. The happy twosome float from the tower window buoyed by the lovely maiden's skirt to live happily ever after—a satisfactory conclusion to the love story.

The *Oswald* cartoons were well-received. *Motion Picture World* wrote, "They are clearly drawn, well-executed, brimful of action and fairly abounding in humorous situations."

For Walt however, Oswald was not to be. In the next round of yearly negotiations with Charles Mintz in New York, he found that Mintz had made a move to take over Oswald himself. Mintz had secretly negotiated with many of Walt's staff to start up another studio and offered untenable conditions in the new contract. In March of 1928 Walt was left with the remainder of the Oswald cartoons to complete for the previous year's contract and no other work. During April, the last month the studio worked on *Oswald*, Ub Iwerks, tucked in behind a curtain set up in the studio so that the defecting animators wouldn't know what he was drawing, animated the first

---

[7] Oswald the Lucky Rabbit was Walt's first character with a distinctive personality and an expressive body. Photo of *Oswald:* https://disney.fandom.com/wiki/Oswald_the_Lucky_Rabbit

[8] *Oh What a Knight:* https://www.youtube.com/watch?v=zums-cxust0 shortID=87. Douglas Fairbanks' *Robin Hood* https://www.youtube.com/watch?v=Rx5QuQcUE50

*Mickey Mouse* cartoon. At the end of the *Oswald* contract, Walt's animators, except for Ben Clopton who stayed for an extra week, and Ub Iwerks who remained loyal, left to join Mintz.

## 3.4    Progress: 1923 to 1928: 57 Alice's Adventures Shorts Followed by 26 Oswald Shorts

Between 1923 and 1927 Disney Bros. produced 57 episodes of *Alice's Adventures in Cartoonland*. Walt had "cracked the market" with a new story idea that appealed to movie going audiences. By placing a real person into a cartoon world Walt was giving the audience an opportunity to identify with the experience of being in an imaginary land doing fantastic things. Walt used a frame narrative with the live action as the introductory main story that sets the stage for the cartoon. The transition from live to cartoon was usually effected by a dream sequence; Alice falls asleep because it is bedtime or she is tired or even because she gets conked on the head, as in *Alice's Spooky Adventure*, and dreams she is in a cartoon. The frame narrative offered ample opportunity to structure a story and in some shorts, such as *Alice's Day at Sea*, Walt did so. But the quality of the *Alice* shorts was erratic; often there was little story line, only a jumbled bunch of gags and events. After Ub Iwerks joined the studio and focus was back on animation, the live action frame story was no longer used. The shorts opened in *Cartoonland* and Alice became just another character. Part of the charm of the original series was in the live action scenes. Without these scenes the Alice series was a more traditional cartoon with fewer opportunities for a range of scenarios and gags that live action had provided. Whether the series would actually have attracted Margaret Winkler's attention without them is a question. Later in the series Alice was often upstaged by Julius, a recurring cat figure that had originally been her sidekick, and the first cartoon character designed by the studio that had a recognizable cartoon personality. With *Felix the Cat* already part of the cartoon scene, the *Alice* series could not be seen to infringe on his territory and so the series suffered from a lack of focus, with either Alice or Julius taking the lead in different cartoons.

Walt spoke about his desire to create a better quality more "dignified" cartoon in which he could develop a character and create a storyline; this did not happen because the distributor (Mintz) insisted on more gags. With a cartoon due every 2 weeks, it was easier to give him what he asked for. Overall (quality of drawing, continuity, gags) the shorts did improve but not significantly and not consistently. Walt wrote detailed scenarios for the shorts but this did not translate into cohesive stories so that while one short may have had excellent gags and a storyline that carried through (*Alice the Jail Bird* for instance) the next would not. The series petered out from lack of interest.

When Universal was looking to develop a new cartoon personality and approached Mintz, Walt took advantage of their directive for the cartoons to have "a real story."

Oswald's face and body were drawn expressively to reflect what he was feeling. Developing Oswald for Universal gave Walt the opportunity he had been looking for to create a distinctive cartoon personality and to create better stories. The studio made only 26 *Oswalds* before Mintz cut Walt out of the picture, but during that time, Oswald was established as a funny, feisty personality. Unlike the flat two-dimensional Julius, he was more three-dimensional with an expressive face and body. The stories, even in the first *Oswalds*, were on par with the best *Alice* shorts, while in the later *Oswalds* the stories are inventive and unfold successfully through events that fit the context of the story. More of the gags are contextual as well; they evolve from the character and the story and move the action forward as part of the storyline (as in the sword fight scene in *Oh What a Knight*). With the *Oswald* series Disney Bros. was able to achieve progress in character and story development that hadn't materialized in twice as many *Alice* shorts. The animators also arrived at a balance between storyline, plot complexity, and gags that had eluded them in *Alice*.

# Chapter 4
# Synchronizing Sound and Character

> *It's a peach of a synchronization job all the way, bright, snappy, and fitting the situation perfectly... . Recommended for all wired houses.*
>
> Variety

> *...an ingenious piece of work... . It growls, whines, squeaks and makes various other sounds that add to its mirthful quality.*
>
> New York Times

## 4.1   From Silent to Talkie

*Plane Crazy*, the debut cartoon for Walt's new character Mickey Mouse, was completed in secret by Ub Iwerks for a mid-May release.[1] With the staff defecting to Mintz still in the office finishing the last three *Oswalds* left in the contract, Iwerks worked behind closed doors during the day and late into the evening. Walt had family and friends helping him out at his garage workshop doing inking and painting but only Iwerks worked on the drawings; the lack of resources and time meant that the new cartoon was hurried through production with little time spent on development. Iwerks set himself the goal of completing 700 drawings a day. For all his skills, the animation could only be simply drawn—Mickey had a stick-finger feel—and consisted of crude gags and a story based lightly on a previous *Oswald* cartoon. The progress the studio had made in improving animation techniques and creating more original gags and storylines suffered in the move from *Oswald* to their new

---

Online photos and graphics provide extra detail and are identified by urls the reader can refer to. This additional reference information will be particularly beneficial as an enhancement for the online version of this book. URLs are current at time of printing.

---

[1] The original Mickey is a dare-devil lothario; in a short time he becomes the gallant, plucky, and optimistic fellow that endears him to everyman's heart. Mickey in *Steamboat Willie* http://www.disneyshorts.org/shorts.aspx?shortID=96. Mickey in *The Klondike Kid:* https://www.youtube.com/watch?v=m24lWIJ5sC8.

© Springer Nature Switzerland AG 2020

K. Madej, N. Lee, *Disney Stories*, https://doi.org/10.1007/978-3-030-42738-2_4

character *Mickey* in much the same way that the progress made with some of the *Laugh-O-Gram*s suffered in the change to the *Alice* cartoons.

Although *Plane Crazy* prompted some interest when Walt did the rounds of the distributors and movie houses, animations were no longer the novelty that had once drawn audiences to the theatre and he had difficulty getting interested buyers. Even so, the studio began on the second Mickey cartoon, *The Gallopin'Gaucho,* and slated it for completion in June. After a number of distribution possibilities fell through, Walt started looking for something new to generate interest, as he had when trying to sell the *Laugh-O-Grams*.

Sound had come to film during the 1920s. Two systems had been developing simultaneously since the turn of the century—sound-on-film and sound-on-disc. The first sound-on-film commercial screening was of a set of shorts by Lee de Forest on April 15, 1923. De Forest had patented a system in which the sound track was photographically recorded on to the side of the strip of motion picture film. He released the first commercial dramatic talking picture, *Love's Old Sweet Song,* in 1924. At the same time as sound-on-film technology was being developed, Warner Bros. was experimenting with the sound-on-disc system. On August 6, 1926, with the premier of *Don Juan*, they introduced their *Vitaphone* system. The film had a musical score and sound effects, but no dialogue. Although both systems had their advantages and disadvantages, sound-on-disc had the edge in early years because it was less expensive to produce and because the audio-quality was significantly better. As sound-on-film improved, these advantages disappeared and eventually it emerged as the predominant technology.

Earlier in the decade Max Fleischer had worked with unsynchronized sound in his popular "following the bouncing ball" series *Song Car-Tunes*.[2] Fleischer was interested in technological innovation and used the de Forest *Phonofilm* sound-on-film system to provide the synchronized sound for his 1926 cartoon *My Old Kentucky Home*. This is his earliest venture into synchronized dialogue—a dog mouths the words "Follow the ball and join in everyone."

When Walt heard *The Jazz Singer* (October 1927), in which Al Jolson and others sing and Jolson speaks the words "Wait a minute, wait a minute, you ain't heard nothin' yet," he turned to this new technology with enthusiasm. "It looks realistic, it'll be realistic. That's what we've got to do," said Walt. He did not think about what could or could not be done or whether the technology that existed could do what he wanted it to, he simply forged ahead with the idea of what he would like to see and broached making a sound cartoon with his staff during a gag meeting for *The Gallopin' Gaucho*. After the disappointment of being unable to sell *Plane Crazy*, everyone became energized by the possibilities of using an exciting new technology. Work on the new film, *Steamboat Willie,* began in July.[3]

---

[2] Fleischer's early use of synchronized sound show the dog in *Song Car-Tunes* instructing the audience to "follow the ball." *Song Car-Tunes*: https://www.youtube.com/watch?v=_wX1_acp53U

[3] Walt Disney's Notes: "Close up of Mickey in cabin of wheel house [sic], keeping time to last two measures of verse of *Steamboat Bill*. With gesture he starts whistling the chorus in perfect time to the music." *Steamboat Willie:* https://www.youtube.com/watch?v=BBgghnQF6E4&t=310s

Walt was not thinking of simply overlaying the film with music or musical effects, like the first experiments with sound. Instead, he planned to use sound as an integral part of the story with the characters' actions synchronized with sound effects, and with music throughout. This would be, as he had shouted when he'd seen *The Jazz Singer*, "realistic." He felt this integration "and not sound alone, would be essential to a sound cartoon's success." Walt was helped in achieving such an integration by his systematic, director-oriented approach to developing animations.

## 4.2   Inventing Sound Production

As part of his production process, Walt wrote out scenarios, made exposure sheets, and timed cartoon action. When making *Steamboat Willie,* his detailed timing of cartoon action afforded inclusion of musical notations. Walt had hired Wilfred Jackson, a recent art student, to join his staff the last week the studio was producing *Oswald.* Jackson played the harmonica and had some musical know-how that he put to use on the new sound short. He developed a method to synchronize the music together with the animation. Using a metronome he created a preliminary score that was a notation of the music Walt had in mind for a piece. For each scene, Walt wrote out in detail how the action and the music were to be combined. When the results were shown, it appeared as if the sounds came from the characters and their actions.

To see how this could work Walt set up a test when the cartoon was half finished. He ran the film in one room while in the other his staff worked from the score to produce the background music (harmonica) and sound effects (pots, pans, slide-whistle) in synchronized time to the action. The result "was terrible, but it was wonderful," he explained later. "The sound itself gave the illusion of something emanating directly from the screen," (Gabler 2006, p. 118) an exciting achievement, even if the cartoon work was not great. When *Steamboat Willie* was complete, Walt went to New York to see about the technology that would integrate the music with the animation.

In New York the studios were taking different roads and either developing, adapting, or licensing sound technologies that they believed most viable for the marketplace. Warner had a sound-on-disc system, *Vitaphone,* Fox the sound-on-film system, *Movietone,* and RCA a sound-on-film system, *Photophone.* When Walt went to see RCA's system, he was shown, *Dinner Time,* the sound Fable that Paul Terry was completing.[4] Terry was not interested in sound and the sound accompaniment was very rudimentary. There was no synchronization or thought of linking the sounds directly to the characters or events: it was a simple dubbing of music and crude sound effects as a background. Walt described it as "rotten." "I'm terribly

---

[4] Paul Terry used the RCA Photophone sound-on-film system for his first sound fable. *Dinner Time*: https://www.youtube.com/watch?v=KLi_CrxwHZM

disappointed," he wrote to Roy, "It merely had an orchestra playing and adding some noises. The talking part does not mean a thing. It doesn't even match. We sure have nothing to worry about from these quarters" (Iwerks 2001). This was an expression of the difference between him and other animated film producers. Although other cartoons being made added sound tracks to their animation, none of the other filmmakers approached the problem of sound as Walt had, with the belief that sound needed to be integrated and carefully synchronized to events.

Walt's choice for a system for *Steamboat Willie* was a factor of availability and cost. He had decided against synchronized recording discs believing that should the recorded discs slip crucial synchronization would be lost. This was not an important factor for other animators, but in the case of *Steamboat Willie* discrepancies would be more noticeable. The demonstration he saw at RCA led him to choose *Cinephone*, which was "absolutely interchangeable" with the RCA *Photophone* system, but was less expensive. The system used a projector with a sound head that read optical impulses printed on the margin of the film. Pat Powers, who owned the company, provided what seemed at the time a reasonably priced, advanced technology to work with. He also helped Walt with organizing an orchestra for the recording sessions, and later, with distribution.[5]

The main technical sound problem for Walt at the time was achieving perfect synchronization of the music with the animation. No one at the time had worked out a solution and the first recording session for *Steamboat Willie* gave Walt an expensive lesson in the difficulties he would have to overcome. Walt knew the importance of following cues in order to achieve perfect synchronization; during the recording, he showed a blank film with marks that provided the tempo for playing the music. The conductor, not accustomed to paying strict attention to a tempo provided by a moving black dot on a screen, ignored it, and predictably, the synchronization suffered. For the second session of the recording, Walt had a ball printed on the sound track as well as on the film itself, which gave the conductor both a visual and an auditory cue (a soft clack). "It worked like clockwork," said Walt of the recording sessions, proving to him that "it can be done perfectly." Walt had spent a considerable amount of extra time (and money) achieving the quality he thought was necessary in a sound film. While in the past he had often made compromises in an effort to get a cartoon out, with *Steamboat Willie*, he pushed the envelope to get sound technology doing what he wanted it to do—create a sense of reality for the animation. He believed the short would "lick them with Quality."

When he had passed through Kansas City on his way to New York, Walt had left *Plane Crazy* and *The Gallopin' Gaucho* with Carl Stalling, a colleague with whom he had worked on several song films years before, with instructions to start writing scores for them. Stalling later joined Walt in NewYork, shared his room with him, and together they finished the scores. These first two Mickey cartoons were not planned as talkies, but even though the sound tracks were superimposed after the

---

[5] Sound for *Steamboat Willie* was provided by Pat Powers' Cinephone system, less expensive than, but interchangeable with, RCA's system.

fact, Walt and Stalling had been able to add more than just noises "without any meaning," and had given the cartoons realistic synchronized sound that put them ahead of cartoons such as Terry's animated short, *Dinner Time*.

The new technology of sound in films was not yet accepted by everyone; the idea of sound cartoons was even more foreign to some—there was, after all, no precedent for animated drawings making sounds or speaking. It was still difficult to sell the idea to theatres and distributors, some of which were holding off a costly upgrade to their equipment for projecting sound as they were not at all certain whether audiences would be interested in sound films other than as a novelty. To help demystify the process not only for the audiences but also for "theatre owners, projectionists, and sound engineers," Max Fleischer made a film in 1929 for Western Electric entitled *Finding His Voice*. Two characters, "Talkie" and "Mutie," represented and explained the two strips of film, one that carried the sound and one that carried the image, that in talkies were merged to create a final film with sound.[6]

Walt had pushed Iwerks to finish the next short, *The Barn Dance,* and send it to New York so he and Stalling could complete the score. The studio had four Mickey Mouse cartoons produced with sound before Walt could convince anyone to preview *Steamboat Willie* to the public. When it finally premiered at the Colony Theatre on Broadway in November 1928, it was billed as the "first and only synchronized-sound animated cartoon comedy" (which, arguably, it wasn't). Other animators had been unable to create the feeling that the sound truly emanated from the characters and their actions as had Walt.

This accomplishment was received with enthusiasm by audiences and critics alike and the short garnered excellent reviews. *Variety* told its readers, "It's a peach of a synchronization job all the way, bright, snappy, and fitting the situation perfectly.... Recommended for all wired houses." The *New York Times* wrote, "an ingenious piece of work... . It growls, whines, squeaks and makes various other sounds that add to its mirthful quality." The short was so successful that 2 weeks after the premiere it re-opened at the largest theatre in the world, the Roxy, which had a seating capacity of 6214 and was considered "The Cathedral of the Motion Picture" (Dercle 1992).

## 4.3  Strategies to Build Character

The technical synchronization process Walt used for creating *Steamboat Willie* helped make it unique, but so did his approach to using the sound with the gags, characters, and story. When Walt was creating a new cartoon he "seemed to have the storyline for the whole picture clearly in mind, as well as the details of each piece of business, and knew exactly what he was after without any reminders" (Barrier

---

[6]"Talkie" and "Mutie" demystify sound film for the audience. *Finding His Voice*: https://www.youtube.com/watch?v=Cg6Ndh34Nxc.

2007, p. 59). From the beginning Walt saw the opportunity to use sound in two ways. He could use sound itself as a gag and in using sound in this way he added a new repertoire to the gag possibilities of animated cartoons. Besides getting a laugh out of the sound itself the animators could add to the comedic quality of the visual gag by adding sound to it. During the gag sessions the animators would not only think about how to add sound to a make a visual gag funnier but about what musical gags were possible as well.[7] In *Steamboat Willie* when Minnie is loaded onto the boat with a boathook and drops her music for the song "Turkey in the Straw," a goat eats not only the pages she drops but her guitar as well. The guitar bounces back and forth in the goat's stomach, stretching it out in funny ways while making musical sounds. The scene both looks and sounds funny. These actions and sounds give Mickey a brilliant idea. He props open the goat's mouth, Minnie cranks the goat's tail, and the goat sings the song.

This is just the first of a series of musical gags that takes advantage of the potential for parts of different animals to make sounds.

In addition to creating sound gags, Walt aimed to make sound a realistic part of the action, as it was in *The Jazz Singer,* the first sound film he saw. Rather than superimposing the music and sounds, Walt conceived them along with the characters, action, and background of the animation, and in this way used them to add reality to the environment in which the characters appeared. He developed a number of different strategies to achieve his desired effect.

Rather than attempting to represent the cacophony of sounds people are bombarded with everyday, Walt used sounds to highlight parts of the scene and denote the action to which he wanted to draw the audience's attention. He has the tugboat chimneys belch smoke as the boat paddles along, the engines make a chugging sound when the boat approaches the shore, and the winch make a winding sound when the cow is being loaded. These sounds are nested within the background music, but do not overlap each other, as they might in reality, rather they stand in isolation. Their sequential presentation also reflects the nature of the recording/filming process. In a live motion picture, the scene was recorded with the sound, while in an animation there is no sound except what is added.

While the background music creates an atmosphere by evoking a mood, the sounds create a spatial environment for the audience as well: they define what the audience can see and imply what it can't see but can hear. In the scene during which the goat is on the deck "singing" *Turkey in the Straw*, Mickey goes into the boat's kitchen where he plays the different kitchen implements and also "plays" a number of animals (this scene is visible) as accompaniment to the goat's singing (the goat is not visible). In the final scene, Mickey has been peeling potatoes and throws one which is half-peeled at a parrot that is standing on the port hole; both parrot and potato disappear and the audience hears the splash of water outside the porthole. These types of "off-stage" sounds add spatial dimension to the cartoon world.

---

[7] Both musical and visual gags were now possible: the goat sings as Minnie cranks its tail in *Steamboat Willie*. Goat, Mickey, Pete, and Minnie in *Steamboat Willie:* http://www.youtube.com/watch?v=RexXDDA8RoI.

Walt uses sounds to announce the presence of individual characters. When we first see Mickey he whistles a cheerful tune while steering a paddleboat, Peg-Leg-Pete growls as he enters stage right, and Minnie, who has to run after the boat to catch it, makes distinctive clopping sounds with her shoes. Through these types of sounds Walt also begins to create individual personalities and make the characters more real for the audience. We first see Mickey as a cheerful devil-may-care enthusiast whistling a popular catchy tune. Peg-leg is a nasty character who bullies others. Minnie is determined to reach her goal.

Walt also creates personality by using story sequences to build up an impression of the character. When Mickey sees the guitar bouncing in the goat's stomach and making musical sounds, a delighted expression appears on his face—he has discovered the goat can make music. He good-heartedly shares this discovery with Minnie. Minnie's next actions are a result of Mickey's disclosure and his enthusiasm to get her involved. By the time Walt gives Mickey dialogue in the ninth cartoon, the cartoon character already has a highly recognizable persona; Walt has made him appealing and winsome like Charlie Chaplin, ingenious and adventurous like Douglas Fairbanks, and an intrepid optimist like Walt himself.

*Mickey Mouse* "became the rage," the character that everyone talked about and wanted to see. When *The Barn Dance* opened at the Strand Theatre on Broadway, the theatre promoted it with a big cutout of Mickey positioned in the lobby. Many opportunities came along through which Walt and Roy promoted Mickey, Minnie, and their friends such as merchandising, vaudeville reviews, comics, and books. The characters quickly become a part of the popular culture, entering people's homes and adding their stories to the daily lives of both adults and children.

Subsequent cartoons the studio made continued to be lauded as "the cleverest sound shorts on the market." Other studios admired Walt's work and tried to emulate it, but because of the system he had developed for synchronization it took a year before any of his competitors could catch up. Even when they did so technically, many would never adopt his detailed approach to creating realistic personalities and environments, and would never catch up to his growing ability to pull gags together to tell a story. Walt continued to build on the strategies that he developed for *Steamboat Willie* in the *Mickey Mouse Series*, and in *Karnival Kid*, the ninth *Mickey* released June 1929, he added dialogue and Mickey spoke his first words—"Hot dog, hot dog." Mickey spoke and sang regularly from then on and the quality of his voice helped structure his personality. Walt had been dissatisfied with the first voice used; he felt it was flat and lifeless. Not able to find a voice that satisfied him, he eventually demonstrated the voice he felt Mickey should have, a slight falsetto that displayed "pathos" and was upbeat and optimistic. Walt would be Mickey's voice until the 1947 release *Mickey and the Beanstalk,* when Jimmy MacDonald, a musician and actor at the Disney studio, took over.

## 4.4  Silly Symphonies: Setting Animation to Music

Although Mickey was a hit, Walt was nevertheless nervous about having the studio dependent on only one series (his past experience with losing his characters showed him how tenuous ownership was), and he wanted to create another cartoon series for his animators to work on. While scoring the earlier Mickey shorts, Carl Stalling, ever the musician, had suggested to Walt that they create a "musical novelty." Rather than using the traditional approach of scoring to the animation, they would begin with the music and animate to the score. Thus *Skeleton Dance*, the first of a series of music-inspired cartoons Walt dubbed *The Silly Symphonies*, was born. Stalling wrote a score using Edvard Grieg's *March of the Dwarfs* as inspiration. Together with Iwerks, whose style of drawing—"smooth and regular and impersonal"—was well-suited to the precise mechanical movement of the skeleton's actions, he produced a cartoon that was "quite out of the ordinary." *Film Daily* said of it, "Here is one of the most novel cartoon subjects ever shown on a screen."[8]

Set in a graveyard the story is slight but complete. Skeletons rise with the moon, dance away the night, and return to their graves with the sunrise. The cartoon sets an eerie mood with the natural events of dusk—owls hoot, the wind whistles, bats flap their wings, and cats screech at each other. The mood sets the scene for the unnatural happenings of a dark night: skeletons rise from behind tombstones and frolic and dance, rattling their bones and using each other as musical instruments. The skeletons change shape, move in and out of the frame towards the audience, become different objects, fall all in a heap, and otherwise change at will to the fantastic sounds. With the cock's crow the skeletons panic and rush to return to their graves to the last of Grieg's score.

Walt created a total of thirteen *Silly Symphonies,* all of which foreground musical scores that created the mood for the short and to which animations were tightly synchronized. In them Walt is "unhampered by the restrictions of early sound-filming procedures.... . Disney combined sound and image in an expressive manner impossible for live action narrative cinema" (Telotte 2008, p. 30). By basing the animation concept in music rather than in a specific character, the animators could be more experimental and fantastical with the direction in which they developed the cartoon and the type of characters they created. Although there were still plenty of gags, the musical scores, with their introductions and endings, led to a cartoon that was based in a traditional story form.

Walt had also decided to ensure that all the Mickey shorts would no longer have just a general musical background but that all action would be tightly synchronized. This emphasis on creating an integration that made the sound and music appear seamlessly synchronized added to the edge Walt's cartoons had over his competition and impressed audiences who continued to flock to see them.

---

[8] Skeletons move and their bones disassemble and reassemble in clever moves that synchronize with Grieg's *March of the Dwarfs*. *Skeleton Dance*: https://www.youtube.com/watch?v=vOGhAV-84iI&t=5s

## 4.5 Commitment to Improvement

More than anything, what differentiated the Walt Disney Studios from other animation studios was Walt's belief that quality would be the source of the cartoons' success. This ethos "permeated the studio." The work had to be better than anyone else's, even if it had be redone repeatedly. This commitment to quality inspired commitment. "We all loved what we were doing and the enthusiasm got onto the screen," said Iwerks (Iwerks 2001, p. 71).

Attaining quality increased the amount of time it took to make each cartoon and Walt developed a production system that more efficiently took advantage of the talent he had available in his studio. To improve his delivery time, he divided his staff into production units that worked on three cartoons at the same time. He wanted his main animators to draw the *extremes* of the action or the *keyframes* and less experienced artists and assistants to draw the *inbetweens*.[9] This would speed up the process, in particular when there was only one senior animator, as was the case when Ub Iwerks did the drawings for *Steamboat Willie*. Iwerks had a prodigious drawing ability and had a preference for doing all the drawings himself, even once the studio had grown to accommodate a significant staff and was working on multiple cartoons at the same time. As Walt wanted to streamline production to ensure the studio was able to work on and deliver more than one cartoon at a time, this approach eventually caused some friction in the studio.

Because of the system of adding music to the shorts Walt (and Jackson) had devised for *Steamboat Willie*, it wasn't necessary to complete an animation before they began to record music for it. As for *Willie*, the drawings and music for both the sound *Mickey Mouse* cartoons and the *Silly Symphonies* were synchronized first on paper—the animator's exposure sheet and the music bar sheet were closely aligned so that the two could easily be synchronized in the finished film.

The tight control required for synchronization as well as the changing fortunes of the studio increased the need of the studio for the skills of a director and strengthened Walt's own position in this role. When the studio was producing *The Barn Dance* Walt was in New York and unable to direct the progress of the animation except on the telephone; the resulting cartoon was not up to his expectations. He learned from this experience that to get what he wanted in a cartoon he needed to provide constant direction and he ensured from then on that he had more control of all aspects of production. When he had to go to New York for another trip, he left 7 pages of single-spaced details that described the scenario for *Skeleton Dance* he wanted the studio to follow.

---

[9] In his book *Animated Cartoons* E.G. Lutz shows how keyframes and inbetweens are drawn. Initially animators drew all the frames for a sequence. As production techniques changed to accommodate producing longer, more complex cartoons and produce them faster, a division of labor evolved which had senior animators drawing the keyframes and junior animators drawing the inbetweens. Photo keyframe in *Animated Cartoons* (Lutz 1998, p. 125).

## 4.6  Sound and Character

While successful in bringing synchronized sound to cartoons, in many ways *Steamboat Willie* was a regression to some of the *Alice* days when the studio had been pressured to turn out cartoons quickly and there was little time to do other then think up gags and animate them. In *Steamboat Willie* the gags were only loosely strung together in a storyline and the animation drawings of *Mickey* were much cruder than of *Oswald*—the mouse was little more than a stick figure. *Steamboat Willie* was a breakthrough film not because of its gags or animation but because it combined sound and pictures in a way no one had ever seen before. Its success however, would allow Walt to move forward in using sound to develop characters with personality and storylines that captivated audiences. And in *Steamboat Willie,* Walt had in fact already begun to use sound to develop personality. The method he used was to make the sound realistic—to integrate sound to movement and to make it contextual to the situation. For Walt, if the sound did not give the "illusion" of coming directly from the screen, it was "merely adding noise." He used the background music to create atmosphere and set the scene and individual sounds to highlight actions. Individual sounds also added definition to and established a character's personality. By making sounds "realistic" Walt created situations the audience could recognize as "real" and characters that the audience could readily identify and even empathize with. Such identification would over time create the affinity the public had for Mickey and make this cartoon character as "real" a personality as any actor of the day.

# Chapter 5
# Drawing and Color: The Language of Realism

*You're going to develop more; you're getting hold of your medium.*

Charlie Chaplin 1931

## 5.1 Pencil Tests and Overlapping Action

When Walt's studio first used sound in the *Mickey* cartoons and in the *Silly Symphonies* most of the animators' time was spent on figuring out the basic synchronization between sound and movement and improving it, less attention was paid to the details of animation and story. For Walt there was always the need to push forward and with the increased success of their sound cartoons the Disney studio turned its attention again to its animation production and drawing techniques and how these could improve how they created the storyline and the character development.

One difficulty Walt and his animators had was knowing whether the way a sequence was being animated was really effective. To know if the action was what they wanted, or if indeed they'd made a mistake of some kind, they would have to wait until the cartoon was filmed and then, an entire sequence might have to be redrawn, inked, and colored. The animators felt they needed an interim stage: they photographed the key poses as drawings and when they had enough for a sequence they developed the film and made it into a loop. These loops, or "pencil tests" as they were called, were previewed on a Moviola, a small projector with a tiny four-inch screen that Walt had first used on his *Steamboat Willie* trip to New York. Later, he had a small room built that became known as the "sweatbox" in which he and his

Online photos and graphics provide extra detail and are identified by urls the reader can refer to. This additional reference information will be particularly beneficial as an enhancement for the online version of this book. URLs are current at time of printing.

© Springer Nature Switzerland AG 2020
K. Madej, N. Lee, *Disney Stories*, https://doi.org/10.1007/978-3-030-42738-2_5

animators would huddle watching the latest tests.[1] Walt and the staff would analyze drawings to find ways to make scenes funnier, run more smoothly, or fit the story more effectively, and make characters move in ways that changed the tone of their personality. The scenes would be drawn and redrawn to make them "the best that we can do." Pencil tests became an effective and timesaving way to see if new ideas worked and caught mistakes.[2] If, for instance, it were part of a cycle, a mistake would be repeated to the annoyance of the audience. Soon the animators began to string the scenes together into longer sequences and eventually they were able to preview the entire cartoon as a pencil test before the lengthy work of clean up, inking, and painting on cels began.

Studying and analyzing their drawings closely in pencil tests led the animators to try new things—they began to think about character movement and to draw it in a way that changed the nature of animation itself. Until that time, cartoon character movement was based on poses—the action all started and ended at the same time. The animator would have a character turn his head or move his arms or legs while the rest of him would just be there. Characters drawn like this had a static feel—they looked like drawings. Disney's animators began to start each new action before the previous one was completed, as happens in real life. This smoothed "overlapping action" made the characters movements appear to flow more and gave them a sense of realism. One of the first cartoons that demonstrated a flow of action was *Frolicking Fish* (June 1930), animated by Norm Ferguson. Walt encouraged his other animators to follow Ferguson's fluid style and his use of "moving holds," a sequence in which, although the character has stopped, some small part keeps moving and creates an illusion that the character is alive.[3]

This was a shift from the more rigid, posed drawings that were a standard set by Ub Iwerks in earlier cartoons and which had allowed the studio to so successfully integrate sound to movement. Ub had left the studio in early 1930. Without his influence in drawing technique, with synchronization of sound now well understood, and with the use of musical themes not set characters as the starting point for the *Silly Symphonies*, the animators had more freedom to experiment with new ideas for developing characters and movement. Walt expected his animators to explore the different dimensions of animation whether in music, drawings, or storyline. He improved the studios production capability and ability to output better work by

---

[1] The Moviola gave Walt and his animators a tool to test the action of their gags and scenes. Walt had a small room built in the Hyperion Studio that became known as the "SweatBox" where he set up the Moviola. The hours spent looking at "pencil tests" led to changes in how the animators approached their drawing and, in the long run, the nature of animation itself.

[2] Pencil tests provided a preview of action that could then be corrected to achieve the desired effect before the expense of inking. Photos of pencil test in *The Three Fairies:* http://www.penciltestdepot.com/2011/06/three-fairies-frank-thomas-ollie

[3] All parts of a body move at different times and speeds. When the action of a character's arms, legs, hair, clothing, etc., overlap, the animation appears more fluid and realistic. Ferguson's "moving hands" in *Frolicking Fish*—Barrier, Michael. *The Animated Man: A Life of Walt Disney.* p. 81. Also called "overlapping action"—Gabler, Neal. *Walt Disney: The Triumph of the American Imagination.* p. 170.

adding inbetweeners and assistants. This gave experienced animators more time to work on key drawings and increased the speed of their drawing while maintaining style and quality. It also provided time for experimentation, even though, occasionally, the inexperience of "apprentice inbetweeners" left animators with little choice but to do much of the work themselves. The end result was that everyone's drawing skills increased. To further improve the animators' drawing technique, Walt organized drawing classes, first at the Choinard Art Institute and then at the studio with one of the Choinard teachers, Don Graham, conducting the twice-weekly sessions.

## 5.2   Gags to Story

From early days on Walt had regularly organized "gag" meetings at the start of a new cartoon. At these sessions the guys would sometimes just start throwing around gags and Walt would later string them together into some kind of story sequence; or sometimes Walt would come with an idea for a scene and everyone would contribute gags based on the idea. He would say, "what gags can we think of?" and everyone chipped in. As the studio grew, these gag sessions changed. During the meetings, which he called "round tables," Walt would provide a detailed synopsis of the story idea he had in mind, often he would act out part of it, then everyone was expected to add to the gags. When the studio was more regularly producing stories (not just gag events) Walt would often act out the story in its entirety.

Walt also took to sending his staff memos before the meeting outlining a plot and encouraging them to submit their gags as drawings. He offered "consultation" prizes and kept track both of the gags suggested and those used. His consultation prize sheet from *The Mad Doctor*, with a total of US\$ 22.50 spent, has 11 people suggesting gags. More money was offered for gags that were actually used so that on *The Mad Doctor* Louie Schmitt earned a dollar for a gag that wasn't used while Harry Reeves earned US\$ 2.50 each for three gags that were used. One of these was "MICKEY ON OPERATING TABLE—WHIRLING KNIVES ABOVE" (Tieman 2007, p. 9).[4]

Although he felt responsible for the stories as a director, Walt began to ask his animators, first Ub Iwerks and Burt Gillett (a well-established animator whom he had brought to Los Angeles from New York early in 1929) to act as directors as well. In this new role they would provide the other animators with the layout drawings for the different scenes and, as Walt had done for earlier cartoons, have the musicians match the bar sheets for the music with the exposure sheets for the animation.

Early on the studio couldn't afford to have anyone devoted fulltime to writing; while experienced animators such as Iwerks created the gags, Walt worked on the

---

[4] Walt offered prizes for suggestions for gags as incentive to his staff; he called these "Consultation Prizes." Photo of consultation prize: *The Mickey Mouse Treasury* (Tieman 2007, p. 9)

continuity. As the animators became more interested in story continuity because of the close analysis they did of their pencil tests, the studio's approach to story changed. In March 1931 Walt hired his first writer/story man, Ted Sears. Later that year he also hired Webb Smith to the staff as a storyman. Walt himself outlined a plot for *The Barnyard Broadcast*[5] on July 20, 1931. Even with these efforts towards acknowledging the importance of story to the success of the cartoons, it still took many years before the *Mickey* cartoons were consistently based in a story; for a long time the stories were still created around gags rather than vice versa.

---

Part of a plot outline by Walt for The Barnyard Broadcast, July 20, 1931. (Thomas, Walt Disney, An American Original, 1976)

Story to be built around a Barnyard Broadcasting Idea. Action will center on the efforts of Mickey and his gang trying to broadcast. Probably work in piano playing, quartet in goofy numbers, the Swiss Yodelers. Mickey could do a solo number on his banjo and Minnie could play a solo on the harp. The barnyard birds come in and sing, whistle and chirp while Minnie is playing the harp. Possible to use the same little canary singing all through the broadcast or the use of the little barn swallows instead.

---

The same is true of the *Silly Symphonies* in which characters dance and move to music. In August 1930 the studio released *Midnight in a Toyshop*, which, more so than the shorts released previously, had a strong storyline.[6] In the beginning of the story a spider hangs from a toyshop sign while a ferocious storm whips around it. Blown from his web, the spider escapes the storm by going through the keyhole into the closed toyshop. Inside, the spider encounters different toys, some of which give it a fright and others that it finds intriguing and plays with. One event in particular provides a new type of continuity that had not been used previously by the animators. The spider finds itself in the dark and lights a candle; a box of fireworks is behind it and there is potential for a firework's gag right at that moment. But the opportunity is not used until the end of the cartoon when the spider is on a turntable and is sent flying into the air. It catches onto a candle to stop itself, the action upends the candle that is standing on the corner of the box of fireworks, and the candle lights the fireworks. They explode and chase the spider out of the store back out into the cold storm. The animators have cleverly planted clues to future action in the scene and created cause and effect sequences that they have encompassed in a traditional story form of introduction, climax, and denouement. The studio would continue to add to its repertoire of story techniques in subsequent shorts in their goal to make all of their cartoons successful stories.

---

[5] *The Barnyard Broadcast*: https://www.youtube.com/watch?v=fjPQUZP1P2E

[6] In *Midnight in a Toyshop* a spider comes in out of the cold only to be blown back out into it by some fireworks it accidently sets alight. *Midnight in a Toy Shop*: https://www.youtube.com/watch?v=QZuxWnX5ido.

## 5.3   Introducing Color

In 1931 Walt signed a distribution contract with United Artists, one of whose partners was Charlie Chaplin. Walt was a great fan of Chaplin's comedies and in many
ways modeled Mickey's actions after Chaplin's. It turned out that Chaplin was an
equally great fan of Disney cartoons and offered Walt advice "... to protect your
independence, you've got to do as I have done, own every picture you make"
(Thomas, Walt Disney, An American Original, 1976). Walt did not want to work for
anyone, not since the *Alice* days when he was associated with Mintz. He had financial struggles with Pat Powers and then with Columbia Studios, which had brought
him around to thinking in the same way Chaplin did. He wanted freedom and independence in his work. During negotiations United Artists offered to sell his cartoons
individually, not packaged with other films or cartoons. Their offer gave the studio
both independence and greater financial stability than he had known previously.
Walt's immediate response to the deal, as it always was with a new influx of cash,
was to set upon making improvements in his animations. The *Silly Symphonies* were
not as popular with audiences as the *Mickey Mouse* cartoons had become and United
Artists only agreed to take them on with the billing, *Mickey Mouse presents a Walt
Disney Silly Symphony*. Walt was looking for a way to make them equally successful. The studio had been discussing the new technology of color that was buzzing
around the film world but as the technology was expensive and not yet proven, it
would be a risky undertaking. Walt believed it would add new creativity and entertainment value and he became determined, whatever the cost, to add color to his
musical "novelties."

Use of color was in its infancy but was used more often in animations before the
1930s than is often cited. As with sound, processes were experimental, expensive
both in cost and in time to process, and progress in development was slowed by the
Depression and lack of financial resources for experimentation. The first color animation, *In Golliwog Land* (1912), was a British production and was a mixture of
live action and puppet animation. A story about the misadventures of a favorite
British comic toy character, the Golliwog, it was later released in the United States
as *Golliwog's Motor Accident.* The film was made in Brighton, England by Martin
Thornton using *Kinemacolor*, an additive two-color process. Black and white film
was used to photograph and project images through alternating red and green filters.
Two frames were filmed at the same time and then projected at the same time; align-
ment of images was difficult to achieve in projection and required constant attention. When the red and green images did not match up perfectly, which was often,
there was a halo effect around figures in the film. As well, because light was being
projected through a filter, the picture was generally dimmer than the black and
whites of the era. In the U.S. the first color animation was made by Earl Hurd for
Bray Picture Corporation in 1920. *The Debut of Thomas Cat*, a story of a kitten that
must deal with a rat when it is accustomed only to chasing mice, was made using
*Brewster Color*, a subtractive process. Subtractive color was experimented with by
a number of film companies including Technicolor, who began making color film in

1916. By 1922 Technicolor had developed a process based on two filmstrips, one exposed behind a green filter, and one exposed behind a red filter, that were glued together and could be projected at one time; this process dealt successfully with problems such as haloing. *Technicolor Process 2* was successfully used commercially, but because of the production cost of the film (three times the cost of black and white) and because of projection problems (the two film strips would sometimes separate), the company continued to experiment with alternatives. In 1928 they developed *Technicolor Process 3*, a two-color dye transfer method that eliminated the need to cement two separate films. The new process had problems with graininess but proved a popular, if still very expensive, means of producing color films.

It was when Technicolor developed a way to record all three primary colors and provided a brighter, truer color, that Walt became interested in their process. His technicians had been experimenting with adding color to films but had achieved little success. He had written to color laboratories searching for a solution that would add to the popularity of his cartoons rather than add problems. When he learned about Technicolor's breakthrough, he felt the truer color they now offered would add to the realism that he was ultimately aiming for in his animations.

The new process required three times the amount of film and significantly more lighting to shoot than did regular film. During the early thirties, the days of the depression, studios found the costs prohibitively expensive. Technicolor was as interested in working with Walt to produce one of his cartoons with their *Technicolor Process 4* as he was in using it. Walt worked out a deal which saw Disney Studios produce thirteen *Silly Symphonies* in exchange for exclusive use of the three-color Technicolor process for 2 years, sufficient time for Walt to build a significant lead ahead of other studios and recoup some of the costs of the experiment.

## 5.4   The Language of Color

When the Disney Studio embraced the experimental innovation of sound and was successful with *Steamboat Willie* and subsequent shorts, its name had become synonymous with technological advancement. New advances were expected of it, both by others and by Walt himself. Roy wrote of Walt at the time that he was, "continually (without letup in the least) always strives for something that has not been done before" (Gabler 179). Even though color was being used in film, Walt did not want to adopt it as a novelty to increase sales. He believed animation was more than mere movement, that it should be an "illusion of life" and he had pushed his animators towards realism in their black and white animation. Walt was keen on his animators understanding the principals of drawing, of movement, of character development, and of writing as he believed that an understanding of these different aspects of production would help them create better animations. The depression had brought to Walt's door many excellent artists who could not find work elsewhere and they shared their skills and techniques with others in the studio. The animators recognized that the approach at the studio—the higher expectations, the drawing classes, the wholistic approach, the sharing of skills and camaraderie—was different from that at other studios. There was a feeling they were creating something new and every advancement aimed at a better product for the audience.

Walt chose as his first color short a *Silly Symphony* that was already in production in black and white—*Flowers and Trees*.[7] The story is about two young trees that fall in love. A gnarled old tree stump is jealous of the young lovers and with malicious glee intends to destroy them by setting the woods on fire. Flames advance on flowers, trees, animals, and birds, causing destruction everywhere. In a concerted effort a flock of birds dive bombs a cloud and the resulting rain puts out the fire, but not before the old tree is caught in it and destroyed. All the woodland flora and fauna celebrate the re-emergence of life with a wedding for the two young trees. The score includes music from Chopin, Schubert, Rossini, Beethoven, and other composers, and ends with Mendelssohn's "Wedding March."

*Flowers and Trees* was not originally designed for color. As with *Plane Crazy* and *Gallopin' Gaucho*, silent cartoons to which Walt had added sound but in which it couldn't be optimized, there was a limitation to what the animators could do with the color in an animation planned in black and white. Even so, the level of realism jumped to a new high with the change to color. Walt had envisioned the power that color had to enhance his narratives and his animators experimented with how to create atmosphere that was right for a character or a scene. The colors used are all part of the natural world that the animators were presenting to the audience. At the start of the short the flowers appear in cheerful yellow and white, brown mushrooms pop out of the ground, a bright orange caterpillar lopes down a flower, red breasted robins spread their song, and the young trees display trunks in a range of browns and sport green "hair." The colors used to represent the young girl-tree are a spring-like tone; in contrast, the old stump is a dark grey. When the fire springs up, a smouldering black is left wherever it touches. When the fire is tamed and the old tree vanquished, color returns to the woods. As when sound was introduced 4 years earlier, this first attempt at using color added more than novelty to the animation: the artists added dimension to the characters and to the atmosphere and mood of the story. They used color to evoke the "personalities of the different" woodland characters, whether flora or fauna, and aimed at directing and heightening the response the audience had to each character. They directed the mood of the story by manipulating colors for the different events and the transitions between events.

Released in July 1932 and premiering at Grauman's Chinese Theatre in Hollywood, *Flowers and Trees* was the success Walt had hoped for, if not anticipated. The story, with its evocative use of the new technology of color, appealed to audiences and the short received as many bookings as even the most popular *Mickey Mouse* cartoons. It was also a critical success and won the Academy Award that year for

---

[7] *Flowers and Trees* is a love story that uses color to present mood and add to character. Photo of poster *Flowers and Trees*: http://en.wikipedia.org/wiki/Flowers_and_Trees. *Flowers and Trees*: http://www.youtube.com/watch?v=bEaW0NX7rvc.

best short subject. Walt determined all future *Silly Symphonies* would be produced in color.

Each subsequent short improved on this first attempt to use color as a language. In *Babes in the Woods*, a retelling of the Hansel and Gretel story released later that year, the animators showed a greater sensitivity to the use of color as a way of engaging the audience's emotions. Here the scene opens on a richly colored meadow scene complete with pretty flowers, flitting butterflies, and twittering birds—the setting is a cheerful riot of color, yet amidst all this color sits a large dark-grey rock signposted "Witch Rock." We are about to be told the history of the rock: two children, dressed in bright colors, walk along a sunlit path that enters a wood. The dark wood frames the warmly lit path; as the children enter further, the colors of the wood become progressively darker and greyer and exude menace. Many scary moments later, the children find their way to a meadow filled with warm sunlight and the noise of working elves who embrace them enthusiastically. A witch dressed in grey and black flies into the meadow and entices the little boy and girl with the offer of a ride on her broom. She brings them to her house that is a wonder of brightly colored candy canes, pies, and sweet treats on the outside, but a dark, dank, cave inside. Black spiders, dark green lizards, and grey rats locked up in numerous cages add to the sense of fear that the place exudes. The witch pours blue potion on the little boy that turns him into a spider; she then chains him up. She is about to change the little girl when a rock hurtles through the window and breaks the bottle. The witch pushes the little girl through a trap door into a dungeon and rushes out to fight the elves who have come to rescue the children. The little boy/spider opens the dungeon and as the little girl emerges, a bottle of green, life-giving potion spills onto the spider and returns him to a boy. The boy and girl quickly use the green potion to change the caged animals back into colorfully dressed children and they all join the elves in fighting the witch. During the fight they drop her into her own cauldron which is filled with a gold potion that changes things into stone; as she attempts to run away covered in the heavy liquid, she changes into the grey rock which we see in the midst of the meadow at the beginning of the story. The bright, cheerfully colored flowers of the meadow entwine and triumph over the dark grey wickedness of the witch.[8]

Walt's animators develop a language with the color they use that creates atmosphere and sets a mood for the story. They have heightened the psychological response of the audience to different scenes by using colors affectively, that is, the color themes are used to help the audience believe the various characterizations and elicit a response by engaging their emotions. Like painters, the animators use color to express a point of view and the changing and contrasting color themes convey a message. The introductory scene, colorful and filled with life yet holds at its heart a forbidding shape and color that portends ominous events. The warm glow of the sun that streams into the woods and heralds the appearance of two children dressed in

---

[8] The dark shape in the centre of a pleasant colorful meadow foreshadows dire events. *Babes in the Wood:* http://www.youtube.com/watch?v=3VFWOHABm0s.

the bright colors of fairytale folk, denotes their wholesomeness and goodness, and invites the audience in; the dark greens, browns, grays, and blacks of the wood are somber and menacing, connote evil, and push the audience out. These dark colors are echoed in the witch's clothes and finally manifest themselves as the grim and unpleasant interior of her house in which we see her malevolent doings—children transfigured into animals and locked up in cages. The fight between the children, their friends the elves, and the witch, is set in the sunny meadow, portending victory.[9]

Color is also used to direct the focus of the audience, to move their attention into a frame, and to change the emphasis within the frame, as in the beginning of the short when the little boy and girl are beginning their walk into the woods. The entrance to the wood and the path on which the children are walking is bathed in sunlight; the edges of the picture consist of the dark and gloomy trees of the forest. The audience's collective eye is directed to the children in the sunlight in the centre of the frame.

Walt did not take color to his star Mickey until 1935 and the cartoon *The Band Concert*. Mickey's popularity was not something he wanted to tamper with and the star was already drawing a very large audience without the extra, added expense of color. In this first Mickey color cartoon the use of color is bright and unambiguous; it is stylized and uniform, less realistic and without the nuances of the impression-istic colors used in the *Silly Symphonies*. Mickey and his friends are painted in rich colors with clean black outlines, true to their black and white predecessors. This is "cartoon color" and reflects the character's personalities which are fixed and larger than life. The color is not intended to make them "real" rather it provides a diffi-dently natural appearance and makes them stand out against a landscape that is uniformly muted and against which they stand out strongly.[10]

Although Walt did not bring color to Mickey until 3 years after his first foray into color, Walt was still pushing the envelope for color films. At the time, only a small number of live action films were produced in color. The heavy cameras and exces-sive heat generated by the light needed for the three strip process made shooting live films difficult. It was easier to produce color cartoons as the cameras was stationary and although the high heat had initially caused a problem with paint on the gels cracking and peeling, Walt's technicians had developed a paint that would withstand the heat of the lights. By 1947 color was used in just twelve percent of films being produced. It was not until Eastmancolor developed a single-strip recording system in the early 1950s that use of color in films became more economical. At the time, television began to vie for film's audiences and the movie industry moved towards color as a competitive advantage. Walt continued to film all their cartoons and later their live films on color film stock even when the work was destined for black and

---

[9] Color sets the mood as the children walk out of bright sunlight into the gloomy woods and later into the witch's dark house where the children's large shadows emphasize the change. Watch the film to see both these effects.

[10] Using "cartoon color" artists painted Mickey and friends bright colors to make them stand out against a muted background. *The Band Concert:* https://www.youtube.com/watch?v=7lz9gxsgAJI

white television. Soon enough color would come to the home screen and he would be ready for the change.

## 5.5  Drawing, Color, and Story

The studio continued to develop techniques that made them more fluent in creating animated stories peopled with characters that had depth and with whom the audience could empathize.

The development of pencil tests gave animators time to consider scenes more closely and analyze what made them successful (or not). It woke them to different ways to make scenes flow more smoothly and draw characters whose personalities had more definition. In striving for realism animators moved away from rigid, posed drawings towards "moving holds" that created an illusion that the character was alive. In *The Silly Symphonies,* animators were not locked into specific characters, locations or appearances; the process of creating visual interpretations of musical pieces encouraged unusual approaches to telling stories and developing characters and provided freedom to do so.

Developing quality stories became noticeably more important at the studio: Walt sent out memos with descriptions of scenarios before "round table" meetings to encourage contextual gags, he made senior animators directors, and he hired story-men to write continuity. Although it was a long time before the shorts were consistently based in stories and not events, the animators continuously added to a repertoire of techniques they developed such as in *Midnight in a Toyshop*, in which early in the cartoon they planted visual clues that would be used in future action.

The studio's move towards color was both cautious and innovative. It did not begin to use color until the process was sufficiently evolved to provide for a quality product. The purpose of adding color was to add to the realism of the story: to create atmosphere, invoke mood, and provide a contextual background for the action. Color helped add dimension to a character, defining it (him/her) in contrast to other characters. It effectively directed the audience's point of view in a scene, both visually and emotionally. The artists learned to manipulate color to achieve characterization, engage emotions, and convey messages.

# Chapter 6
# Capturing Life in Animated Film

*I think we have made the fairy tale fashionable again.*
*That is, our own blend of theatrical mythology. The fairy*
*tale of film—created with the magic of animation—is the*
*mode equivalent of the great parables of the Middle Ages.*
*Creation is not the word. Not adaptation. Not version. We*
*can translate the ancient fairy tale into its mode equivalent*
*without losing the lovely patina and the savor of its*
*once-upon-a-time quality.*

Walt Disney

## 6.1 Creating Believable Personalities

The studio had steadily been moving towards creating characters that would invite audiences to suspend their disbelief about the reality of its animations. In *The Silly Symphonies*, unrestricted by the need to work with established characters or traditional subject matter, Walt continued his exploration of uncharted territory. He used each symphony to experiment with different animation and sound techniques and to try out new forms of storytelling.[1] While the *Skeleton Dance* exemplified Walt's perfecting the technique of applying animation to music, and *Flowers and Trees* showed the way to using color to create atmosphere, it was through characterization and storytelling that the *Silly Symphonies* became a household word. In *The Three Little Pigs*, released in 1933, Walt and his animators "put real feeling and charm in our characterization" (Barrier, Hollywood Cartoons: American Animation in its Golden Age 2003). Changing the traditional fairytale's storyline so no little pigs

---

Online photos and graphics provide extra detail and are identified by urls the reader can refer to. This additional reference information will be particularly beneficial as an enhancement for the online version of this book. URLs are current at time of printing.

---

[1] *The Silly Symphonies* experiment with different animation and sound techniques and to try out new forms of storytelling. *The Silly Symphonies, Music Land:* https://www.youtube.com/watch?v=dihJ1w48Jh0

© Springer Nature Switzerland AG 2020
K. Madej, N. Lee, *Disney Stories*, https://doi.org/10.1007/978-3-030-42738-2_6

were eaten, the studio took the three pigs and the wolf and gave them realistic appearances and a sense of life; out of their drawings they created actors who reached out, and engaged the audience emotionally by encouraging it to really feel the situation and root for the little pigs.

Walt was passionate about getting the audience emotionally involved with his characters and their story, whether a *Silly Symphony* or a *Mickey Mouse* cartoon. During a studio session of *Mickey's Mechanical Man* that was being animated at the same time as was *The Three Little Pigs*, he shouted,

> You know what's wrong with this? You don't know anything about psychology.... It's feeling. You've got to really be Minnie, you've got to be pulling for Mickey to beat that big lunkhead. You've got to hit that mat hard, you've got to stretch. (Barrier, The Animated Man, A LIfe of Walt Diseny, 2007, p. 99)

Walt was pulling animation up by its bootstraps from its origins in crude drawing and trivial unrelated gags, and making it a vital representation of human feelings and stories. He wanted not to reproduce life exactly but to create a caricature of life that people could recognize and relate to: "an exaggeration of an illusion of the actual, possible or probable" (Thomas, Walt Disney, An American Original 1976). He wrote of the three pigs that "They will be more like human characters," (Ibid). each would have a personality that was created by their rounded forms, their voices, their facial expressions, and in particular by the way they moved.[2] The animators created actors of the characters because they effectively made their movements reflect emotions, such as joy, confidence, or fear that the audience could empathize with, laugh at, love, or in the case of the wolf, hate.

Much of the pigs' and the wolf's personalities was created by the music that accompanied their actions and by the way they spoke in rhymes and/or sang. As a *Silly Symphony* the cartoon was expected to be musically based, but progress had been made in how the music was used and the cartoons became more like musicals or operettas: music was not only the background but also took on an acting role. In *The Three Little Pigs*, unlike the previously released *Symphonies* such as *Noah's Ark* in which the songs are descriptive but incidental to the story moving forward, the songs the pigs sing do help to move the story forward. This is particularly notable in the verse that Practical Pig sings in which he foretells the action that will happen in the next few scenes:

> You can play and laugh and fiddle
> Don't you think you'll make me sore
> I'll be safe and you'll be sorry
> When the wolf comes to your door

The complete song, *Who's Afraid of the Big Bad Wolf*, became a nation-wide hit during the Great Depression, and, everywhere it was heard, provided a message of hope. The approach to using songs and lyrics to support the script can be seen again in the short *The Wise Little Hen*, in which the hen sings her request for help. Using

---

[2] The two littlest pigs were appealing fellows whose faces and bodies reflected their feelings. *The Three Little Pigs:* http://www.youtube.com/watch?v=VHJ0L6DftGg.

music this way became a standard for Disney animation, particularly for its longer features. To give the animation a story that people could relate to Walt also looked for every opportunity to add meaning and depth to the narrative. In the outline he sent his staff to help with developing gags and a storyline for *The Three Little Pigs* he wrote:

> ... . Might try to stress the angle of the little pig who worked the hardest, received the reward, or some little story that would teach a moral... . This angle might be given some careful consideration, for things of this sort woven into a story give it depth and feeling. (Thomas, Walt Disney, An American Original 1976)

By providing deeper reasons for the character's actions the animation moves away from being just "a bunch of situations thrown together in any form just to allow an opportunity for action." Instead, the story tells "something interesting which leads up to a climax that will have a punch and impress an audience" (Barrier, The Animated Man, A LIfe of Walt Diseny 2007, p. 106). Later, in his quest for good story ideas, Walt would use *The Three Little Pigs* as an example of a simple story with only a few characters that nevertheless has enormous impact precisely because it is a morality tale that engages the audience through the personalities that populate it.

His instincts to create an animation based in personality and story proved right as *The Three Little Pigs* became the studio's greatest success, filling theatres across the country and touching people with its positive, upbeat message. "At last we have achieved true personality in a whole picture!" he wrote to Roy (Thomas, Walt Disney, An American Original 1976).[3]

## 6.2  The Challenge of *Snow White*

Walt knew that he wanted to move ahead and develop a more substantial project for the studio to work on. Eight-minute cartoons did not provide the right setting for the realism he aimed to achieve. Later, in looking back, he would say, "... we had gone about as far as we could in the short subject field without getting ourselves into a rut" (Gabler 2006, p. 214). By the time he was reaping success for *The Three Little Pigs*, he was already planning on a feature length animation of the fairytale *Snow White*. He saw the story as the perfect vehicle for animation. It was well known and had all the important elements he needed to work his magic: "an appealing heroine and hero; a villainess of classic proportions; the dwarfs for sympathy and comic relief; a folklore plot that touched the hearts of human beings everywhere" (Thomas, Walt Disney, An American Original 1976). He introduced the idea to his team during an inspirational two-hour storytelling session in which he acted out all of the

---

[3] Each of the characters in *The Three Little Pigs* had a personality that was strongly projected and affected the audience. Poster of *The Three Little Pigs:* Big Bad Wolf's Hut, http://kayaozkaraca-lar2.blogspot.com/

scenes for them so effectively that they would refer to this performance even in the later stages of production of the features.

Walt's vision for *Snow White* was to create an animation to compare with live action film in artistic expression and ability to engage an audience through believable actors. To achieve his vision of *Snow White* Walt's team needed to change the way his animators thought about and created animations; he wanted to strip his animators of complacency and stir up in them, old hands and new alike, an enthusiastic interest that would push them to experiment and learn. His insistence on realism and depth became a driver for breakthroughs in the technology of making animation. In the end he showed that animation could create characters and scenes as believable and engaging as in any live action film. Walt wrote in one of his memos "I honestly feel that the heart of our organization is the Story Department" (Thomas, Walt Disney, An American Original 1976). Walt put together a small group of artists and storymen to work together and by 1934 they had an outline of a plot and the main characters for *Snow White*. He believed they needed a story that had a well worked out storyline to put over their animations. The temptation of making a series of cute gags, however, was always there. This was especially true because of the gag possibilities the seven dwarfs provided—each was a funny character that could be exploited for laughs. Initially, the story leaned heavily on the dwarfs' comic scenes, but by working through the different scenes over and over again as the feature evolved, Walt came to the realization that much of the comic business that involved the dwarfs did not add to the story. As he watched and analyzed pencil tests and finished scenes, he saw that to make a feature that could compete with the best of live action film his story needed to move away from a storyline dependent on a series of great gags towards one that was a more serious reenactment of the original Grimm's Brothers fable about youth and age. As he had so often talked about, what was needed was emotional and psychological depth. Much as he was loath to give up the type of comedy that was at the heart of the animations he had been producing, it was equally important for him to create the most credible and realistic animation possible. As the work of creating a real story progressed, he dropped many funny but unnecessary pieces of business, even though the work on the scenes had been completed and it was costly to discard them. Instead, each action chosen for use in the feature built on the characters' signature behaviors and reinforced the storyline without reliance on the often-exaggerated approach used in cartoons to milk the audience for emotional effect.

The studio's first realistic animation of a human figure in a short was Persephone in *The Goddess of Spring*, released in November 1934.[4] Walt had asked for a pretty, believable girl to portray the goddess. The animators, unfamiliar with drawing realistic humans, provided a stretchy, flexible figure that had grace and rhythm but was not realistically alive. In addition, Persephone's face did not provide the range of emotions that would be necessary to show in *Snow White*.

---

[4] Persephone was a first attempt at a realistic human. The result: an elastic body and a face lacking in emotional range. These had to be overcome to achieve a more realistic look. *The Goddess of Spring:* http://www.youtube.com/watch?v=JuVRi9XzNpk&feature=related.

*Snow White's* heroine was a real girl and she needed to be portrayed realistically if she was to be believable. The animators needed more than the drawing lessons they had been taking to interpret Snow White's movements and achieve a realistic look for them. Walt hired a dancer to act out the live action in the different scenes and filmed her to get key poses for the animators to work with. Each scene was directed to achieve a feeling of innocence, sincerity, and feminine appeal. The animators scrutinized every scene and began to give as much attention to the movement of Snow White's eyes and mouth as to her other movements; this gave her a new range of emotions with which to engage the audience. Having a live action model helped the animators to keep Snow White's movements accurate and genuine and her character consistent throughout the length of the feature. They paid attention to each scene in the feature equally intensely, and worked and reworked their drawings until each character had his/her/its own persona that moved fluidly through the scenes, always *in* character, and each scene accomplished its goal without undue exaggeration.[5] Since *Flowers and Trees* Walt's animators had been working on different types of color effects and had used colors more expressively than realistically. For the later *Silly Symphonies*, and for the *Mickey* shorts when they were finally in color, the animators consistently used pure hues; the images were filled with bright, candy colors that were poster-like and very cheerful to the eye. To make *Snow White* realistic, the palette they used would have to be changed to one closer to what existed in nature. In some cases the palette consisted of the more muted colors of a forest or of the interior of a woodsy cottage, in other cases it would have darker values that could provide for the mood in the darker scenes. The technical department had 1200 colors it worked with. The film reproduction of these colors wasn't exact and the studio had a wall-sized reference chart for artists to refer to when they wanted to see how the colors they were using would reproduce in the film.

In addition to the change in color palette, realism required that the animators apply that color differently. Rather than a flat application of bright colors outlined with a clean dark line, they experimented with a more painterly approach using a chiaroscuro effect, modeling with lights and darks to create a sense of volume.[6] This created an effect of realism distinctly different from traditional animation.

Walt also wanted to achieve backgrounds that had visual depth. The animators began to work on larger paper (12.5″ × 12.5″ rather than 9.5″ × 12″) and to use it like watercolor paper, dampening it to be able to layer washes. They painted their backgrounds with tremendous attention to detail: shadows under the leaves of trees in the forest, different types of mushrooms beneath the trees, reflections in the water on the ground. Each scene became a small painted masterpiece. This attention to realistic detail needed perforce to be reflected in perspective and movement. To have figures move in a changing perspective would require constantly changing

---

[5] Snow White's features presented genuine feeling without "undue" exaggeration. Animators used painterly techniques such as chiaroscuro to model volume. See in *Snow White* Trailer: https://www.youtube.com/watch?v=IfePzXxIuvc

[6] Animators used painterly techniques such as chiaroscuro to model volume. *Snow White*: http://www.youtube.com/watch?v=K3PDHAN9ed4.

backgrounds. The studio produced *The Three Orphan Kittens* in October 1935 to show some of the effects that could be achieved and in this short there is an exceptional use of perspective for animation at the time. In one particular scene a shiny tile floor reflects the kittens movements with extraordinary clarity and delightful humor. The background in a number of the scenes is not stationary, it moves with the point of view. However, producing such effects was excessively time consuming and would very quickly become prohibitively expensive. Even if used it would not achieve the realistic depth that exists in live action and that Walt was searching for. No matter how fine the work, it was impossible to achieve the realism Walt wanted for his full-length feature with the traditional animation techniques they were using at the time.[7]

## 6.3   Multiplane Camera

Since the nineteen-twenties, animators had been looking to create depth in their backgrounds by moving away from using painted flat scenes and towards using layers of images. In 1926, German filmmaker Lotte Reiniger devised a multiplane camera to film layers of paper and glass for her 65 minute film *The Adventures of Prince Achmed*. Reiniger used cut-out silhouettes of figures that she placed on a glass plate and illuminated from below. The entire scene was moved past the camera that was in a fixed position above the plates. The film, championed by Jean Renoir, premiered at the Cannes Film festival and was a success critically and with the public. Reiniger followed it with *The Adventures of Dr. Doolittle* in 1928.

In 1934 Max Fleischer created the Stereotopical Camera or Setback. This three-dimensional system consisted of a twelve foot diameter turntable on which was placed a miniature set built to the scale of the animation. Painted animation cels were place in front of or behind objects and filmed as a stereoscopic image to create an illusion of depth. The *Popeye* short *For Better or Worse* was the first of the *Popeye* cartoons to use the process for the backgrounds. Fleischer used the process for his *Popeye, Betty Boop*, and *Classic Cartoon Series* shorts. Then in 1935, Ub Iwerks built a horizontal multiplane camera with four different levels of drawings/paintings through which the camera lens could move when scenes were being filmed. Built out of the chassis of a Chevrolet pickup truck at the cost of US$ 750, the equipment was heavy and awkward to use; one of the few animated shorts Iwerks made was *The Headless Horseman* for P. A. Powers.[8]

---

[7] Even a semblance of realistic perspective such as achieved in the short *The Three Orphan Kittens* was excessively time consuming and expensive for the studio to produce. *Three Orphan Kittens*: https://www.youtube.com/watch?v=wo8hbZkscGw

[8] German filmmaker Lotte Reiniger moved silhouettes in the multiplane camera to create the feature-length film *The Adventures of Prince Achmed*. Photo of Lotte Reiniger and multiplane camera: https://imgur.com/gallery/vkDd6. Photo of title screen for *The Adventures of Prince Achmed:* http://en.wikipedia.org/wiki/The_Adventures_of_Prince_Achmed.

Walt's animators and technicians had also started testing different ways to achieve depth. For one test they devised a horizontal process similar to the one Iwerks had developed for filming layers of action: they created a foreground that consisted of trees modeled from clay, behind it three planes of animated trees were mounted on glass plates. The different elements were placed on sawhorses that could be moved back and forth to create distance between them and provide for different focal planes. The action simulated the effect of using a camera dolly to move in and out of a live action scene. The difference between using a zoom lens and using a dolly movement is that when a camera is dollied into a scene, the movement allows you to see things the camera is moving past in perspective... there is a realistic feeling of moving through space into (or out of) the scene.

The size of the multiplane camera they needed to build was dictated by the camera optics available at the time; Walt's chief engineer Bill Garrity and his crew built a camera that was 12 feet high and could accommodate four different layers for background paintings and overlays. Each layer could be cranked up and down to move through different levels or pan sideways to simulate trucking. It took four men to operate the camera and there were often up to eight men changing the levels of the glass plates or moving them forward or backward incrementally (For Fantasia they would build a camera that could accommodate seven levels).[9]

Walt liked the results from the tests the animators made and thought the process would work for *Snow White*. After a second test of a scene that included the Dwarfs' cottage and Snow White, he decided to develop the technique using one of the *Silly Symphonies*.

## 6.4   *The Old Mill*

Walt chose *The Old Mill* on which to test his new multiplane camera before using it on *Snow White*. This was a poetic short without dialogue that was conceived to show what could be done with mood and visual imagery. Like *Flowers and Trees* before it, the studio had already begun production on the short with traditional animation when Walt decided he could use it to experiment with the multiplane and had the animators begin again.

The story of the *The Old Mill* begins quietly and serenely with the camera slowly dollying towards the mill through the leaves of bushes and a spider's web and past ducks and their young leaving the pond and waddling their way towards the mill. The camera dollies inside the mill towards a bluebird sitting on her nest with her mate feeding her worms, past mice on a ladder, then trucks past a pair of lovebirds in the window, an owl on one of the mill cogwheels, and bats hanging from the rafters.

---

[9] Disney's multiplane camera was 12 feet high with four moveable levels. It required four men to operate the camera. Walt Disney on the multiplane camera: https://www.youtube.com/watch?v=YdHTlUGN1zw.

The dollying and zooming in and out of the scene and the trucking and panning across the scenes captures and highlights details and creates an exceptional sense of three dimension and perspective. The activity of the scene, accompanied by the music, escalates as a storm moves in, and changes the mood from one of serenity to one of growing anxiety. The mill wheel is inactive and is tied down by an old rope. The main focus of panic is the bluebird sitting on her nest of eggs. The bluebirds have built their nest in one of the gaps into which fits a mill wheel cog. Now, the mother bluebird and her eggs are in a precarious position as the rope that holds the wheel slowly frays. Panic begins to take hold as the rain arrives and the wind howls fiercely against the windmill's blades. The rope breaks and the great arms of the mill begin to move. The mill wheel approaches the bluebird's nest and the mother bird cries in fear... only to be saved as the wheel rumbles over them because a cog is missing—the nest is safe. Tension mounts again as the storm rises, scenes change faster and faster, and the mood becomes frenzied until lighting strikes the mill. Spent, it tilts over on its side, blades awry.[10] Morning breaks with a glorious light, we meet again all of the animals of the night before, and newly arrived ones as the eggs in the bluebird's nest hatch. We leave the mill, moving backward along the path we arrived, dollying out past the pond, the spider's web, and back into the bushes.

*The Old Mill* was superb in its detailed approach to mood and atmosphere—it gripped the audience in the small drama of the animal's lives and the windmill's life as they are caught up in a violent storm. The animation won awards for Best Short Subjects, Cartoons as well as for Technical Achievement at the 1937 Academy Awards. That year it also won the Best Animated Film award at the Venice Film Festival.

Walt used *The Old Mill* to experiment with more than the multiplane camera for *Snow White*. The animators approached drawing different animals and birds both realistically and anthropomorphically. They tried out a variety of ways to depict water, to show it rippling and splashing, to show rain falling, and lighting flashing.[11] They explored movement in great detail, zooming towards and away from objects and scenes, going around them and through them. They tried new, complex lighting effects to create and change mood. They experimented with timing to see if they could create more drama and elicit stronger emotions by slowing down, speeding up, or abruptly stopping the character's actions. They did the same within the scenes and with scene changes. There was not a detail that was not analyzed and experimented with in order to understand it better and improve it, if possible. Without the multiplane camera the animators would not have been able to achieve an illusion of visual depth. Without experimentation on other aspects of the picture, the animators

---

[10] The multiplane camera moves through the scenery to arrive at the windmill, enters, and zooms in on the bluebird's nest. Animators experimented depicting many characteristics of water: raging and powerful, calm and picturesque. *The Old Mill:* http://www.youtube.com/watch?v=MYEmL0d0lZE.

[11] The animators experimented depicting many characteristics of water: raging and powerful, calm and picturesque. *The Old Mill:* http://www.youtube.com/watch?v=MYEmL0d0lZE

would not have been able to achieve the complexity of mood and the differently toned scenes that would be required to give *Snow White* the emotional depth of a live-feature and the ability to engage an audience intensely.

Ultimately *Snow White* would draw in the audience by giving people an opportunity to identify emotionally with the characters. It conveyed feeling by depicting characters that showed emotion through their every movement and facial expression, drawing viewers intimately into every scene, and creating an immersive experience in which they shared the emotions characters were experiencing. The audience is brought into Snow White's world and enticed to embrace the feelings of the moment: in the gentle scene by the castle well when, as the scullery maid, she sings her hopeful song *I'm Wishing* to an audience of white doves, in the frightening scene when she runs frantically from the woodsman through the dark and menacing forest, in the happy dancing scene when she smiles at Dopey's new height and sweetly accepts his dance.

The scene in the forest makes particularly effective use of the multiplane camera's ability to provide the audience two ways to participate in the action. The audience is swept up by the music and movement as it follows Snow White into the woods and as it sees what she sees and feels what she feels. But the audience is also the voyeur and watches through the woods to see her frightened escape. The dual role the audience is given—to both feel part of the action and to view it from afar—encourages the audience to share Snow White's state of mind—her fear, her panic, her aloneness—and creates an edge-of-the-seat experience.[12]

## 6.5  *Snow White's* Success

*Snow White* premiered at the Carthay Circle Theatre in Los Angeles on December 21, 1937 and instantly became a classic. *The New Republic* wrote it was "among the genuine artistic achievements of this country." The National Board of Review named it one of the outstanding pictures of the year while the New York Film Critics awarded it a special citation. A week after the premiere, Walt and the Seven Dwarfs appeared on the cover of *Time Magazine* and in February 1938 *Snow White* received an Academy Honorary Award "as a significant screen innovation which has charmed millions and pioneered a great new entertainment field."[13] By May 1939 it had grossed US$ 6.7 million in the United States and Canada at a time when average ticket prices in the United States were 23 cents, and children's admissions even less, proving to be one of the most popular films ever made enjoyed by both adults and children. It was equally popular around the world, playing in 49 countries and in 10 languages by the end of its run in 1939. The dwarfs became immediate folk heroes

---

[12] The audience's runs through the woods with Snow White, feeling her confusion and panic. *Snow White:* https://www.youtube.com/watch?v=Z4zQ1txgD94

[13] A full-size Oscar statuette and seven little ones were awarded to the film in 1938. Photo of the 1938 *Academy Award:* https://www.youtube.com/watch?v=

and, although all the songs were played on popular radio, *Heigh Ho, It's Off to Work We Go* and *Whistle While You Work* became hits. With *Snow White*, Walt Disney had achieved what he had aimed for. He had created a feature animation that was as engaging as a live action film, that created characters that were not artificial but real, that engaged audiences in a story that touched their hearts as any real life story could. What had been dubbed "Disney's Folly" at the outset had instead become an unprecedented exploration of technology and storytelling as Walt instituted a scientific approach to exploring all aspects of the animation realm.

# Chapter 7
# Learning to Navigate *Features*

> *By nature I'm an experimenter. To this day, I don't believe in sequels. I can't follow popular cycles. I have to move on to new things.*
>
> Walt Disney

Walt's next feature would come about because he was looking for a new vehicle for his favorite compatriot, Mickey. In the years leading up to *Snow White,* the *Silly Symphonies* shorts were used as testing ground for experimentation. There was no expectation from the audience that these shorts would be about the studio's stars and for the most part, stars went their separate ways (excepting appearances by Donald and Pluto). Each *Silly Symphonies* was a novelty, intended that way, and appreciated for its innovation. This can be seen in the shorts leading to *Snow White. Babes in the Wood* had used color and light to highlight and set the emotional tone of the "good" children and woodland elves in contrast to the dark and brooding colors of the "bad" witch. *The Three Little Pigs* had explored personality, both through the animation of each pig and of the wolf, and by associating music with each character. This short also used song for the first time to move the story forward by previewing the disaster that was coming to the first two Little Pigs. *The Three Kittens* had taught them what they could achieve with perspective, *The Toyshop* about how to hint of future action with clues imbedded in background settings, *The Old Mill* about depth and perspective through manipulation with the multiplane camera. *The Old Mill* had also been a practice ground for new ways to use lighting, sound, and movement to create mood and engage the audience's emotion in the story. Water effects pound our senses until, finally when the great mill wheel stops abruptly because a windmill arm has broken, a little family of birds is

---

Online photos and graphics provide extra detail and are identified by urls the reader can refer to. This additional reference information will be particularly beneficial as an enhancement for the online version of this book. URLs are current at time of printing.

© Springer Nature Switzerland AG 2020, Corrected Publication 2021
K. Madej, N. Lee, *Disney Stories*, https://doi.org/10.1007/978-3-030-42738-2_7

shown to be safe: the tension is broken, and we sigh a great sigh of relief. Each of these shorts is noted for adding to the increased knowledge about story and technology.

In the decade it had taken to make *Snow White,* the studio had released 183 shorts; many more were worked on that never made it to the theatres. Shorts—seven-minute films—were a mainstay of the motion picture industry when going to the movies was akin to attending a vaudeville show and meant settling in to watch a feature, a comedy, a newsreel, a travelogue, and perhaps more. Of the 183 shorts released throughout the 1930s, 69 were *Silly Symphonies*, 83 featured Mickey and Minnie, with various of their friends playing smaller roles in the stories. The remaining shorts featured Pluto (1930), Goofy (1932), and Donald Duck (1934) in their own series.

The series shorts, with Mickey in the lead, continued to bring storylines filled with comic business to audiences. Making shorts was of ongoing importance to the studio, both financially, and as a means to maintain and evolve the Disney Master Narrative. In the early 1930s Mickey was as important as many of the leading actors: "The Most Popular Character in Screendom" both in North America and internationally (Gabler 2006, p. 150). As it turned out, as his light began to wane at the end of the decade, the *Silly Symphonies* came to the aid of the Studio's first Star.

## 7.1   Mickey's Dilemma

When *Steamboat Willie* was released (November 18, 1928) Mickey was set on his way to stardom. Before this, two other films featuring Mickey, *Plane Crazy* and *Gallopin' Gaucho*, had already gone round the distributors and been rejected. *Plane Crazy* harked back to the animations of the early *Alice* series, with its repetitive gags, simplistic backgrounds and actions, and barely-there story line. *Gallopin' Gaucho* used similar scenes to those in the *Oswald* short *Oh What a Knight*, such as the tower scene and aspects of the sword-fighting scene. The studio was completing the last of the *Oswald* series and Ub Iwerks, as the only animator who was working on the new Mickey, had very little time for coming up with innovative storylines and creating a complex character. Another Mickey short, *The Barn Dance*, was begun while *Steamboat Willie* was in production and, as with Steamboat Willie, much of the attention was on how to add sound to the animation. The story and character development were kept simple as the innovation of adding sound kept attention on how sound could be added as gags or comic business.

In these first four shorts Mickey's personality was just beginning to form. He is an adventurer who wants his way with the ladies in *Plane Crazy,* a smoking, drinking, braggadocio who saves the lady from the bad guy in *Gallopin Gaucho*, a generally nice guy who can smile through his troubles until it all gets a bit much in *Steamboat Willie*, and a traditional guy who drives a horse and cart rather than a roadster and loses out to a competitor for Minnie's hand because he tries to be too wily on the dance floor in *Barn Dance*. A slightly disreputable character with a tendency for the crude move was perfectly acceptable in the second half of the 1920s.

Times changed and a concerned public began to see movies as contributing to the violence and loose morals of society. From 1930 onward, the Motion Picture

Production Code provided guidelines for what was acceptable and not acceptable content in films for North America. The guidelines, which became known as the Hays Code after the lawyer Will H. Hays, its creator, were set in place in 1930 but not strongly enforced until 1934. As a member of the Motion Picture Producers and Distributors Association, Walt preferred to forestall criticism and work with the code rather than oppose it. His interest in depicting family values evolved as the studio grew and he wanted to ensure that very little in his shorts was offensive. Many of the broad gags that brought laughter to audiences but might be deemed inappropriate (those for instance to do with cow udders) were modified as the studio worked towards developing shorts that relied less on slapstick and more on engaging stories. The characters in the shorts underwent a fundamental change. Mickey had been patterned a winsome scamp, after Charlie Chaplin (as Walt saw him) and as a swashbuckling adventurer, after Douglas Fairbanks (as Ub Iwerks saw him) (Gabler 2006). When Mickey first appeared on the screen his character was drawn as an unconstrained bachelor. As he became more popular in a time of cleaned-up values in Hollywood films, he was changed into "a nice fellow," (Surrell 2014). He became an all-around good guy in which characteristics from both of these forbearers, Chaplin and Fairbanks, melded to create an amiable character always prepared to try something new. On November 16, 1930, The New York Times ran the following notice in the regular article "THE CENSOR," which identified movies in contradiction of the code (Times 1930).

---

**THE CENSOR!**

ALTHOUGH there is no morality clause in the contract of Mickey Mouse, that vivacious rodent of the animated screen cartoons must lead a model life on the screen to meet the approval of censorship boards all over the world. Mickey does not drink, smoke or cut any suggestive capers. Walt Disney, his creator, must be hypercritical of his own work to avoid wounding various national dignities.

---

In making Mickey an "everyman" Walt wasn't simply creating an animated character who could pratfall his way across a scene, rather he was instilling in Mickey the psychology and emotions that would make him a personality that everyone would want to identify with and believe in. Mickey is invariably cheerful and optimistic; he's reliable but still adventurous and even a bit mischievous and scrappy; he loves and is faithful to Minnie. Above all he's a wholesome character who is pretty level headed. While Mickey was a mainstay of the studio, other characters who appeared in both the early Mickey Mouse and Silly Symphony cartoons began to enjoy a following of fans as well. If they became very popular, a series was developed around them. First Goofy, then Donald, and then Pluto appeared under their own headings during the 30s and 40s and even into the early 1950s. Figaro (the cat) who first appeared in Pinocchio, accompanied Mickey, Minnie, Donald, and Pluto (plus other characters) on a regular basis, and appeared in three of his own shorts. At the same time new characters would be tested and series created that might only last a few years, as was the case with the chipmunks Chip and Dale. With each of these characters, stories specific to their identify were written and played out.

Animators and storymen got into the spirit of each picture by analyzing the character, understanding what made the character tick, and the creating a story that displayed the feelings of that character (Walt Disney Productions 1984).

It was Donald Duck who was first a foil to Mickey and then replaced him in popularity during the 1930s and then 40s. They made 26 cartoons together between 1935 and 1942, cementing a friendship that in each short had its ups and downs. Donald was able to display the range of extreme feelings largely removed from Mickey's personality now that he was "everyman." Donald was a show off with an outsized ego. He reacted aggressively to frustration: ranting and raving, getting mad and blowing his top. When he was happy, he was exuberantly happy. His was the perfect squash and stretch body that allowed the animators to show frustration, anger, or happiness in their most exaggerated forms. In many ways he was the bad boy that Mickey could no longer be (Walt Disney Productions 1984). Audiences loved him for being audacious, for venting so vociferously, and his popularity steadily increased. While in the 1930s Mickey featured in 83 shorts and Donald in 14, in the 1940s Mickey featured in 16 and Donald in 72.

As Donald Duck began to replace Mickey as the top billing animated star in the Disney panoply, Walt wanted to boost his first star's popularity and looked around for something special to bring to audiences. Mickey's stories were based in the activities of Mickey and his friends and heavily reliant on gags and traditional cartoon storylines. There weren't many ways that Mickey could shine and counter the antics of Donald. The *Silly Symphonies*, the other main series of animated shorts the studio made throughout the 1930s, did not "pile up one comic situation on another to a smashing climax," rather they were artful explorations into animation and music that took many directions (Thomas 1958). Walt himself had a large collection of music and was always on the lookout for something new, and possibly different. It was here that he found his solution.

## 7.2   From *The Concert Feature* to *Fantasia*

When Walt heard *The Sorcerer's Apprentice*, the symphonic poem written by composer Paul Dukas, he felt he'd found the right story vehicle for Mickey's comeback. Dukas's music was based in "an ancient fairy-tale motif" made into a popular poem by Goethe in 1797 (Finch 1975). In the poem, an old wizard leaves his apprentice to clean up the spell room in his castle. Using a spell he finds in the wizard's magic book, the apprentice summons a broom to help him clean up. He cannot control the magic and the broom soon has the room flooded. In a desperate attempt to stop the magic, the apprentice resorts to chopping the broom in half. Each half rises to continue the work set at an even faster pace until the wizard returns and stops the spell. The music is dramatic; the story perfect for the adventurous mouse. It fit comfortably into a storyline common in the Mickey shorts and also fit his personality perfectly: he was an adventurer, often getting himself into a scrap from which he gets extricated (or extricates himself), and in the process learns a lesson.

The length of the music and the story that went with it made the short twice the normal length, fifteen minutes instead of the usual six or seven. Cutting the music was not possible. The solution came when Walt met the populist conductor Leopold Stokowski and they began discussing working together. Stokowski became enthused about conducting the music for the short. Out of their conversations came the idea of producing *The Concert Feature* "an anthology of music illustrated with animation" of which *The Sorcerer's Apprentice* would be one segment. Walt's enthusiasm and ambition for bringing classical music to the public in a new way, grew and took over his usual view that story was key to a successful animation. Walt wanted to create an entertainment event rather than an animated film—he was again reinventing animation.

By 1938 the film was renamed *Fantasia* and Walt had determined it would be an all-encompassing sensory experience for film goers—a delight to the eye and the ear. He wanted dimensional visuals and dimensional sound to envelop the audience. The final film consisted of eight classical compositions, each animated in its own style, and each introduced in live action scenes by music critic and composer Deems Taylor. Challenge was heaped upon challenge for the animators as Walt wanted the animations to respond to the compositions innovatively and distinctively. Each scene demanded something extraordinary: some effects that Walt wanted, such as 3D or widescreen, were not possible or too expensive. Others, such as the bubbles boiling in *The Rite of Spring* were "invented on the spot, scene by scene," (Barrier 2007, p. 147). For sound, Walt envisioned the feeling that a symphony orchestra was playing in the theatre and pushed existing sound technology to new limits to achieve this effect. New recording techniques and a surround sound system with three-channels, left, center, and right (Fantasound) were designed to place the audience in the midst of the music. Theatres had to be refitted with the new sound system in order to achieve the full effect.

For the original release of the film (November 13, 1940) Walt had leased the Broadway Theatre for a year and a half and had it specially outfitted in order to bring the film to audiences as the entertainment he had envisioned. The film was difficult to show in all its glory except in 12 theatres across the country where Walt had sound surround systems installed at great cost to the studio. The audiences reserved tickets and came from miles to see the special show, all to mixed reviews. Some thought the presentation of classical music too pretentious for an animated film, some thought the animation sequences were inappropriate for the classical music. The film became popular in larger centers but in smaller centers, without sound surround to engage and impress, it became a shadow of itself. The animation, superb as it was with each segment done in its own expressive style, did not have a satisfying storyline that "everyman" could enjoy. *Fantasia* lacked the human appeal of a *Snow White,* despite its many technological accomplishments.

Bob Thomas in his 1958 book *The Art of Animation* shared how Stokowski described what the studio achieved in visualizing the music through its explorations in animation techniques.

> In making 'Fantasia' the music suggested the mood, the coloring, the design, the speed, the character of motion of what is seen on the screen. Disney and all of us who worked with him believe that for every beautiful musical composition, there are beautiful pictures. Music by its nature is in constant motion, and this movement can suggest the mood of the picture it invokes.

While *Fantasia* received two Academy Honorary Awards for its achievements, one for advancing the use of sound in motion pictures, and another (to Stokowski) for adding visualized music as a new language for motion pictures, Walt himself felt that his vision for the film wasn't achieved. He had wanted both dimensional sound and a wide screen. He said in particular of his idea of wide screen "I had *Fantasia* set for a wide screen… But I didn't get to building my cameras or my projects because the money problem came in…. It finally went out standard [screen dimensions] with dimensional sound. I think if I'd had the money and I could have gone ahead I'd have had a really sensational show at the time" (Barrier 2007, p. 162).

What had been started as a simple vehicle to bring Mickey back to the public eye in 1937 had become a very costly experiment in pushing the limits of sound and art in animated film. In much the same way that Walt had learned an important and costly lesson about the fickleness of distributors from his dealings with the Winklers over *Oswald,* he learned an important and costly lesson about what American movie audience were prepared to accept in an animated feature when he stepped out of *SnowWhite's* limelight and pushed the limits of innovation without considering the basic premises about story and character he'd used to create his successful first feature: the audience needed an engaging story with believable characters.

## 7.3  *Pinocchio*

In 1937, when *Fantasia* was added to the studio's work load, other features were already in various stages of production and planning. *Bambi* and *Pinocchio* were in the works with production starting that fall. Preliminary work was being done on *Alice in Wonderland* and *Peter Pan.* Ideas for other features such as *Jack and the Beanstalk* with Mickey and Donald, *The Reluctant Dragon,* and *The Wind in the Willows* were floating in the air. Walt continued to encourage his animators to be innovative in their approach and pushed to add subtlety to both the story and the animation for all the films in production. Walt had had very clear cut objectives for what he considered the perfect story for *Snow White:* well-known heart-warming theme, appealing heroine, classic villainess, and some comic characters for relief. The stories Walt chose for his next animated features, however, were more complex than the Snow White fairy tale. The challenging problems this brought could have been worked out with time; instead they became obstacles as the films' much shorter deadlines, set both by Walt and the need for an ongoing supply of funds to keep the bills paid, put pressure on the studio to produce quickly. Predictably, difficulties ensued.

Work on *Bambi* had started with a formal story conference in September 1937 and the movie was already in production when the idea of making an animated feature from Carlo Collodi's novel *Pinocchio* was presented to Walt. *Bambi* had come to a standstill in December because of difficulties with the storyline and the character animations. The storyline had to be less violent but still maintain emotional depth and the deer needed to look less like "'sacks of wheat'" (Gabler 2006, p. 319). Walt embraced the idea of doing *Pinocchio* enthusiastically. He believed it would be an easier story to work with then *Bambi* and immediately made it the studio's priority.

*Pinocchio* had originally been released in serial form at the end of the 1880s and has a predominant characteristic typical of serial stories: a wandering story line with many events that often seem unrelated. The main character *Pinocchio* is not a human but a puppet, who does not know or even understand human boundaries. As a result Pinocchio is often cruel, makes poor decisions, and at the end of the series is hanged for his faults. Because of its popularity, the series was made into a book in which the events were more continuous, characters such as the Blue Haired Fairy were added to help Pinocchio, and he ends up being better and turning into a real boy. Even streamlined, the book's storyline was convoluted and an underlying cruelty in the puppet remained.

The story of the transformation of a puppet into a real boy through the act of overcoming his own personal failings appealed to Walt and he set a short deadline of Christmas 1939 for release of the movie. Once production was started, two main difficulties arose with the main character Pinocchio. The animators found that creating a physical appearance for a wooden puppet, one that would be jerked about by strings in the first scenes, but would soon need to be an appealing almost-boy, proved difficult. Directing the story around a character who the audience didn't sympathize with and who they weren't prepared to root for (as they did for Mickey) seemed impossible (Sorrell). Walt stopped work on production between February and September of 1938 because the story and his main character could not be defined to his liking (Gabler 2006). He was committed to getting the story right.

The special effects animators, who handled all of the animation except the characters, continued to push innovative ideas to new heights. Special effects were being created for *Fantasia* at the same time. For both these films animators experimented with ways to create atmosphere and the multiplane camera operators worked to achieve movement through unusual camera angles. The results in *Fantasia* pushed animation to tell visually dramatic musical stories. In *Pinocchio* they made a fantastical story believable. A studio was built to make 3D models of Jiminy Cricket, Pinocchio and other characters so the animators could turn the models to see how they would look from all sides. Scenes in which movement of complex action needed to look realistic, such as the racing wagon and coach, required live action shots that animators could follow in their drawings. Great attention to detail was paid in layout drawing that benefited the sense of lush reality of the final background paintings. The multiplane camera was used to great effect in its use of panning, zooming, and pulling back from a scene to "capture our imagination and draw us into the atmosphere of the story without a single word..." (Finch 1975).

When production on the film started again the studio had come to some decisions about its direction. First it gave Pinocchio a conscience in the form of Jiminy Cricket to help him over the rough spots when his own lack of conscience inevitably led him into bad situations. Then the animators worked on the drawings of Pinocchio from the human side rather than the puppet side, and created a successful animation of a likeable-looking boy with puppet joints. Animators were put under great pressure to complete the film and still maintain an extraordinary level of innovation. In the end the film missed the 1939 Christmas season and was not released until February 7, 1940. It received good reviews, but did not prove as popular with the public as Walt had hoped, certainly not as popular as *Snow White*. Walt was an innovator, always moving forward, never satisfied with what had been accomplished. Once something had been done he wanted to move onto the next exciting, wonderful thing. Audiences on the other hand, proved to prefer the familiar, the stories they had come to expect in watching Mickey and Minnie shorts and in seeing his first feature, *Snow White,* which had at all times considered how good the story was for the audience and used technology to tell that story, not to impress.

## 7.4 *Dumbo*

*Dumbo* released in October 1941, was Disney's 3rd film. *Bambi* was in the works and had been planned for release, other stories were in various stages of discussion. Finances were tight, other stories weren't working, and Walt needed a quick fix. The publisher of a delightful story about a little elephant who is born with extraordinarily big ears (intended as a "Roll-a-Book,"[1]) approached Walt, who thought it would make a good 30 minute cartoon that could pull the studio out of financial doldrums. Walt explained how it grew to a feature length, "'But I got developing and we got new things in there… I kept expanding and before I knew it, I had a 62 minute picture….'" (Martens 2019). In contrast to the other features in production at the time, *Dumbo* was intended to be a shorter, less complex animation, more like the cartoon shorts the animators were so accustomed to making rather than an innovative supernova. To this end, the character designs were simpler, the background paintings were less detailed and used the same watercolor technique used in *Snow White*, and the run time was only 64 minutes. While there was much less concern about complex animation effects and more about telling a heartwarming story, the effects achieved by cost savings, such as depicting people occasionally only as shadows against tent walls, added to the emotional nuances being built up in the story. Even on a strict budget, Walt believed in authenticity and went so far as to bring elephants and other animals into the studio so animators could study their movements. The film touched people's hearts and proved a great success with audi-

---

[1] There were only 2–3 copies of the Roll-a-Book and all, at this time, are lost. http://www.michael-barrier.com/Essays/DumboRollABook/DumboRollABook.html

ences. It was regarded as a return to Walt's ability to tell a good story using the traditional cartoon medium at which his animators were so accomplished. It is now seen as classic of animation. In the case of *Dumbo,* the familiar won out over experimentation, and story trumped technology.

## 7.5  *Bambi*

*Bambi,* on which the studio had started work in 1937, was finally released as Disney's 4th film in August 1942. When Walt had originally read the novel *Bambi: A Life in the Woods* (1923), he'd felt it was a story worth telling. Intended for release as the studio's 2nd feature after *Snow White* in the winter of 1939, it went through many changes and many difficulties before it was completed.

The movie tells the story of Bambi, a male deer, as he is born, through his young childhood, the unfortunate loss of his mother when she is killed by a hunter, the finding of a mate, Feline, and his growth into adulthood. He learns lessons along the way from his father and gains experience of danger from hunters. The story is told from Bambi's point of view, and the topic is quite dark. From the beginning the studio had difficulties with how to represent the death of Bambi's mother and the presence of "man the hunter" as a danger to Bambi and his loved ones. As the story continuity developed the storymen and animators created scenes and discarded them in their attempt to depict complex emotions. Working on the story and how to visualize it "'...showed us a new dimension that was possible for animation: real drama with the communication of an idea that would move the audience'" (Gabler 2006, p. 290). In 1939 the studio was only slowly gaining the experience to make the film with the sensitivity needed to bring the intensity of the story's real-life emotions to audiences. It would take many months, and eventually years, before they finally got it right enough for Walt. He explained that he didn't want to hurry the film because he "... wanted those animal characters in Bambi to be actors, not just cute things. I wanted acting on a plane with the highest acting in the finest live action pictures" (Bambi World Premiere in London, 1942).

Problems arose not only with the script but also with the animators' ability to depict animals in a life-like and believable way. Disney set *Bambi* in the animal world and didn't intend it to be overly anthropomorphized. Unlike the look of *Snow White*, which is a stylized fairytale, the goal was to achieve a naturalness with a look and feel of real animals in a natural setting (Sorrell 32). To create the right atmosphere he felt his artists needed more instruction as well as practice and brought them to forest environments to soak up the atmosphere and to work on how to represent a true forest environment in an animation. Walt had thought that his animators' experience with drawing animals in *Snow White* would have prepared them for doing so in *Bambi*. Instead when he took a second look at *Snow White* he decided all the deer looked like "... big flour sacks" (Hill 2017). In his usual quest for excellence, Disney challenged the animators to draw animals more realistically. They spoke to animal experts, spent time at the Los Angeles Zoo, watched nature films, and spent considerable time studying animals, including two deer donated to the studio. More than usual, the animation became tedious as every spot on the fawns had to be replicated perfectly. This attention to detail meant that animators could not maintain the daily output of drawings as on other films. The work progressed, but very slowly. They were also using oil painting, a technique Walt felt would help create a more realistic world because of its quality, but it was something new to the studio and perfecting the technique added to the time they spent on each scene. Walt explains

> We took some of our top artists who worked in oils for their own enjoyment in their leisure time. They taught their technique to the watercolor men. There's a vast difference in the two techniques, but I was set on oil painting, because of its quality. I figured oils would give a sheen to the forest and accentuate the depth. It worked, too, but perfecting a technique takes time." (Bambi World Premiere in London, 1942)

When completed, the emotional depth and quality of work was evidence of the continued growth and sophistication Walt's studio brought to developing stories. It also set him on the road to thinking about nature films which resulted in the creation of the *True-Life Adventure* series (Wills 2019). Unfortunately *Bambi* was not a financial success. In the 1940s Walt had to look to making features that were not as experimental, time consuming, and expensive to make.

# Chapter 8
# Live Action and Animation Hybrids

> *In this volatile business of ours, we can ill afford to rest on our laurels, even to pause in retrospect. Times and conditions change so rapidly thatwe must keep our aim constantly focused on the future.*
>
> Walt Disney

## 8.1 Live Action Animation

One story genre Disney evolved that led directly to the development of Computer Graphics in films in the early 1980s is the hybrid movie—a combination of live action and animation. *Alice's Wonderland*, the pilot made for the Alice series in 1922 which Walt successfully sold to the distributor Margaret Winkler (discussed in an earlier chapter), is Walt's first use of the combination. The technique had worked successfully for Max Fleischer's *Out of the Inkwell* series—it featured Koko the Clown jumping into the real world from the cartoon world—and Walt had wanted to emulate that success. Rather than copying, he took the idea of hybrid in a different direction —bringing a live action Alice into the cartoon world. Walt hoped this innovation would be appeal to audiences and help him break into the industry: it did. Live action took less time, less skill, and less money to produce, and in those early days when he and his brother Roy were the only company employees and were struggling financially, the technique became the go-to mainstay for their shorts. As the studio hired more animators and became more stable financially, animation replaced live action so that it became almost non-existent in later Alice shorts.

---

The original version of this chapter was revised. The correction to this chapter is available at https://doi.org/10.1007/978-3-030-42738-2_18

---

Online photos and graphics provide extra detail and are identified by urls the reader can refer to. This additional reference information will be particularly beneficial as an enhancement for the online version of this book. URLs are current at time of printing.

© Springer Nature Switzerland AG 2020, Corrected Publication 2021
K. Madej, N. Lee, *Disney Stories*, https://doi.org/10.1007/978-3-030-42738-2_8

The studio did not use live action together with animation again until the production of *Fantasia* in 1940. Live action was an important part of the production of *Fantasia* in both the introduction and in the interstitial scenes in which the Master of Ceremonies, Deems Taylor, introduces each of the symphonic pieces. *Fantasia*, however, was an anthology of musical animations, without a traditional storyline for audiences to engage with. Integrating live and animated characters to tell a good story in an animated feature was a challenge that would yet need to be addressed.

Walt had developed a system of working that he refined over time: script was written, storyboards created, music either drove the idea or was integrated into the story, directors together with layout men worked out how the film would look, sketch artists and draftsmen sketched out the scenes, background men painted the settings, special effects department produced all the visual effects, ink and paint department prepared cels for the camera, voice actors spoke for the characters. The studio had a large group of talented individuals prepared to tackle any challenge, but in the early 1940s it was struggling after the financial failure of the first post-*Snow White* features *Fantasia* and *Pinocchio* and the closure of the international market because of WWII. To add to difficulties, as America mobilized for the war, studio staff (along with thousands of other Americans) were drafted, many of the studio buildings were appropriated by the military, and, as a final blow, a labor strike at the studio caused discouragement and alienation among the artists.

The very modest finances now available to the studio, and the smaller number of animators working, resulted in live action again being used as a convenient and inexpensive way to produce features. When the last of the studio's "blockbuster" efforts, *Bambi*, proved not to be a financial success, the studio started to look to modestly priced hybrids. The first of these was *The Reluctant Dragon* (1941), a documentary feature about the studio that combined a live action studio tour together with four animated shorts that showed off the skills of the different departments. The story was slight and carried by the live action: the shorts were not linked in any way other than as a demonstration of the studio's abilities. The studio continued to explore combining live action and animation in a number of different ways throughout the 1940s. They followed two main roads in their exploration, Package Films, and story features such as *Song of the South.*

## 8.2   Package Films: *Silly Symphonies'* Successors

Between 1942 and 1949 the studio released six features that became known as Package films.[1] Committed to releasing "feature films" yet without the resources to complete them on the scale of *Pinocchio* or *Bambi*, Walt used the Package films as a vehicle to provide a feature-length structure for shorter animation sequences that in an earlier decade might have been released as Silly Symphonies. In the 1930s the studio had released 69 Silly Symphonies using this series to experiment with animation, sound, and production techniques. In the 1940s it released none. Innovation and experimenta-

---

[1] *Saludos Amigos* 1942, *The Three Caballeros* 1945, *Make Mine Music* 1946, *Fun and Fancy Free* 1947, *Melody Time* 1948, *Adventures of Ichabod and Mr. Toad* 1949.

tion continued at the studio—the outlet was now the sequences created for Package films.[2] As features, these films moved far from the ideal "illusion of life" Walt had worked to achieve with *Snow White;* they reverted, some more than others, to a vaudeville form of entertainment, a variety show of music, short animations, and live action, that were often only loosely supported by storyline. All except one of the Package features (*Make Mine Music*) incorporated live action and each did so in a different way, in fact, each sequence within the feature, was often treated differently from the next.

Limited manpower and funds did not halt the studio's experimentation and innovation with animation, music, and hybrid techniques. Each new sequence provided an opportunity for the character and special effects animators to try new things, and they did so with gusto. *Saludos Amigos* (1942) was the first of these films. It was a documentary travelogue of the goodwill tour Walt had made of South America at the behest of the U.S. Government in 1940 and consisted both of footage filmed of local scenes and of the animators' drawings of local scenes. These drawings framed four animation "shorts" that reflected the local lifestyle: the transition from live action to animation was a simple cut with no attempt to integrate live action into animation, or vice versa.

## 8.3   *The Three Caballeros*

The animators took a major step forward with live action animation sequences in *The Three Caballeros* (1945), the next Latin-American inspired Package film. The trailer for the feature importantly announces "Walt Disney actually combines for the first time on the screen cartoon[s] with flesh-and-blood personalities."[3] It is for this film that animators developed new technology that would be used in future hybrids and in which we first see the potential of technology that is fulfilled two decades later in the very successful *Mary Poppins* and portends the use of CGI in *TRON* two decades after that.

The studio began compositing animation cells onto live action film footage with optical printers and using rear-screen projection for fantastic animation backgrounds behind the live actors and dancers. Of special note was a new color removal/transfer process in which "a dark background, when duplicated onto black and white negative film, would hold a luminance matte of the actor from the color film" (Foster 2010, p. 6). The film was then composited with animation cells and color overlays to achieve the exuberant results that *The Three Caballeros* became noted for. Compositing is when different layers of film are produced and then filmed together as one. It was done through optical printing which used a number of projectors linked to a camera to combine different strips of film.

The feature was planned as seven different animated sequences. The story was introduced by Donald Duck who received a large parcel of presents from his friends in South America and in opening them was able to revisit past events. Studio animators experimented with different hybrid styles from the simple to the complex in the different sequences: they used simple superimposition scenes such as those in which

---

[2] Trailer: https://www.youtube.com/watch?v=OaAkRqo65rw, Movie: https://www.dailymotion.com/video/x6kdr3d

[3] Trailer: https://www.youtube.com/watch?v=vxn0VVtUwec

the actress Dora Luz's face appears as Donald's eyes and in which performers appear as the center of flowers; they experimented with integration of animated characters and live action scenes such as the one in which Carmen Molina sings on a set in which space is left for animators to later insert Donald; they constructed many sequences in which real life performers sing their way through brilliantly colored, unusual animated sequences of flowers and lush greenery; they made collages of exploding lights and flowers—a pastiche of animation/live action in which there is a constant movement; they surrounded performers' faces in haloes of sunrays or flower petals as they sang tenderly to Donald, or to all three Caballeros. In one scene reminiscent first of *Alice Under the Sea*, then anticipatory of *TRON*, bright green bathing beauties seem to fall through the water as did Alice only to reappear on a toboggan sliding back and forth across the scene as rapidly as did Kevin on his cycle. Some scenes are gag-based such as one in which the three Caballeros are joined at the waist with "real female legs which walk off, leaving the characters without lower halves" (Watts 1997, p. 248). Most scenes, however, are less literal experiments, seemingly of every kind the animators could imagine, with little regard for the story.

So many different techniques, styles, and perspectives were piled one on top of the other that cumulatively they created a sense of frenzied action, more in keeping with the most exuberant and frantic of the Donald shorts than with a well-told story. The "technological razzle-dazzle" was seen as being too frenetic and a move away from Disney stock in trade of good storytelling: "Disney… confuses creative artistry with technical developments" (Watts 1997, p. 248). In the Silly Symphonies of the 1930s the studio special effects animators would experiment with a few new techniques that would be presented in a 7-minute short. Audiences could appreciate the innovation and become accustomed to it. In Donald shorts, they enjoyed frenetic activity and exuberant overacting, again for a short 7 minutes. The 72-minute feature threw so many different special effects at the audience all at once, seemingly without purpose, that they simply became confused by it.

These two films were also unusual at the time because they represented South American culture. Most films of this era had European roots: the fairytales, fables, poems, short stories, or novels that Disney would have been raised on. His goodwill tour for the American government opened the studio up to new influences.

The remaining Package films included live action in more traditional ways as an interstice and as framing stories. Only *Melody Time* (1948) was used to show off innovation; it did so in only one of its sequences. In its trailer, *Melody Time* was billed as being in the "grand tradition of *Fantasia*." It consisted of seven "musical classics" that at least one reviewer saw as acts in a "variety show" (Scheuer 1948). The *Pecos Bill* animation sequence was introduced and framed by a very traditional live action cowboy scene featuring Roy Rogers. But the *Blame it on the Samba* scene on the other hand, drew on the exploration and innovation audiences had seen in *The Three Caballeros*. The scene begins with a depressed Donald Duck and Jose Carioca walking into a bar; the bartender wants to cheer them up. He does so with a cocktail, and the action moves into the cocktail glass. Here we find an organ playing Ethel Smith; Donald Duck and Jose Carioca first dance on top of the organ amidst floating bubbles and then get swept up in an exuberance of changing special effects that stem from the music. They then find themselves in a dream sequence signified by a white eye mask that Ethel finds herself wearing. The scene ends with the bartender closing the door on a scene of exploding keyboard fragments.[4] The sequence is short and the exuberant action and innovative animation/live action mix is in context of the song. This makes it more fitting than the lengthy onslaught of innovation in *The Three Caballeros*. As part of an anthology of seven songs, the innovative sequence was so negligible it warranted only one line in a 1948 newspaper column: "Near to this, [Bumble Boogie] and yet different because it shows organist Ethel Smith in the flesh, is "Blame it on the Samba."

In the final Package film, *The Adventures of Ichabod Crane and Mr. Toad* (1949), the use of live action was limited to a library framing scene in which the stories were introduced to the audience. With this short, Disney was back to telling longer, better structured stories, in which the techniques the animators used supported the building of characters and creation of atmosphere that made for an engaging story. At each short just over 30 minutes, they could not be fitted into the distribution patterns of the film industry. Together they were just long enough to make a feature film. The feature won the Golden Globe award in color cinematography. The need for an inexpensive coupling of live action and animation ended when the success of the animated feature *Cinderella* allowed the studio to again give all its attention to creative storytelling through animation. The idea of combining the two in inventive ways was never abandoned; the different roads taken met again in *Mary Poppins*.

## 8.4   *Song of the South*

The first full-length feature after *Alice's Wonderland* in which live action and animation worked together in a symbiotic relationship to create a story was *Song of the South* made in 1946. Walt had come to the conclusion that it was no longer financially feasible to make animated features as he done previously, paying attention to every detail, testing every story sequence and character, changing entire sequences at great cost because they did not fit. But the Package films only provided a satisfactory answer to one of the studio's needs—how to show audiences the innovative ideas his studio continued to experiment with at a reasonable cost (and make some money). Walt still wanted to tell a feature length *story,* and hybrid films provided the answer to his desire to do that as well.

> I wanted to go beyond the cartoon. Because the cartoon had narrowed itself down. I could make them either seven or eight minutes long—or eighty minutes long. I tried the Package things, where I put five or six together to make an eighty-minute feature. Now I needed to diversify further, and that meant live action. (Thomas, Walt Disney, An American Original, 1976, p. 204)

---

[4] *Blame it on the Samba* video: https://www.youtube.com/watch?v=hn22ofUCNvs

While he considered making Lewis Carroll's *Alice in Wonderland* as a hybrid, the story was too much like a variety show and difficult to script (it would have made a good Package film). Instead, the inspiration for his next feature, *Song of the South*, came from Joel Chandler Harris's *Uncle Remus* books. The folk tales of Brer Rabbit, Brer Bear, and Brer Fox had become very popular since their first release in the late 1800s and were a fixture on children's books shelves across the US and around the world, including Walt's: "I read everyone" (Gabler 2006, p. 273). The stories had been under consideration as an animated feature at the studio since the end of the 1930s (Maltin 2010). The books' own frame story, about the young son of a plantation owner who is captivated by Uncle Remus's stories, could easily be translated to film, with the live action of the storyteller framing the animated sequences of the folktale characters and their doings. Now their time had come and script work for the film, titled *Uncle Remus* at the time, began mid-1944.

The film was planned to have live action, animation, and scenes in which live action and animation were combined. Combining live action with animation meant the live action was constrained and required careful planning as scenes had to accommodate later additions of, not inanimate objects, but moving characters. The live action was filmed on sets that were built to look like they were cartoon animations, saving the time and cost of animating the background for these scenes. These scenes were filmed first, edited, and then animators filled in the characters similar to the way in which Donald Duck is drawn into Carmen Molina scenes in *The Three Caballeros*.

The studio had little experience with shooting live action and relied on assistance from Samuel Goldwyn. Goldwyn loaned Disney one of his most talented and well-known cinematographers, Gregg Toland, who had shot the award-winning *Citizen Kane*. This was the first color work for Toland, and his sensitive treatment of close-ups and visually arresting panning shots added to the emotional tenor of the film's live action, which was a significant percentage of the film (Lingan 2013; Gabler 2006).

While less than 30 minutes of the film was animation "that limit allowed the animation to be done as painstakingly as in the old days" (Gabler 2006, p. 437). Disney's animated characters had been evolving—they were becoming more fluid as animators made the thought process going on in their head, and the purpose for their moves, more evident, mimicking live acting (Watts 1997). Brer Rabbit, Brer Fox, and Brer Bear were lively, interesting characters for the animators to work with, their antics filled with fun, and in some cases wisdom. The new naturalness animators could give them made the juxtaposition of animated character and live actor appear congruent, and so, more life-like. Animators had experimented with combining cartoon character with live actor in *The Three Caballeros* (1945). While that hybrid had a cartoon, fantasy feel about it, *Song of the South* in contrast, was planned to have a real-life feel, in keeping with Walt's "illusion of life" credo, in which a close, warm relationship was created between "the critters" and "the folks" (Thomas, Walt Disney, An American Original 1976).

The resulting excellence in cinematography and animation created a seamless blending of technology and story. The interaction of the fantasy figures and real-life people in a smooth, coherent, and consistent manner was an unprecedented and noteworthy accomplishment that astounded audiences of the time. The techniques used would not be improved upon for decades.


## 8.5  *So Dear To My Heart*

Walt Disney's only other hybrid feature made in the 1940s that was not a Package film was *So Dear To My Heart,* based on the book *Midnight and Jeremiah,* a heartwarming story about a young farm boy who adopts an unruly black lamb and with his uncle trains it so he can keep it. Walt had originally considered the story for his first all live action feature. Contractual obligations to RKO, the possibility that audiences wouldn't be interested in a Disney film without animation, and his unhappiness with the results of the live action footage when it was complete, encouraged him to change his mind and make it a hybrid film instead (Gabler 2006). "He knew he had a problem. And that's when he went back and started building those little vignettes in there in animation. He was working to improve it, to make it better" (Barrier 2007, p. 203). Four vignettes were eventually added to the story; these consisted of a total of 12 minutes or 15% of the film (Sampson 2010). As it had not been planned from the initial scriptwriting, the animation and live action were not as integrated as they were in the preceding hybrid film *Song of the South.* However, they weren't only tacked on cut scenes, rather they helped build up the nostalgic tone of the film, and reinforced the lessons Jeremiah was learning as he raised his lamb.

The feature was introduced with a two minute animation sequence which used the multiplane camera to great effect. A scrapbook lies neglected in the attic of the old homestead. As the cover opens and the pages begin to turn, the audience is drawn into pictures of nostalgic scenes, going past trees, leaves, birds that twitter, and eventually coming to a romantic view of the old farm house. Another sequence places the wise old owl and Danny, the lamb, in Jeremiah's bedroom, mixing animation and a live scene momentarily before the animation sequence takes over. In one clever animation, the frisky lamb bounds through an animated fence only to appear on the other side breaking through Granny Kincaid's actual screen door. Except for the introduction, the animations were planned to fit into the live action as Jeremiah's daydreams. Walt later noted, "I saw the cartoon characters as figments of a small boy's imagination, and I think they were justified."

*So Dear To My Heart* was a nostalgic look at the small town life that Walt envisioned as being the heart of the American Midwest. During its filming Walt wanted to get back to some of the hands-on he'd had during the early days of his career. He began to make miniatures of the scenes he dearly loved and had scenes drawn of life in an early American town. He built "Granny Kincaid's Cabin" first and then planned a barber shop quartet that would sing, his first interest in what would become an abiding interest in animatronics (Snow 2019; Barrier 2007).

The success of the all-animation feature, *Cinderella,* brought the studio back to a strong financial footing and reminded Walt of the importance of satisfying his core audience, yet the studio completed only five animation features during the 1950s in addition to *Cinderella*: *Alice in Wonderland, Peter Pan, Lady and the Tramp*, and *Sleeping Beauty*. Walt was distracted by his interest in live action films; in this he was helped by the studio's international sales problem. During and immediately after WWII proceeds of film and product sales in foreign countries, including Great Britain, were stranded in those countries. In addition European countries were setting quotas for the number of foreign films to be shown in their theatres. In Great Britain, 45% of films had to be of British origin. Setting up an animation studio was fraught with issues such as hiring the right animators—live action was the easier route to take. Walt set up Walt Disney British Films Ltd. and (in association with RKO which also had stranded funds) began to make live action films in Britain (Barrier 2007; Gabler 2006). Although the first film produced, *Treasure Island* (1950), used almost all the funds held back (Barrier 2007), together with RKO, Walt went on to make *Robin Hood and His Merrie Men* (1952), *The Sword and the Rose* (1953), and *Rob Roy* (1954). Through these films he cemented his relationship with British filmmaking, and continued to use British stories for many of the studios animated, hybrid, and live action films (Walt Disney and Live action Films 2011).

In the 1950s the Disney studios made 5 animated features, 18 live action films, and 5 nature documentaries (*True-Life Adventures*). Walt was very busy with other ideas, ideas for Dislandia that had started with building Granny Kincaid's Cabin became ideas for Disneyland, building Disneyland needed the funding brought to the studio through *Walt Disney's Disneyland*, the weekly television program Walt agreed to host in 1953, animated figures that had their start with the barbershop quartet for Dislandia became a major interest.

In the 1960s Disney made just 3 animated feature films out of a total of 52 films. The studio also produced *Mary Poppins*, which brought a number of Walt's interests together: live film, animation, animatronics… and a great story that he had been chasing for 20 years. *Mary Poppins* was the studio's return to the hybrid film, and developed technology that would help the coming transition to using computer graphics and the move to digital stories.

## 8.6   *Mary Poppins*

Walt's interest in new ways of approaching telling stories governed his attraction to different technologies. *Mary Poppins,* released August 27, 1964, is one of the best known Disney live action/animation film. The film received 13 Academy Awards nominations, including Best Picture—a record for films released by Walt Disney Studios. The movie won 5 Oscars awards, including Visual Effects. This award was predominantly for the work undertaken by engineer and inventor Petro Vlahos in merging animation and live action. For while the final visual effect was similar to the blending of live acting and animation drawing Walt's animators had achieved in

*Song of the South* almost twenty years earlier, the technology used to achieve the effect was revolutionary.

Disney had used mattes in the original Alice hybrid's he had made in the 1920s. To help eliminate some of the shimmering around Alice, Ub Iwerks had created a matte that was placed on the camera lens to provide a constant position for Alice as she acted against a white background. The studio worked with mattes again in *Song of the South* when they used the blue screen and traveling matte technology introduced in the 1940 film *The Thief of Bagdad*. The first work on blue screen and travelling mattes was done in the 1930s at RKO Radio Pictures by Linwood Dunn. Dunn created special effects by exposing film twice, once with the matte on one area, then the second time with the reverse matte on the second area. Larry Butler, who had worked at RKO at the time, moved to London and worked with Alexander Korda for London Films. He developed these effects further and created the technique of travelling mattes to move objects photochemically. *The Thief of Bagdad* was the first movie in which this special effect was used. Butler also used travelling mattes in technicolor for the first time (Alexander 2015).

Innovative and revolutionary at the time, the limitations of blue screen for moving figures was apparent in the dark line around Ahmad, the King of Bagdad, and his flying carpet. Other problems that directors worked around was the blue cast created on characters and their costumes. Each scene had to be lit carefully to avoid the blue cast and only certain colors were used in the costumes actors wore. Vlahos eliminated the blue screen and instead used the yellow hue from sodium gas because the gas produces light at a very exact wavelength, 589 nanometers, and he could improve the accuracy of isolating actors or objects. He had created a special, one of a kind prism that when used in the filming camera would isolate the hue. Actors stood in front of a white background lit by sodium vapor lights. The method was completely within the camera and simplified the matting process by creating a more accurate silhouette of the image. In using such a narrow color wavelength he solved many problems for filmmakers. Above all they didn't have to light the scenes as perfectly. Suddenly any colors could be used both in the costumes the actors wore and in the props they used. Bert, the chimney sweep, could be resplendent in white, red, and blue stripes, and with yellow socks to boot (the yellow in the sodium gas was in such a narrow field that it did not affect most yellows). Because the process created a more accurate matte, it gave the animators the ability to isolate intricate objects and gauzy fabrics. Mary could, on her days off, of course, wear frilly dresses and hats with elaborate gauze veils, with disdain. No more crude black line was visible around these objects as with blue screen.

Walt had invested much personal energy into bringing his vision of *Mary Poppins* to audiences. Although the movie was a triple threat success, applauded by critics, loved by audiences, and financially successful, surprisingly, the hybrid genre was little used in the next few years, or indeed over the next few decades. When Walt passed away on December 15, 1966 two years after the film made its debut, he was involved in many other innovative technologies besides hybrid films that had caught his interest, including designing and building EPCOT.

Computer technologies were beginning to enter the scene, CGI was being developed and would enter the movie scene with TRON in 1982, and would change the way animated films were made. However, throughout the 1970s and 80s Disney animators were still looking at new ways to combine live action and animation through animation technology that did not include digital methods; they made *Bedknobs and Broomsticks* in 1971, *Pete's Dragon* in 1977, and *Who Framed Roger Rabbit* in 1988.

*Bedknobs and Broomsticks,* released in 1971, was a story that had at one point been considered as an alternative to *Mary Poppins*. The film employed the sodium vapour process invented by Vlados to combine live action with animation. Sets were put up in front of a yellow screen, lit with sodium lights, and actors were filmed doing their scenes with a camera that used Vlados's special prism camera to capture the images. The film had extensive special effects throughout and had to be tightly scripted to ensure the live action and animation sequences would be completed as scheduled. In one scene, the witch Eglantine flies through the air on her broom to lead the armor in the museum, brought to life by the "Substitutiary Locomotion" spell, to fight against the Nazis (shades of Professor McGonagall in the *Harry Potter* series). The film was nominated for five academy awards and won for Best Visual Effects.

*Pete's Dragon* in 1977 turns tables and in it is a magical animated dragon, Elliot, who finds himself in a live action adventure. It is the first time since *Alice's Wonderland* that a Disney hybrid film put an animated character into the real world as a main character. Initially Elliot was only going to appear in a short scene and would remain invisible in the rest of the movie. Animators thought the audience would question where the Dragon was in a film with the title *Pete's Dragon* and convinced Disney management to make the film a combination live action animation (Korkis 2016). A full-size mechanical model (19 ft.) of Elliot was constructed to help the animators visualize how Elliot interacted dynamically with people and his environment. Making Elliot move around buildings and play with his live friend so the action appeared realistic added to the animators techniques and set the scene for creating life-like interaction in *Who Framed Roger Rabbit* more than a decade later. They were so successful that reviewers stated that Elliot "trumped the film's script and actors" and that the film "suffered 'whenever Elliot is off screen'" (Buhl 2019). Sodium vapor mattes were used for the live action animation sequences in which Elliot appeared. For some frame sequences animators used compositing and sandwiched an animation layer between two layers of live action film so that Elliot appeared with a live foreground and a live background (Korkis 2016). To help the animator, frames of the live action were enlarged so that the animated drawings were done directly on the live action images and the lines were again drawn in ink rather that photocopied, as a clean, crisp line fit more naturally with the live action than did sketchy photocopied lines.[5]

---

[5] Photocopying draughtsmans' and sketchers' work started with *101 Dalmations,* and became a standard, reducing costly inking of each scene.

## 8.7  *Who Framed Roger Rabbit*

Following in the footsteps of *Pete's Dragon* was *Who Framed Roger Rabbit* (1988) which took the integration of live action and animated characters to a new level with its "realistic" portrayal of interaction that was fluid and dynamic. Rather than looking as if they simply shared the screen together, both live and animated figures interact freely with each other on screen. Even though the camerawork is complicated, there seems to be nothing they don't do together: actors perform as if the animations are real and the animations are given a real three-dimensional presence on screen (Cho 2018).

All of this was created with traditional animation techniques, albeit with a few innovative twists and a lot of time, harking back to when Walt Disney was prepared to give the time necessary to create the quality of the studio's first features. There were three main areas of work: live action, animation, and compositing. "'We were making a live action, an animated and a visual-effects movie. Bob [Zemeckis] would shoot with the actors and cut the scene in London. We'd send the cut footage to ILM [Industrial Light and Magic] in San Francisco, where they'd make a print of each frame, and those prints would go back to the animation studio in London, where they'd draw in the cartoon characters. Then they'd go back to ILM to be composited as a visual effect'" (Higgins, 2017).

In order to film live action that would be useful to the animators, each scene had to be meticulously planned with space for the cartoon characters' actions. Once the live action was complete, black and white print outs of each frame were made and the animators and layout artists drew their animated characters on these printouts. The drawings were used in the pencil tests to ensure the action worked and then completed as cels for filming. The resulting footage was sent to Industrial Light and Magic for compositing which was done through optical printing. With CGI this work would be done digitally. The cartoon characters were given a 3D appearance through the use of three lighting layers that added shadows, highlights and tone mattes. These lighting effects gave the characters an actual real presence: it appeared they were being affected by the lighting in the scene. An example is a scene in which a hanging light is bumped. As the light moves back and forth, the lighting on Roger Rabbit changes in concert giving the sense of reality not found in simpler composites like the ones in which Elliot the Dragon appears. Once these lighting effects were created they were composited together with the animated character footage onto the live action footage.

Building the fantasy that the animations were truly actors in the live space required they look eye to eye with humans, and interact with all the objects around them. To help the performers act as if they were really interacting with the animated characters, life size rubber puppets were used as props (Welk 2018). To provide real action that would be done by toons, the mechanical team made robots that performed them, like when Roger smashed a load of plates one by one. The robot picked up each plate then smashed it over itself. For other objects with which performers interacted, the puppet team dangled stage props in the air (Wong 2017).

The intent of the film was not to create human figures out of the cartoons but to give them reality as toons in our real world, to create an illusion. To this end, they used a 2.5D effect rather than a 3D one. Animated characters were made to look like the traditional cartoon characters audiences had grown up with, but with lighting and texture providing a little extra depth that made the illusion just that little bit more substantial.

It's not likely that a similar world could have been created with CGI and motion capture, with its push towards complete versimilitude. Reality, as Walt so often stated, was not the purpose of his animations. The CGI world, often misses the point that to be a successful illusion of life, it isn't a necessity for an animation to appear completely realistic, but it is necessary for it to have believable characters with purpose within an engaging and satisfying storyline. The caricature of animation, which helps define a character, adds considerably to telling the story, as some of the most recent live action remakes of animated features have shown us. Animation can provide the face and body nuances, adding just the right amount of exaggeration to an otherwise authentic movement that puts over the thoughts and emotions the story hopes to share.

In the 1980s, computer graphics changed the way Disney produced films. The traditional studio had to adapt to advancements in technology, conceptually and organizationally. Key moments and technologies that helped the studio evolve towards digital storytelling were the use of CGI in the film *TRON* in 1982 and the use of the Computer Animated Production System, CAPS, which was used for the entire production process starting with *The Rescuers Down Under* in 1990. *TRON* paved the way for CAPS, as Disney was not ready to adopt CGI. CAPS was the easier way to introduce computer graphics to their process—it improved two time-consuming and expensive processes in traditional animation, handpainted cels and the multiplane camera. It did not change the notion of what animation was, but in becoming a mainstay of the studio's animation process, changed the underlying technology.

The next chapter tackles CAPS first and then CGI. While not chronological, this order situates CAPS as a system that had a finite life, both at Disney, and as an animation system. It's capabilities were eventually replaced by other systems within the CGI world.

# Chapter 9
# CAPS, CGI and the Movies

> *I could never imagine making movies without it today. Has it made it easier? I don't know. It's made it more fun. It's made it more fun because you can do so much. As an artist, you can conceive of something and go do it.*
>
> Peter Schneider, President of Disney
> Feature Animation 1985–1999

## 9.1 From Hand-Painted Cels and Multi-plane Cameras to CAPS

In 1924, the early *Alice* days when he was young and struggling to establish his animation business, Walt hired his first inker; he could only afford one.[1] When the studio was in production for S*now White*, 158 inkers and painters sat at desks pushing out cels at an incredible rate to complete the movie on time (Disney 2012). The well-trained inkers and painters (mainly women)[2] were the muscle of the animation industry, they prepared the animators concepts for the camera work; without them, there would have been no animated films. An inker traced drawings created by sketchers and draughtsmen onto one side of a celluloid sheet using a range of nibs for the black lines. When the tracing was complete the cel went to the painters, who completed the image by painting on the reverse side of the black line and using colors mixed especially for the

---

[1] He happened to hire Lillian Bounds with whom he was later married.

[2] In 1935, five months of training were required before trainees were considered for hiring. Then few made the cut. Out of the 1935 class of 60, only 3 were hired (Zohn 2010).

---

The original version of this chapter was revised. The correction to this chapter is available at https://doi.org/10.1007/978-3-030-42738-2_18

---

Online photos and graphics provide extra detail and are identified by urls the reader can refer to. This additional reference information will be particularly beneficial as an enhancement for the online version of this book. URLs are current at time of printing.

---

© Springer Nature Switzerland AG 2020, Corrected Publication 2021
K. Madej, N. Lee, *Disney Stories*, https://doi.org/10.1007/978-3-030-42738-2_9

film. The celluloids in *Snow White* consisted of painted details "requiring the precision found in the finest machine manufacture" (Boone 1938).

> For a full-figure shot, Snow White appears in fifteen tints, selected from among 350 standard colors available in the studio paint shop. These vary from tint 685-1/2 (yellow shoes) to pastel 23 (cheeks). When she sings, six colors are added to her eyes and mouth for close-ups, these ranging from orange-yellow on the lids to light red for the lips. Upon each drawing is noted the particular colors to be added to the several areas, and thereafter scores of girls complete the many paintings by spotting colors according to number (Ibid).

Colors painted on a cel appeared differently from colors in film. When working on features like *Snow White* painters had a chart posted above their boards to show them how each color would appear once captured by the camera. The cels were stacked one on top of each other to be shot. Because even clear celluloid is not completely transparent the same color would look different on the different layers. This meant the color needed to be adjusted for each layer. It also meant that the number of layers that could be used was limited (five) as the change was too great if more were used. With a film like *Snow White*, which consisted of 362,919 frames and required "more than 1,500,000 individual pen and ink drawings and color paintings..." these adjustments added significant time and cost. "'Ink and Paint' represents the manufacturing bottle neck, for a movie cartoon can progress no more rapidly than skilled hands complete the multitude of drawings. Since this cartoon required an average of 22 individual painted cels for each foot of completed picture, 166,352 finished paintings were exposed to the camera" (Boone 1938). "Ink and Paint" as a manufacturing bottle neck would be done away with by CAPS.

The earlier chapter on *Snow White* in this book discusses the different innovative technologies developed for the feature, one of which was the multiplane camera. The multiplane was developed to allow camera angles that created a sense of movement and depth not possible filming a 2D piece of artwork on an animation stand. The multiplane built for *Snow White* was 12 feet high, with a camera at the top of the unit and four levels below, each of which held an animated piece of art. Camera operators needed to climb a ladder to get to their camera and shoot as technicians operated each layer below independently. A multiplane camera with seven levels was constructed to achieve the special effects for *Fantasia*. The multiplane was used for later movies like *The Three Caballeros*, *So Dear to Our Hearts,* and *Peter* Pan—when Peter teaches Wendy, John, and Michael how to fly over London and then takes them to Never Land (Deja 2016). Camera operators were able to give scenes a sense of depth and movement with camera moves that included zooming past objects into a scene, and panning across scenes that could move in opposite directions. Each sequence was complex, time consuming and expensive to produce, so they were used sparingly for effect. CAPS would do away with the need for the multiplane as well.

## 9.2  The Road to CAPS and CGI

In the early 1970s it was still difficult to get any kind of a colored picture on a computer screen. *SuperPaint* had been created in 1972–3 by Richard Shoup at Xerox PARC where many talented researchers got their first taste of what was possible in graphics. *SuperPaint* was the first program that could be used to create art work, edit video, and make computer animations. It had virtual paint brushes and pencils and could autofill images from a preset color palette; from this palette it could also change hue and saturation as well as graphical data of an image that it either imported or that it created. In 1974 Xerox canceled Shoup's color project (not useful to industry research) and he left a year later to create his own company, Aurora Systems, where he continued to develop digital animation software as well as hardware (Sito 2015). Shoup had brought in Alvy Ray Smith as a contractor on the project and when the color project was canceled, Smith went on to work at the Computer Graphics Lab at the New York Institute of Technology (NYIT). NYIT, along with University of Utah, was home to researchers working on leading edge computer graphics. At NYIT he joined a team headed by Ed Catmull[3]; innovations at NYIT included Smith's *BigPaint*, the first RGB paint program, and Catmull's *Tween* 2D animation program that automated producing inbetween frames. In 1979, taking with him a number of the computer scientists from NYIT, Catmull left to work as vice-president of the Graphics Group at Lucasfilm. Smith joined him in the early 1980s. George Lucas was not interested in graphics and expected the Graphics Group to work on hard-ware and software that controlled visual and audio editing; the group continued its work on paint programs and digital compositing within this framework.

## 9.3 CAPS

In the early 1980s Disney became serious about developing a more efficient way to handle their ink and paint, multiplane, and compositing. They approached Lucasfilm and a competitor, Digital Productions[4] for proposals.[5] The Graphics Group's understanding of traditional animation and Smith's early work with paint programs at NYIT convinced Disney they understood the problems inherent in the production process and had the creativity and technical skills to come up with a successful solution. Lucasfilm was having financial issues and had considered divesting itself of the Graphics Group. With this as impetus, the Graphics Group purchased the technology, left Lucasfilm, and established Pixar (Mason 2007; IEEE 2008; Seymour 2012).[6] In May 1986, Pixar signed a contract to develop an operational system for Disney in under 4 years.[7]

CAPS would soon do all the traditional, time consuming work of the inkers and painters in the studio and, in addition, all of the camera work of the multiplane.

---

[3] Ed Catmull became president of Disney Animation Studios when it acquired Pixar in 2006 and remained president until he retired in 2018.

[4] John Whitney, Jr., and Gary Demos worked for Triple-I, one of the four computer graphics companies that worked on *TRON*. They left in 1981 and started their own company, Digital Productions.

[5] As noted later in the chapter, Disney had met these companies when it was producing *TRON*.

[6] Podcast of Interview with Alvy Ray Smith at https://www.fxguide.com/fxpodcasts/fxpodcast-alvy-ray-smith/

[7] http://alvyray.com/Pixar/documents/CAPS_ExecSummary_AlvyToPixar_4May86.pdf

It provided a new palette of tools for the animator. Rough sketches for a pencil test could be scanned into the system and run to make sure the scene worked; changes could be made and the roughs printed out so animators could complete the pencil drawings which were then scanned back into the system. Inking could be done in any style. When making *101 Dalmations,* Disney revolutionized the look of its animation by introducing the process of photocopying pencil sketches on cels that gave the animations a rougher, less polished look, and was a much less expensive and time consuming technique than inking clean lines. CAPS could reproduce this sketchiness. It could also reproduce any other line quality the animator might want to represent, and draw the line in any color.

The computer's paint application offered unlimited possibilities: transparent shading, blended colors, and other techniques not previously available. The studio no longer had to mix paint colors in their paint department, or be limited by what was possible to mix. There was no longer a concern about layers of cels changing a color and having to compensate for it, or about the difference in color between the color the painter was applying to the cel and what the camera captured. CAPS could give a princess soft pink glowing cheeks that would always be that color, and could be tweaked to look a little pinker without the need to mix a new batch color or repaint all the work done previously. Because each inked or painted section was a separate layer, the work could be done in any order. The completed layers (or now digital cels) once assembled in the planned order, were composited with background paintings to create a final image. In hybrid films, the digital animated cels were composited with the live action images. Pixar's Tom Hahn (software engineer), said of the CAPS program "There are dozens and dozens of graphic operations. It can do virtually all the useful 2D operations we know about for films" (Robertson 1994).

In addition to the new flexibility with color, CAPS provided a new flexibility with the camera. The program could simulate any camera movement, pan across a scene as in traditional 2D animation, multiplane zoom into a background, create optical effects such as rack focus in which we first see the foreground in focus, then the focus changes to reveal the background. Complex multiplane shots could incorporate dozens if not hundreds of layers of artwork—which were no longer restricted in size. Using the multiplane, animators had new freedom to make their characters movements more integral to the environment around them, giving a seamless look and a greater feel of naturalness almost impossible with traditional animation.

The completed composites were recorded onto film and edited into the final form of a movie. The entire process, every bit of work completed, was based on exposure sheets, originally hand written and then digitized, which provided meticulous direction for each shot (Robertson 1994).[8] The first proof of use for the paint system was a sequence of Mickey standing on EPCOT's Spaceship Earth for *The Magical World*

---

[8] Although Disney's CAPS had received numerous Academy Awards in 1992 for the CAPS system, it was not until the company invited Computer Graphics World on a tour that the public was offered a glimpse into how it worked. The article *Disney lets CAPS out of the bag,* by Barbara Robertson, was published July 1, 1994. See at https://groups.google.com/forum/m/#!topic/rec.arts.anime/WOkkuV0Yr7w

*of Disney* titles.[9] The first feature in which CAPS was used was *The Little Mermaid* when Ariel and her newly-wed husband Eric are sailing off and Triton and the mer-people wave goodbye (Robertson 1994).

The original goal for the project was to return to the quality of animation of the 1930s and 1940s but avoid the time and cost it took to achieve that quality. Instead, the technology went a step further and gave animators opportunities to add unimaginable effects to their animation. "Anne Tucker, supervisor, Scene Planning, who worked on Disney films using traditional methods before CAPS, put it succinctly. 'Now. I'm Free'" (Robertson 1994). The technology changed the way animators could work because it made non-standard effects not only easier to accomplish but affordable. "In *Little Mermaid* there are three [traditional] multiplane shots because that's all we could afford and all we could really manipulate. In *the Lion King* [released in 1994] there are hundreds," Peter Schneider, president of Disney Feature Animation told Computer Graphics World in an exclusive interview about CAPS (Robertson 1994). In that interview as well, Robertson goes on to say that "The people at Disney emphasize that CAPS is not just technology, it's the process of making the film, and it's the people" and expressed the importance of the integration of new technology into the culture of how the studio crafted the story, the characters, and the final movie. This process of integration of new technology into how the studio functioned was a legacy of Walt's enthusiastic embracing of innovation, but even more so of his constant demand for using innovation to make the story better. Occasionally, however adopting new technology meant some initial kinks for the storyline.

Even though CAPS was only tested in a short sequence of *The Little Mermaid*, Disney took the risk to make their next film 100% CAPS. It was the start of a new era of creativity: every film the Disney studio made after that used CAPS. With each film the studio learned how to use it more effectively as a technology for special effects, if not always, as a way to make a better story. *The Rescuers Down Under* (1990) was planned as a sequel to the successful 1977 feature *The Rescuers*, whose hero and heroine, Bernard and Bianca, work for the Rescue Aid Society. They are called to Australia to rescue the young boy Cody who has been kidnapped by a poacher. Cody has rescued a Golden Eagle from the net in which it was caught, and they are now friends. The poacher and his evil cohorts want to capture the eagle and intend to use Cody as a lure to a trap. Animators experimented with all their new toys in this film, in particular the multiplane. It is first used in the introductory scene to draw the audience into the landscape: the camera moves through the tiny world of insects crawling through the grass before it goes on a head-long rush skimming the ground towards Ayers Rock, an isolated red mountain in the midst of Australia's bleak outback. It finally comes to a stop at the isolated home of the film's tritagonist (third lead), Cody. In a later sequence the camera follows the eagle, Marahute, on great heart stopping swoops from tops of mountains up into the clouds and down to rushing waterfalls. "We were told to pull out all the stops in the eagle sequences,"

---

[9] Numerous sources, but none seem to be primary.

one of the animators explained—the animators spent a year completing seven minutes of film in which Marahute starred (Barret 2016). In Disney tradition, the animators ensured accuracy in depicting the animals and their movements by observing them directly: visiting Australian animals at the San Diego Zoo, eagles at the Peregrine Fund in Idaho, mice at the studio, and created a mix of animal realism (Marahute is never cute) and anthropomorphized animals, such as Bianca and Bernard.

The film won accolades at the time for its technology and inventiveness, particularly in the spectacular flying scenes and the adventurous "Indiana Jones" scenes. It engaged its audience by emulating the live action adventures popular at the time, yet it seemed to miss the mark for good storyline: it was praised for daring, even audacious scenes, but faulted for its story inconsistency; it had a strong beginning and ending but a weak middle; it had too many characters, some of which were given too much screen time for their value in the story; it had too many gag filler sequences that did not further the storyline (Rotten Tomatoes 2016; Barret 2016). As with previous films that adopted challenging innovative approaches using new technology (whether *Fantasia* or *The Three Caballeros*) it seemed to demonstrate the common missteps that come with the introduction of new technologies: having fun trying all the new toys while forgetting the tenets of the best animated films: well-developed characters that engage through a solid storyline. In *Rescuers Down Under* CAPS had proven itself as a technology that could enhance both paint and multiplane movement in movies, that would make the animation process more efficient, and that would free animators to be more creative. CGI had by this time been used to create special effects successfully and Disney took advantage of both new technologies to add innovation to its next feature, *Beauty and the Beast*. CAPS was used in all of Disney's features until 2004 when new studio management believed audiences were no longer interested in 2D animation.[10] At that time all of the CAPS systems were dismantled; for traditionally animated films made after 2004, Disney used other software by then available.[11]

## 9.4   Early CGI at Disney

Before its initial exploration of CAPS in the second half of the 1980s, Disney had embarked on using computer graphics in the 1982 film *TRON*. The movie is important for being the first to make extensive use of CGI imagery—fifteen minutes of the

---

[10] Management at Disney at the time (Jeffrey Katzenberg) was not supportive of 2D animation and the film's marketing budget was cut back rather than increased after its first weekend because of a less than stellar showing against movies such as *Home Alone* (Stewart 2006).

[11] Disney used Toon Boon Harmony.

film consists of images generated entirely by computer but also for using it in a way that accentuates the presence of technology through CGI within the story.[12]

Disney movies depicted robot technology and computers before TRON because as story material, these had possibilities. In the early 1930s technology—automation and the robot—had come to be feared by the common man. After the Wall Street Crash, the Depression had hit hard. Robots were seen as a threat, taking factory jobs that were being automated for efficiency and cost cutting. In 1932, sensationalized reports of Alpha, the Robot, shooting its inventor during a demonstration (gun discharged accidently while being loaded) increased negative attitudes that the mechanical man was something to be feared. At the time, talk about robots was everywhere: science fiction magazines and books, radio serials such as *Flash Gordon*, and even in the boxing ring. *Modern Mechanics* featured an actual event in January 1931 about two robots controlled by short wave radio that were built for a boxing match. "...the wires got crossed... smoke rising from their innards... one robot went down and the other collapsed on top of him" (Novak 2011). Jack Dempsey, boxing champion in the 1930s, spoke about why a robot had no hope of winning against him in the ring:

> The reason is simple: Engineers can build a robot that will possess everything except brains. And without brains no man can ever attain championship class in the boxing game. It is true enough that we have had some rare intellectual specimens in the higher frames of boxing glory, but I can truthfully say that no man ever attained genuine boxing recognition without real headwork. The best punch in the world is not worth a whoop if the boxer doesn't know what to do with it. (Novak, 2011)

Both the boxing event and Dempsey's comment show the comeuppance of technology. One because of technological complications, the other because of intellectual limitations. In 1933, Walt put Mickey to work to reflect current attitudes and calm them in *Mickey's Mechanical Man*. Mickey trains a robot to box the giant gorilla, Kongo Killer.[13] It is well mannered and civilized in its boxing style, which

---

[12] The first film with a CGI human character was *Looker* released shortly before *TRON* in 1981. The main character, Cindy, a model, has her body digitally scanned to create a 3D computer-generated model of an entire human figure. Polygonal models obtained by digitizing a human body were used to render the effects. The CG was done by Information International Inc. (Triple-I) which was one of the companies that worked on TRON. Reference lines were drawn on Actress Susan Dey's head to digitize it for Cindy's head https://ohiostate.pressbooks.pub/graphicshistory/chapter/14-1-introduction/. In researching the film I found a 2014 response to a YouTube video of the film from creative supervisor Richard Taylor. He wrote about the experience, "I enjoyed designing this sequence. The CG elements of her being formed were difficult to do at that time, but the team at Information International Incorporated (III) did a terrific job. You have no idea how crude the hardware and software were in those days compared to where we are today. Super labor intensive, one of a kind software and hardware. This was a great warm up for Tron. The reason the CG didn't get the attention it should have in this film is because all the CG images appeared on monitors in the lab. None of the CG images were projected full frame." The film clip and comment are available on the YouTube Gorkab Channel which has it as an age-restricted video. Search the quote to be able to see the clip and comments on YouTube. I have screen shots in my research files in the event the clip is removed completely.

[13] The movie *King Kong* had been released in March 1933.

only results in a trouncing. Minnie recalls that the honking of her horn drives the robot into a frenzy. She honks her horn, the robot goes beserk, and beats Kongo Killer. It wins but shatters as a result and ends in pieces of metal and springs on the boxing ring floor, a one-time wonder. The robot has no real control over its responses and when it wins, it is only a temporary win; ultimately it has no hope to succeed. Walt was putting robots in their place, giving the upper hand to man.

This is also the short in which Walt exhorts his storymen and animators to think more about creating real characters and stories not just gags (see Chap. 8): "You know what's wrong with this? You don't know anything about psychology…. It's feeling. You've got to really be Minnie, you've got to be pulling for Mickey to beat that big lunkhead. You've got to hit that mat hard, you've got to stretch." Understanding the psychology of a situation and imbuing characters and story line with this understanding to touch audiences was of paramount importance.

In 1967, with the world on the cusp of a new age of computers, Disney made *The Computer Wore Tennis Shoes*. Again, society was concerned about human/computer interaction. The live action, light weight, movie lampooned society's concerns: during a thunderstorm, a Medfield College student, Dexter, runs through the rain into the school to replace an actuator on a donated computer[14] (the school is too poor to purchase one). Sopping wet, he receives an electric shock when trying to connect the computer to a power source and, as the official trailer tells it, "… [the] campus computer accidently drains its brain into a campus clown who becomes a socket-shocked human computer."[15] To set the tone for the movie, the introductory credits used "binary visual metaphors and punch card aesthetics"[16] with numbers, letters, and punched hole sequences. Presciently, they included rows of disappearing dots that would later be the basic graphic for the popular Pac Man arcade and home video game. Reflecting the common skepticism and fear the general public had towards the computer's potential to overtake man, the story made fun of the professor's attempt to consider using it as an assist to living and working. In the end, man's intellect trumps machines at a national trivia competition, during which Dexter slowly loses his superbrain because of an earlier concussion, and the school goes on to win as a team member, without computer super brain power, answers the final question correctly (Anderson 2013).[17] Again, the computer is shown to be inadequate when pitted against human ability, and fears are laid to rest.

---

[14] In Medfield's computer, already old in 1969, the actuator would have been the part that carried out the action required by the control system.

[15] Official trailer, https://www.youtube.com/watch?v=nBkw65BYj6o

[16] http://www.criticalcommons.org/Members/ccManager/clips/computational-kitsch-in-opening-titles-of-the-computer-wore-tennis-shoes/view

[17] The movie's reflection on technology and the man=machine brain swap is made current in a 2013 mashup of Radiohead's song Idioteque and sequences from the film. YouTube Channel PaulGuitart: Radiohead Idioteque + The Computer Wore Tennis Shoes, https://www.youtube.com/watch?v=X3asaPmvapg

## 9.5 *TRON*

During the late 1960s, when Dexter was acquiring computer superpowers, computers were mainly used by industry and research. They sold in the tens of thousands, many of them as kits that had to be assembled. By the second half of the 1970s, with the introduction of pcs and lower prices, computers began to sell in the millions. By the late 1970s the growth in video gaming, use of personal computers, and interest of a generation of researchers in developing computer graphics (such as those at Xerox PARC) had leaped forward. Video games were on their way to becoming ubiquitous, whether played on the computer, console system, or handheld device. As noted in Chapter 12, by 1981, Disney had already released its first video game *Mickey Mouse* for Nintendo's *Game and Watch*. Disney was no stranger to where computer technologies were going, it simply needed a nudge to look at using them, and *TRON* was that nudge.

*TRON* was brought to Disney by its writers Stephen Lisberger and Donald Kushner. It is a story set both in the real world and in the world of computer games. Even more so than the surreal musical worlds of *Fantasia,* the landscapes in *TRON* are unfamiliar to us, the objects and vehicles that inhabit those landscapes are ones that don't exist in our world. They needed a new technology to bring them to life. *TRON* had its genesis when Lisberger and Kushner were working on the NBC specials *Animalympics* for the 1980 Olympics. Bill Kroyer, who had worked as an animator at Disney (*Fox and the Hound*) before he joined Lisberger Studios, talked about how the idea got started: "We were playing video games, and that's when he [Lisberger] first started pitching the idea to us about a guy who gets lost in a video game. We thought that was an original idea, so as we were wrapping up *Animalympics,* we were boarding and developing *TRON*"" (King 2017). John Norton, who worked with them, drew a neon warrior throwing a glowing disc that inspired the TRON character (Smith 2017). Lisberger and Kushner attempted to produce the film on their own, then tried to interest a number of other studios in making the film, and finally brought it to Disney. By the time they got to Disney "we had it storyboarded, we had designs, we had budgets, we had staff, we had schedules, we had sample reels. I mean we had everything except money" (Konow 2015). The game world the story inhabits is essentially an animated one, and its best home ended up being at Disney.

At the time the 2D animators at Disney were concerned about maintaining the family-oriented approach they believed was Walt's legacy and were not tempted to move out of their self-proscribed limits. Kroyer remembers his studio space at Disney from his time as animator there: "The only thing in my room that was not there during *Snow White* was the electric pencil sharpener. In 40 years, literally nothing had changed in the pipeline" (Kroyer 2012). Tom Wilhite, who had joined Disney in 1977 and was at the time Vice President of Creative Development for motion pictures and television, *was* interested in introducing some change. He believed the company should take on the challenge of telling a story that was different from their norm and use leading edge computer technology to help tell that story in ways that traditional methods could not.

Except that all of the technology did not yet exist. Reminiscent of Walt's approach to taking on challenges, Kroyer says, "Nothing we needed existed... . We didn't come up with the movie to exploit technology. We came up with the movie and then we said, 'We believe we can make the technology as we make the movie" (King 2017).

"We had this gut feeling because all of us had some experience with these techniques in small amounts," says Lisberger, "... if we set this up correctly and had the right team of people, that we could turn this into a process that would be able to handle this quantity. And we did... ." Because of the extent of the CGI planned, much of it specialized, the worked was divided among four different companies: Digital Effects, Robert Abel & Associates, Mathematical Applications Group Incorporated (MAGI), and Information International Incorporated (Triple-I).[18] Each had their own expertise and way of working. One of the difficulties became merging the different ways the different companies interpreted the characters and objects. Together with merging live action with animation, ensuring a smooth integration so all the scenes appeared seamless was one of the greatest challenges. Richard Taylor of Triple-I, who was overseeing design and programming for the film commented, "As a design problem and as a film-making problem, I think that was the most difficult thing to do" (Carlson 2017).

Fifteen minutes of the final film consisted of moving images that were generated entirely by computer programs. While the more traditional techniques, such as matte painting, predominated, a further two hundred background scenes were also generated with computer graphics. Backlit optical effects played a major part in giving the game world its neon look. Lisberger brought his experience with backlit optical effects developed for *Animalympics*. In *Animalympics's* introductory credits, Tie Fighter-like shapes (*Star Wars*), their frames glowing, fly at the viewer, morph into triangular shapes that send a blast which explodes into stars and transforms into an outline of a dynamic super-human figure who throws out glowing discs that fly across the screen. These discs were predecessors to the glowing concentric identity discs in *TRON*, an important piece of multi-functioning equipment used by the players. The disc housed personal data and was used in battle as a shield or as a boomerang. Backlit optical effects created the glowing circuitry on the costumes of the characters and, as CAPS was a ways in the future, each glowing bit had to be painted on each frame by hand.

A major limitation at the time was that computers were able to generate only static images and not moving images. The work to animate the images was not

---

[18] MAGI and Triple I were given most of the work in computer animation because of their expertise in creating motion and 3D graphics. MAGI had responsibility for creating work mainly for the first half of the film "in the game grid area where they created such vehicles as the Lightcycles, Recognizers, and Tanks." Triple I's work was seen more in the second half and their work on the MCP and the Solar Sailer is some of the most complex graphics work in the film (Carlson 2017, pp. 442–4).

unlike traditional animation in its heavy requirement for painstaking, and infinite, detail work: as example, the camera coordinates of the lightcycle sequence were inserted by hand for each frame. It took approximately 600 coordinates to create just four seconds of movie. Those who worked on the film emphasize just how little technology the animators started out with, "they would wake up and there would be some new digital inventions…. The momentum was there. During the course of the production it was changed radically… this excitement of being able to be out in the frontier of something brand new is something that didn't happen all the time" (King 2017).

The film created great excitement in the CG world. In a reminiscence on the development of *TRON* Kroyer says "The minute the word got out that Steve had this idea [making a film about computers] people just started coming to the studio. I remember Alan Kay would come down from Xerox PARC every week to consult with us on our story sessions" (Kroyer 2012). The film attracted not only people from the outside but also those who worked in the traditional arm of Disney. While many Disney animators were adverse to CG, more came by to see the work once it was underway. One of those intrigued was John Lasseter who "used to come and sit behind me all the time and watch. That's where he really started to get hooked on computer animation" (King 2017).

The film's use of technology ultimately eclipsed its story. With so much emotion and enthusiasm invested in the technology, the story was bound to get short shrift and reviews at the time extolled the technology but not the storyline.

> … this movie is a machine to dazzle and delight us. It is not a human-interest adventure in any generally accepted way. That's all right, of course. It's brilliant at what it does, and in a technical way maybe it's breaking ground for a generation of movies in which computer-generated universes will be the background for mind-generated stories about emotion-generated personalities. (Ebert 1982; Price 2009)

To the film's great credit the CGI and VFX technology used today is a direct descendent of what was created in *TRON*. As John Lasseter put it, "Without *TRON* there would be no *Toy Story*" (King 2017). The industry would learn to use CGI technology as an effective technology to enhance the telling of a good story only in future films. And John Lasseter would be one of the people who would help ensure that the story stayed key.

## 9.6   *Computers Are People Too*

From early in the studio's career Walt had promoted the technology he loved and the studio's animated stories through promotional films, from the 1941 *The Reluctant Dragon* that takes the audience on a tour through the new Burbank studios, to the final film he shot for his weekly television program *Wonderful World of Disney* in 1966 about EPCOT. The studio continued this tradition and in 1982, just before *TRON* was released in theatres, Disney brought *Computers are People Too* to its television audience.[19] This TV movie celebrated the future of computers as a partnership and captured both the general public's concerns of man being replaced by technology as well as the enthusiasm, in particular of a younger generation, for what technology promised. A kaleidoscopic montage of vintage and contemporary images, the TV movie described leading-edge advances made in computer graphics, computer camps, interviews, and featured scenes from *TRON*. Among other images of the evolution of computer animation, it included clips from the film *Looker,* released before *TRON* in 1981, which showed head, eye, and complete figure of a model being digitally scanned to create a 3D computer-generated character.[20]

## 9.7   *Where the Wild Things Are*

While at Disney, Lasseter and fellow animator Glen Keane worked on a pioneering film test of digitally composited traditional 2D characters and 3D computer graphics backgrounds. Using Maurice Sendak's story *Where the Wild Things Are* (1982–83) they generated a model of Max, his dog, his room, and parts of the house. Max is scratching his name on the wall when the dog comes and jumps on the bed. Max chases the dog down the stairs and runs out of the door knocking a lamp down in his haste. The tricky dog has hidden around a corner and once Max is gone, sneaks back up the stairs. A Disney docushort shows the vector test and then the modeled results.[21] The test was featured in the in-house newsletter, *Disney Newsreel*[22] in which Lasseter comments, "In five years these tests will seem so primitive, they'll look like *Steamboat Willie* does today" (Amidi 2011).

## 9.8   *Black Cauldron* and *The Great Mouse Detective*

In 1985 Disney released its first animated film that used computer-generated imagery, *The Black Cauldron.* The film, 5 years in the making, was planned as a return to the Disney tradition of grand storytelling. It was filmed in 70 mm for widescreen and there was a plan for "special holographic sequences to bring the deathless swordsmen into the theatre" (Kois 2010). As with *Fantasia,* the studio set out to consider an older audience, although in this case it was interested in attracting the youngsters that had grown up with its cartoons and were now teenagers. The story

---

[19] Complete movie from Museum of Classic Chicago Television, https://www.youtube.com/watch?v=Poc-zDWz8FU

[20] https://www.youtube.com/watch?v=Poc-zDWz8FU, minute 14:22. Richard Taylor notes that the reason the computer graphics weren't given more attention was because the storyline has them shown on the laboratory monitors rather than full-frame (Taylor 2017).

[21] Disney docushort showing test: https://www.youtube.com/watch?v=LvIDRoO8KnM

[22] Experimenting with Computer Generated Graphics, Vol.12. No. 23, June 10, 1983. (Amidi 2011)

is based on Lloyd Alexander's YA (Young Adults) books *The Chronicles of Prydain*. It is a dark fantasy and the imagery used throughout is dark and frightening, much in the vein of *Night on Bald Mountain*, rather than the comic approach taken in Disney's typical animation treatment of stories in the 1960s and 1970s, such as *Jungle Book*, *The Aristocats*, and *Robin Hood*. It is noted for being the first Disney animated movie that received a PG rating because of its frightening depictions of evil and violence, even though a number of scenes were cut for the final release.

Unlike in *TRON* where CGI was evident as a feature of the story, in *The Black Cauldron*, CGI was used to add special effects to traditional animation, such as making the bubbles, the floating orb of light, and the realistic flames at the end of the movie. It was also used for objects such as the escape boat and the cauldron itself. The Animation Photo Transfer Process, APT, was another technology introduced to help the production process. This was a new photographic way for animators sketches to be transferred onto cels that Disney had developed and which its animators used for a number of films. It was subsequently replaced by CAPS in 1990. The CG enhanced the look of the scenes in which it was used, but neither of these technologies had a major impact on how the story was told. While the film used gruesome scenes similar to those in live action films like the *Indiana Jones* series, the effects were all accomplished with traditional animation techniques.[23]

The story is complicated and difficult to tell. The final script was sufficiently different that the author, commented, "… I have to say, there is no resemblance between the movie and the book…. I had fun watching it…. The book is quite different. It's a very powerful, very moving story, and I think people would find a lot more depth in the book".[24] Reviews praised the movie's visuals but the story received mixed reviews. Interestingly it was used by Disney as the basis for a video game and, in that genre, proved to be ahead of its time in storytelling. The game designer Al Lowe created six different endings and offered players choice in their decision making, unusual and progressive at the time. Unfortunately the movie was very expensive to make, and a financial drain on the company.

The next film to use computer graphics, *Great Mouse Detective* (1986), used it in a way that assisted animators to create a more exciting and dynamic chase scene in Big Ben's clock tower. The animators designed Big Ben's gears on a computer and printed out wire frames to use as references for the chase. This gave them reference points for visualizing Basil swooping in and out of the gears. The final scenes were, however, traditionally hand-drawn as at the time the CGI was still limited in its capabilities. The gear chase, helped by the complex views the wireframes provided, did rivet audiences with reviewers noting, "As usual with film noir [...] it is the villain who steals the heart and one is rooting for in the breathtaking showdown high up in the cogs and ratchets of Big Ben" (Peachment 2008, p. 426). The reviews also

---

[23] The atmosphere of terror was heightened and maintained by the musical score.

[24] https://www.scholastic.com/teachers/articles/teaching-content/lloyd-alexander-interview-transcript/

rated the story as one of studio's stronger efforts and reiterated the importance of engaging the audience through well-developed characters: "The key to good Disney animation is character and facial expression, and *Detective* abounds in both" (Steinmetz 1986).

## 9.9  *Beauty and the Beast*

On September 29, 1991, Disney premiered an unfinished, work-in-progress version of *Beauty and the Beast* "in what at the time seemed like the unlikeliest of venues, the New York Film Festival, America's most prestigious showcase of international and art-house fare" (Ebiri 2019). At the time, Disney animated features were thought of as fare for kids, with parents tagging along. This had changed from 50 years earlier when Disney's features, *Snow White, Fantasia, Pinocchio,* appealed to all members of the family, and to adults possibly even more so than to children. Showing the preview was a risky decision for both the studio and for the Festival. The studio had never shown a work in progress, the festival's audience was unaccustomed to being shown mainstream animation. Production on the feature had already been in the works for 4 years, and although only three-quarters complete, Disney marketing wanted to create early interest in it. The animators created a seamless story for the festival from the work in production: the preview began with black and white drawings, animators' versions of sketches, and actual footage of "a babbling brook." Only when the "windows open up and townspeople start greeting her [Belle] with a series of bouncy bonjours do we witness the final animation in all its breathtaking, full-color glory" (Ebiri 2019). The audience reacted with enthusiasm and wild applause throughout. The films co-director Kirk Wise says of the screening, "I really do feel that screening represented the real turning point in terms of the audience perception of these movies. From *Beauty and the Beast* onward, I think animation managed to escape the kids' movie ghetto we'd been consigned to for so long. It made the audience look at it as not just cartoons, but as film" (Ebiri 2019). The movie began an era of Disney animation that actualized Walt's dream of animated features holding a rightful place as equals with live action in the film world.

It was also finally in *Beauty and the Beast* that CGI began to take its place as a technology that could strengthen and elevate story in Disney's animation movie pantheon. As in *The Rescuers Down Under,* the movie used CAPS. Every frame of the film was scanned, created, or composited using the computer system and animators were able to create a world with the look of Disney's exquisitely hand animated first features. By far the most famous computer-aided scene in *Beauty and the Beast* is the sequence of Belle and the Beast waltzing through a computer generated ballroom. The studio had only created wire-frames in CG prior to this; Jim Hillin, who supervised the CG animation, had only nine months in which to ensure the CG sequence was completed on time, "we had to set up a whole software pipeline for getting this done" (Failes 2016). Hillin used technology familiar to him, RenderMan and the modeler Alias (precursor to Maya), "there were finally beginning to be standards for how to do this stuff—how to put together a scene, how to create material that responded the same way every time" (Failes 2016). Complex perspectives were very difficult to achieve with traditional animation techniques. In *Beauty and the Beast* the animators composited hand-drawn traditional character animation, CG imagery of the ballroom created by CGI artists and engineers based on a concept painting made by the background department, and complex multiplane camera moves to do so. As Mrs. Potts, the teapot (Angela Lansbury) sings the signature song *Tale as Old as Time* and looks on with her son Chip, the camera takes the audience on a slow sweep from the couple, around the ballroom, to high above the chandelier, then back down through it, to join the couple again as their dance takes them to the patio doors and they begin to walk out. The scene ends with Mrs. Potts giving Chip a kiss goodnight; he takes a last look from around the corner as he heads for bed.[25]

The sequence marries hand drawn animation with CGI seamlessly creating a powerful visual as well as an emotionally engaging moment. Complex perspective had been experimented with by the studio's animators as far back as *The Three Kittens* in 1933 when kittens scampering across a black and white tiled floor was a scene too complex and time consuming to create realistically. Now the camera swooped around a room which consisted of hundreds of windows, tile patterns, and chandelier crystals, all of them changing with each frame, to create a scene of wonder and romance around the hero and heroine.

In the 1980s the studio had made 5 animated films, in the 1990s they went on to make 15, all of them made completely with CAPS and using CGI in sequences that benefitted scenes by its use. Among these were *Aladdin, The Lion King, Pocahontas, The Hunchback of Notre Dame, Hercules, Mulan, and Tarzan*. In addition to these, a partnership began with Pixar to make *Toy Story*, and added *A Bug's Life,* and *Toy Story 2* later in the decade. That alliance brought with it Pixar's more advanced CGI capability to the Disney studio.

## 9.10   *Lion King*

In the 1990s Disney used hand-drawn animation and enhanced with CGI only when a director wanted a special effect or when a scene proved beyond the capability of the combination of hand-drawn animation and CAPS. In the *Lion King* (1994) CGI was used during the wildebeest stampede scene in which Mufasa, Simba's father, was killed. The storyline depended on the wildebeest stampeding. There had been no occasion in previous films where a crowd scene was as significant a plot point as was this one. There was no reference for and no CGI tools to create crowd action that also showed individual movement which is shown in this sequence. Scott Johnston, the artistic supervisor, clarified the process in a docushort about the scene:

---

[25] Ballroom scene: http://www.youtube.com/watch?v=9qtTPTxvoPA

a hand animator provided reference artwork of a wildbeest as well as of one galloping. The CG artist matched the image as closely as possible then extrapolated it in
3D so it could be rotated and filmed from all angles as the scene required. Johnson
and his fellow animators wrote their own software for planning the trajectories of
the stampede which they based on key animal's movements. They choreographed
the overall crowd action and then created modifications for individual animals for
actions such as leaning into curves. They color coded each wildebeest for all of the
planning and once the action was in place they colored each animal realistically,
giving each individual characteristics (Johnston 2012).[26] The stampede is one of the
most riveting in the movie; CGI was used successfully to move the story forward
visually and emotionally.

## 9.11  Connecting with Pixar

Disney and Pixar came to know each other's strength's through the CAPS Project.[27]
The creation of Pixar had been financed primarily by Steve Jobs whose intent was
to build a hardware company. As under Lucasfilm, where their job was to use computers for editing audio and video, not to create graphics, the team's interest in making animations was concealed as making experimental films to show off the
capabilities of the imaging equipment the company sold, the Pixar Image Computer
(Price 2009). Among the employees that left Lucasfilm to start Pixar was John
Lasseter. John had worked at Disney as an animator, had been let go, and had subsequently been hired by Catmull and Smith to join the Graphics Group because of
his storytelling and animation skills (Seymour 2012). He was the only animator at
Pixar: with him he brought his interest in story and his talent in storytelling.[28]

   To promote Pixar in their first year of business, Catmull and Smith wanted to
have a film to show at the 1986 SIGGRAPH show, an important industry conference
and show that featured new ideas and products in computer graphics.[29] Lasseter
developed a self-shadowing sequence around his Luxo lamp in which the light from
the lamp created its own shadows, a test to show how shadows could be created
using the company's PhotoRealistic RenderMan software. Happenstance in the
form of a coworker bringing in his little boy led to Lasseter creating a smaller, child
version of the lamp, Luxo Jr. He designed the sequence as a motion study and

---

[26] Scott Johnston on how the stampede was made in CGI at https://www.youtube.com/watch?v=
HLmAT6t5kL0

[27] There are many histories of Pixar's start. Alvy Ray Smith's takes the story back to NYIT. It is
found at https://www.fxguide.com/fxfeatured/alvy-ray-smith-rgba-the-birth-of-compositing-the-
founding-of-pixar/

[28] Lasseter speaks about the excitement during the early formation of Pixar when he was "the only
animator" in a talk about the making of *Toy Story* (Pixar 2010).

[29] Started in 1974, SIGGRAPH is the premier computer graphics conference and industry show
held in North America. Since 2008 a second conference has taken place yearly in Asia.

showed it at the Anima Festival in Brussels (Neupert 2016). There he was reminded by the award winning animator Raoul Servais that any animation "No matter how short it is, it should have a beginning, a middle, and an end. Don't forget the story" (Price 2009).[30] Lasseter's training at Disney, where story and character integral to telling that story came first, his inherent storytelling skills, and his abilities as an animator, led to his redeveloping the sequence as an affectionate storyline about a dad (or mom), their kid, and a bouncing ball. The story was etched into the objects' movements and engaged the audience, not only intellectually, but more importantly, emotionally. "There's curiosity, there's dismay, there's sympathy, there's amusement, a whole range of things that he was able to get through to the audience using just a few triangles" (Luxo Jr. (1986), 2018).[31]

Lasseter knew that his skills lay in telling the story; he worked with Pixar's graphics experts and showed them how to bring personality and emotion to characters through movement while they helped him with model making and rendering. Other tests done at the company included *Flags and Waves,* that experimented with water reflecting sunlight as it lapped against a shore, and *Beach Chair,* in which an object, a beach chair, displays a personality as it tentatively approaches the water (Price 2009).

It was Lasseter's responsibility to take the technology the company was developing and tell stories they could use to promote it. His next short, *Tin Toy* was officially a test for the PhotoRealistic RenderMan software and was completely animated in CGI. The story again revolved around objects, this time it referenced his love of classic toys and showed a small musical toy, a one-man band, attempting to save itself from the enthusiastic attention of an infant. Hiding under a sofa with other terrified toys, it feels badly when it sees the infant fall and begin to cry. It goes out to distract the infant, and when it loses the infant's attention to the very box it came in, the toy is annoyed, wants to be the center of attention again, and follows the infant about playing its instruments. The short was shown at SIGGRAPH, and as with *Luxo Jr,* received accolades from the industry and later won the 1988 Academy Award for Best Animated Short Film, the first computer-generated film to do so. It gained Disney's attention and led to a movie collaboration between Disney and Pixar that was the beginning of Disney's, now enduring, commitment to CGI, and telling stories digitally.

---

[30] Raoul Servais went on to say, "You can tell a story in ten seconds" when Lasseter complained of how little time they had for the film. Servais is noted for his live action animation short Harpya (1979) which won the Palme d'Or for Best Short Film at the 1979 Cannes Film Festival.

[31] This clip about the making of *Luxo Jr* shows the excitement the short created at the 1986 SIGGRAPH screening. Comment is from Jim Blinn, from NASA/Jet Propulsion Labs, https://www.youtube.com/watch?time_continue=206&v=MJQRVKtwr70&feature=emb_logo

## 9.12  *Toy Story,* Disney's Digital Leap

> Working on the production, Andy Stanton, who rewrote the script said "it's not a widget you're making. It's not a product" (Zorthian 2015).

In 1991, all Disney's animation production used CAPS but the company only used CGI as a technology aid when directors wanted something special. Through the development of CAPS Disney and Pixar had grown to know each other well and Disney began to show interest in making a feature with Pixar. Pixar suggested a half-hour Christmas special based on the *Tin Toy.* In response Jeffrey Katzenberg, head of Disney at the time, offered them a contract for a full-length feature film, with an option to make two more (Price 2009). Pixar had the technical expertise and Disney had the filmmaking expertise. The first film they collaborated on, *Toy Story,* was a buddy film about two toys, one a pull-string cowboy doll and the other an astronaut action figure, who are first competitors for their "boy's" attention but through adversity, end up friends. The movie brought advancements in CGI that captured the "illusion of life" and showed a growing industry that technology in animation did more than bring toys to computer-generated life, it also offered new storytelling opportunities.

The Pixar team anticipated learning from Disney about filmmaking and envisioned working with an experienced group who could guide them through the process of making an animated movie. This did not work out as hoped. The first year Disney and Pixar would fly back and forth to LA to discuss progress, Pixar provided storyboards of the storyline and the character development, Disney made changes, Pixar reacted to the changes and made new storyboards to discuss. The last person to see the work was always Jeffrey Katzenberg, the head of the studio. He was very interested in animation and in the film, and pushed constantly for it to be "edgier." Rather than undergoing a thoughtful evolution, the constant reacting to criticism morphed the story into something unexpected. Lasseter talks about the day they were ready to present about half the film; after the fact, they called the day Black Friday, "I sat there and I tell ya' I was pretty much embarrassed by what was on the screen... it was a story filled with the most unhappy mean people" (Pixar 2010). Through the back and forth process the movie had changed and was no longer the movie that Lasseter and his team had envisioned. Disney shut down production and wanted to start laying people off but Lasseter said no, he wanted two weeks to go back and rework it. And the team did. Back at their studio he said, "Let's just make the movie we want to make." The group "really bonded" as they worked as a team to return to the original ideas, built up the characters, and created a story that had conflict but was also a buddy film. Pictures of them working with their storyboards, evoke the exciting moments depicted of Walt and his crew working on *Snow White* in a similar setting (Pixar 2010).

"Our goal was to make Woody so likeable then when he started kinda becoming a jerk it was like, 'Oh Woody, don't make those choices,' instead of 'what a jerk, I don't care about this guy'." Lasseter goes on to say, "After this experience... the most important thing we learned was to trust our own instinct and to make the movies we wanted to make" (Pixar 2010). If Disney could not provide advice on a process, and considering the complexity of integrating the needs of CGI and film-making perhaps Pixar's hope of that happening was ingenuous, then they would develop the pipeline as they went, on the fly, something they were already accustomed to doing when new technology was needed to bring an idea to reality.

As a pioneer film, *Toy Story,* had no graphic assets. One of Disney's advantages in producing animated films was the extensive archive of images the studio had developed. Common objects abounded as did rotoscoped figures of characters in motion. Snow White dancing in 1937 was still used more than 35 years later as reference for Maid Marion dancing in *Robin Hood* (1973). Christopher Robin and Mowgli shared a throwing arm between 1967 and 1977. The ballroom dance scene in *Cinderella* in 1959 was repeated in *Beauty and the Beast* in 1991. Everything in *Toy Story* had to be constructed from scratch, not only the characters but every chair, every flower, every blade of grass had to be visualized, drawn first in 2D and then constructed in 3D so it could be walked around, moved, used in combination with other objects. Given the state of CG at the time, the film was fortunate in its choice of subject. Toys are made of plastic or metal and could be made to look realistic more easily than could humans, who in the film were purposefully stylized and appeared only minimally (Snider 1995).

One of the goals for the technology for *Toy Story* was to give animators software they could learn to use on their own without being or becoming computer graphics experts (Zorthian 2015). Central to the project were Menv and RenderMan. The Menv modeling environment gave animators the tools to articulate 3D models of characters. Menv was develop specifically with the traditional animator in mind when Lasseter was working on *Tin Toy.*[32] It was designed in modules so one tool could be used at a time and new tools could be designed and added when needed. It supported secondary animation (ripple effects of water), procedural animation (define a set of rules to repeat), and it had articulation controls so an animator could isolate and plan movements—the shoulder, elbow, and wrist of an arm throwing a ball for instance—as key frames and have the computer complete the action (Pak 2015; Snider 1995). Each character was given their own set of behaviors, Eben Ostby, one of the modelers on the film says, "I work a lot with the lead animator to find out what he needs to know about a character, how he expects it to behave, how the wrist should bend, or how we should make the face smile or frown. This takes months for each character" (Snider 1995). This early work provided flexibility downstream and meant each character could be animated doing many different kinds of movement. If the animator wanted to change a movement even fractionally, in 2D cell animation, the key frames and all the in-betweens would have to be redrawn; in Menv, a key frame would be changed and the computer would take care of the rest. Lasseter preferred not to assign a character to each animator in the traditional Disney sense; once character behaviors were completed, animators could

---

[32] Menv replaced Motion Doctor, a less nimble software used before Lasseter's input.

work on more than one character without concern that the nature of the character's movements would change (Price 2009).

RenderMan was the studios shading and rendering tool. It had been developed at Graphics Group to create realistic images and lighting so characters would move in believable ways. At the time, the group wanted to convince Lucas he should use CG in his films (think *Star Wars* with its host of interesting unusually colored aliens). The software was used in all Pixar experimental shorts such as *Luxo Jr* and *Tin Toy* and would be essential for rendering the much longer *Toy Story*. When a need appeared, Pixar created additional software, such as *Unwrap* which helped with complex surfaces. The program would take a curved image, like a face or a ball, flatten it so animators could add details, then wrap it back on the model (Snider 1995).

The pipeline for the film went something like this:

*Creative development*: The script was "locked down." Early sketches, story-boards, were drawn of each of the movie shots. These were scanned and mixed with preliminary dialogue and music in Avid Media Composer to create video storyreels and begin the iterative process of view, change, approve that continued until the final approval.

*Artistic Design*: An art director was brought in to create a visual feel. Character designs were created and changed as the story evolved. Spaces and objects (Andy's room, the bed, the desk) were designed. Lighting was considered for mood and tone of shots. A design document was created for characters and objects. Reference photo files were created.

*Production*: Actual models or 3D computer models of the characters were made. The real models were digitized and made into 3D models. The 3D models were then articulated. Animators choreographed character's movements. Voices were recorded. Backgrounds were designed. Models were placed in shots for the virtual camera to film. Standard camera moves were programmed (so it appeared as if a live action movie was being shot). Rough animation shots went onto storyreels to replace the original storyboards: the movie could be seen in rough form for the first time. Experienced animators refined the rough animations. Shading began, surfaces were textured (color, pattern, texture, dirt). Background paintings were composited with computer images to get the results visualized in the storyboards. Preliminary lighting was refined to complement each scene, provide interest and ensure continuity. As shots were approved they went to be rendered. As rendered sequences become available sound effects were added, color corrections made. The editing system was used to assemble the sequences as the final version that would be used for the 35 mm cut (Henne 1996; Snider 1995; Price 2009).

The work was ambitious: 27 animators built 400 computer models of the characters. Each was articulated: Woody alone had 723 motion controls, with 212 for his face and 58 for his mouth (Henne 1996). Characters' mouths and faces were synced to their voices, which took animators a week for each 8 seconds of animation (Snider 1995). The final rendering was completed with 117 Sun Microsystems computers running 24 hours a day. A total of 800,000 hours of machine time was required for the final render of 114,240 frames (Snider 1995; Price 2009).

Although the film was produced completely by computers, Catmull noted on its release that "almost all of the reviews only mentioned in one sentence that it was done on computer. We took incredible pride in that. We had succeeded because we hadn't made it about the technology. We made it about the story, which is what our goal had been" (Pixar 2010).

There are many comparisons with Disney's early history. With the "folly" *Snow White,* no one had ever made a feature length animated movie; with *Toy Story,* no one had ever made an entire animated movie using CG. Disney went from making 6 and 7 minute shorts to creating an 83 minute feature. Pixar went from making commercials and 5 minute shorts to an 81 minute feature. Both companies invented technology as they needed it, and possibly more importantly, developed the process of making features. *Snow White* received an Academy Honorary Award for Walt Disney "as a significant screen innovation which has charmed millions and pioneered a great new entertainment field." *Toy Story* received an Academy Special Achievement Award for Pixar "for the development and inspired application of techniques that have made possible the first feature-length computer-animated film." Walt Disney talked about a new kind of believability, "The kind of animation we were after was entirely new. Before that, it had been done by stunts: limber legs moving in trick runs like egg beaters. But in *Snow White,* we wanted our action believable. We were after drama and pathos as well as laughter" (Miller 1956). Lasseter tells us, "When we were working on this film, what kept pushing us was that we were doing something that's never been done. With these tools of computer animation, you can make things look so real that people believe whatever you've created really exists" (Snider 1995).

Disney and Pixar went on to make *A Bug's Life* (1998) and *Toy Story 2* (1999) before the end of the decade. Disney eventually purchased Pixar in 2006. Since *Toy Story*, Pixar has made 20 feature film and dozens of shorts and has received many accolades for its consistent excellence in telling stories that engage their audience, and for its continued development of innovative graphics technologies.

## 9.13   After *Toy Story*: New Lighting Technology

The intent of this history is to stop with Disney's first major CGI film. *Toy Story* is however, a Pixar film. Disney's animation arm, Walt Disney Feature Animation, did not release a full computer-animated feature until *Chicken Little* in 2005. When Disney purchased Pixar in 2006, Ed Catmull became President of Disney and John Lasseter became Chief Creative Officer. They set a direction for repositioning and reviving the animation house, and changed its name to Walt Disney Animation Studios. This section will end with short descriptions of three directions that technology and story are currently taking that have potential for being historical points as Disney moves forward.

The fairy-tale inspired *Frozen* brought the studio back to its blockbuster status but it was *Big Hero 6* released in 2014 that showed that Disney still had the drive to develop leading-edge technology as well as brilliant storytelling. In much the same way that *TRON* was a love letter to the technology of the computer game, *Big Hero 6* is a love letter to the science and technology of the robot. Based in one of the Marvel franchised stories Disney had acquired in 2009, it is the story of a young man, Hiro, who with the robot Baymax and four of Hiro's nerdy friends come together to make a high-tech band of heroes. For the movie, Disney developed the light rendering software Hyperion, which it has used in subsequent films.[33] As with earlier new technologies, it wasn't a sure thing, and represented the studio's greatest and riskiest commitment to R&D in animation technology. In a docushort explaining the process, Disney's Chief Technology Officer Andy Hendrickson says, "It's the analog to building a car while you're driving it," and required use of a 55,000-core supercomputer spread across four geographic locations. Hendrickson goes on to explain, "light gets from its source to the camera as it's bouncing and picking up colors and illuminating other things," instead of the one-bounce indirect lighting normally used in animation, Hyperion uses 10 to 20 bounces. "This movie's so complex that humans couldn't actually handle the complexity. We had to come up with automated systems." To put how big the task was into perspective, Hendrickson says that Hyperion "could render *Tangled* from scratch every 10 days."[34]

Disney animators went on trips to MIT, Harvard, Carnegie Mellon, and Tokyo University in Japan, researching both the latest, and what was coming, in robotic technology. The result was a movie in which Hiro used the latest technology, such as a 3D printer, as part of the story and the robot, Baymax, was ahead of the curve in robotic possibilities. The movie brought technology and story together and offered the audience "something for everyone: action, camaraderie, superheroes and villains. But mostly, Baymax offers a compassionate and healing voice for those suffering, and a hug that can be felt through the screen" (Estrella 2014).

## 9.14  Virtual Reality

In 2018 Disney married cutting-edge virtual reality (VR) technology with its own classic art style in the three minute short *Cycles*. First time director, Jeff Gipson was inspired to tell the story of his grandparents living in their home before his grandmother had to move to assisted living after his grandfather died. He visualized the story standing in the living room and sharing the experiences his grandparents had enjoyed. The studio had not worked with VR before. A new process had to be integrated into the existing animation pipeline and a motion capture stage was built so the filmmaking team could visualize the story (Pobletein 2018). At its debut at SIGGRAPGH, participants stood on a plush rug, donned a VR headset, and were

---

[33] *Big Hero* Teaser Trailer https://www.youtube.com/watch?v=OvgyXKDXdZY. *Big Hero* Trailer https://www.youtube.com/watch?v=z3biFxZIJOQ

[34] https://www.engadget.com/2014/10/18/disney-big-hero-6/

invited into a 1950s home. The story begins at the end, when the house is dark and the two main characters are discussing the necessity of the grandmother moving out of the house (Snetiker 2018). The movie then turns to flashbacks to show the house as it was lived in over the years. The viewer is free to look around in any direction throughout the experience although the majority of the experience requires the user to pay attention to specific locations in order to follow along with the plot. To help guide a user's gaze towards the action, *Cycles* automatically fades to gray whenever the viewer breaks general eye contact with the focus point of the scene: an intuitive way of redirecting attention without taking the viewer out of the experience. The happy moments in the movie and the ending are filled with a sense of poignancy made more authentic by the VR. The poster for the movie takes advantage of augmented reality (AR): if viewed through an iPad or iPhone the door opens up to show scenes from the short. In a short documentary about the film Gipson talks about the personal meaning the story has for him and how important it was to marry that story with the technology he envisioned for it.[35]

Virtual reality requires headgear that is only beginning to make an impact with the general audience of Disney viewers. As research into the technology makes it more affordable, as more young people who are familiar with the technology through video games take an interest, more stories such as *Cycles* that have animation potential and benefit from 360 degree participation will surface.

## 9.15 Live Action, Photorealistic Remakes

Disney began to remake its classic animations as live action films with *The Jungle Book* in 1994 (remake of the 1967 movie). With the successes of a second remake of *Jungle Book* in 2016 and of the remake of *Beauty and the Beast* in 2017, Disney moved forward to create a new canon of what it calls live action from a long list of its animated features. The new films use real actors and CGI effects to bring characters or animals to life and create or augment the story settings. The latest offerings have received a mixed reaction, with the audience often comparing the new versions against the old, CGI not always able to simulate live action as expected, and animals not able to demonstrate the same quality of expression that an animation brings. Walt's purpose in his animated features was to create an illusion of life, not real life, but rather the essence of characters and situations. Animations bring expressiveness and personality to depictions of animals and objects, and even people. Treated with care, the live action versions may rise to new heights when aided by CGI technology but critics worry that the creativeness for searching out enchanting new stories is now buried beneath the rush to use CGI technology in a way that doesn't benefit the story. One convincing argument was presented by a Disney fan and reviewer writing in Forbes, "... photorealism is not inherently superior to 2D animation; those old

---

[35] https://www.youtube.com/watch?v=bh648H4S7Y4

Disney animators didn't draw cartoon lions as a backup plan because they couldn't train an animal to say lines. They chose that medium to tell a beautiful, stylized story, a story that resonated with children and adults alike" (Placido 2018).

## 9.16   Going On to Walt's Master Narrative

The next section returns to Walt Disney's earliest days to look at his process of creating the Disney Master Narrative. Walt's purpose was not only to create the best in animated stories but also to bring the stories and their characters to everyman, everyday, and, eventually, across all media As part of the company's growth and popularity—a result of *Steamboat Willie* and their star attraction, *Mickey Mouse*—Walt and his brother Roy were able to take advantage of other media to bring Disney stories to the public, and to build a Disney Master Narrative that would help maintain their continuous presence in the public eye. The next section briefly describes the first journeys across different media they embarked upon to feed the voracious appetite their audience had developed for all things Disney in just a brief period of time. The model of cross-media storytelling and marketing they developed and then embraced benefits the company to this day.

# Part II
# From Watching to Experiencing Across Media

**The Mickey Mouse Yell**

Handy! Dandy!
Sweet as candy!
Happy kids are we!
Eenie! Ickie!
Minnie! Mickey!
M-O-U-S-E!

*Walt was determined that his cartoon Mickey Mouse would be "as well known as any cartoon on the market." Soon after he first appeared in "Steamboat Willie" Mickey and then his friends made their appearance in all manner of merchandise. Mickey's popularity crossed boundaries from books to Mickey Mouse Clubs to television and, ultimately, to Disneyland, a themed entertainment environment that brought Mickey and friends to real life.*

# Chapter 10
# Creating the Disney Master Narrative

*My husband is one of the devotees of Mickey Mouse.... .*
*Please believe that we are all of us most grateful to you*
*for many delightful evenings.*

Eleanor Roosevelt

## 10.1  Establishing a Cultural Icon Within Popular Culture

*Steamboat Willie* came to the screen on November 18, 1928 at the Colony Theatre
in New York and became an immediate sensation, winning accolades for its sound
innovation and for keeping "the audience laughing and chuckling from the moment
the lead titles came on the screen" (*Weekly Film Review*). Walt's love of animation,
and his understanding of the nature of stories, determined the push towards exploration of the expressive nature of the new technologies he worked with. This was one
of the reasons for the constant exploration for ways to present his characters and
stories in animation. But it wasn't the reason for his interest in increasing the scope
of the characters he had created and shaped.

Over the years Walt's name came to be associated with many different characters
and stories. Ultimately, however, the Disney name was built on the little mouse
Mickey. Early on in his career Walt had been stung by Charles Mintz's underhanded
business dealings. After his problems with the *Alice* series and then the *Oswald* character, he was determined that his cartoon *Mickey Mouse* would be "as well known as
any cartoon on the market" so that his position would be completely invulnerable.
Walt understood that stories lived in many media worlds and he would make Mickey
popular in all of them. When entering the medium of television in the 1950s he said,
"I've always had this confidence since way back when we had our first upsets and
lost Oswald and went to Mickey Mouse. Then and there I decided that in every way
we could, we would build ourselves with the public and keep faith with the public."

---

Online photos and graphics provide extra detail and are identified by urls the reader can refer to.
This additional reference information will be particularly beneficial as an enhancement for the
online version of this book. URLs are current at time of printing.

© Springer Nature Switzerland AG 2020
K. Madej, N. Lee, *Disney Stories*, https://doi.org/10.1007/978-3-030-42738-2_10

As a model Walt would take the animated character *Felix the Cat*, the most popular character at the time, with a song, comic strip, books, and merchandise from figurines to pencils depicting his likeness. Unfortunately for Felix, his creator did not share Walt's interest in new technology and was slow in moving into using sound; when Felix cartoons finally did incorporate sound they did so poorly and were a flop. Mickey soon replaced Felix as the people's favorite animation character. Throughout 1929 Mickey Mouse became a national craze, a familiar site not only in the U.S., but also in the capitals of Europe and the Americas.

One correspondent who went around the world shortly after the premier of *Steamboat Willie* said, "After a quick trip around the world… I have returned to New York to say that Mickey Mouse has been with me most of the way" (Finch 1975, p. 88). From England to India, Singapore, Japan, and even the South Sea Islands, Mickey entertained movie-goers who watched as many as seven cartoons in one sitting. The Germans called him Micky Maus, the Hungarians Miki Eger, the Finns Mikki Hiiri, and the Swedes Musse Pigg. The French say his name with a strong accent on the Me-KAY! In China he is 米奇老鼠 or mi qi lao shu, while in Russia he is микки Маус and in Greece Μίκυ Μάους. In Italy a publisher started a comic book featuring Mickey as "Topolino," and Topolino he has been ever since.[1]

Walt took full advantage of the popularity Mickey enjoyed in the U.S. and around the world to make Mickey's story, everyone's story. He orchestrated a Master Narrative, a system of interrelated stories he developed with the purpose of establishing audience expectations for entertainment that was the image of happiness and based in the family values which Mickey, whose character was still evolving, eventually came to represent. Each new manifestation of Mickey and friends, each new appearance of Walt together with his creations, was planned to reinforce the overarching story he was establishing to provide permanency for his ideas.

The varied media that Walt used to build his Master Narrative offered him different types of opportunities to extend or add to the Disney story. Some, such as the merchandising and the *Mickey Mouse Clubs*, brought the animated characters to peoples' homes and communities and became a part of their daily lifestyle. Adults and children incorporated Disney objects and events into their activities in ways that added to their own life stories. In doing so they made them a part of popular culture. Other media such as comics and books were more suitable for or more easily accommodated transmedia storytelling. That is, they told a story across media in ways that both extended the story and gave the audience new ways to engage with it.

---

[1] Photos of international comic covers: http://www.comicvine.com/mickey-mouse/29-39413/issues-cover/. Mickey entertained fans around the world. In 1935, the League of Nations presented a special medal to Walt Disney "for the creation of Mickey Mouse as a 'a symbol of universal good will'." Reference url. http://kpolsson.com/disnehis/disn1935.htm

## 10.2   The Disney Master Narrative and Popular Culture

### 10.2.1   Merchandising

Mickey's story was adapted into a medium other than animation very early in his career. Although Walt was familiar with the financial potential for merchandising a character, merchandising Mickey first happened by chance. In 1929 when Walt was in New York he was pestered by an entrepreneur who wanted to put the image of Mickey Mouse on a school writing tablet. Offered $300 dollars and desperate for the money at the time, Walt said yes. Mickey's first modest presence on a simple school tablet was an inauspicious beginning to what creative merchandising would help him become—not only a character that entertained adults but also a favorite character of teens and children and a ubiquitous presence on the American landscape. He would become a familiar image within the family home, a part of many moments in the day for all family members, no matter what age and no matter what activity. Mickey was more than an image however, as he evolved into an optimistic, cheerful and whole-some character, Mickey would be the key to building the Disney Master Narrative.

As *Steamboat Willie* took on steam and made Mickey a "national craze," Walt and Roy found there were many ways in which they could take advantage of Mickey's popularity to help with their finances. More offers for merchandising contracts arrived; the first that Roy signed was with George Borgfeldt Company in New York. The company was licensed to manufacture and sell "figures and toys of various materials" that used designs based on Mickey and Minnie. One of the first products Borgfeldt produced were Mickey and Minnie handkerchiefs that were manufactured by Waldburger Tanner in Switzerland. 8.5″ × 8.75″ in size, each corner of the hand-kerchief had a different Mickey scene: Mickey and Pluto going for a walk, Minnie running towards them, Mickey and Minnie talking while Pluto looks on, and Mickey drawing a heart on the ground that reads "Mickey Loves Minnie." Even as little a thing as a handkerchief was used to tell a story. These handkerchiefs were a hit and became the most wanted Christmas gift of 1930.[2]

Walt and Roy became dissatisfied with early licensing arrangements: the manufacturers didn't provide products of sufficient quality and the financial arrangements were difficult to deal with. When an enterprising department store sales promotion man from Kansas City, Herman (Kay) Kamen, came to them with a proposal that emphasized the quality of the products that would bear the Disney name and suggested that he could also handle the payment of royalties, they were convinced. A contract was signed on July 1, 1932 and immediately Kamen began to license Mickey's image to appear on all manner of merchandise from watches to children's undies.[3] His ideas proved to be financially lucrative to the Disney studio as demand for Mickey products escalated. For instance, within 2 years of the first Mickey watch being introduced at "Century of Progress," the Chicago Exposition of 1933, two and half

[2]Even as little a thing as a handkerchief told a story. Photo of Mickey and Minnie Mouse Handkerchiefs: https://www.pinterest.ca/pin/569916527834902194/

[3]Mickey's image was both on the product and used to sell it. Display for the first Mickey Mouse Watch: https://www.collectorsweekly.com/stories/217858-the-three-variants-of-the-1933-34-mickey

million watches had been sold. In 1934 Kamen published the first of seven illustrated catalogues that described or showed all the Disney-licensed merchandise available.

As had all animations at the time, Mickey started life as a cartoon targeted at adults. His appeal to children, however, had grown rapidly. Although many of the products licensed by Kamen were intended for children, Mickey merchandise crossed all boundaries, whether it be age, finances, or countries. Businessmen took Mickey satchels to work and children took Mickey lunch boxes to school. Mickey Mouse toothbrushes could be had for a thin dime, Mickey Mouse sweaters sold at three-dollars, while a Cartier's diamond bracelet might be had for $1150, an extravagant amount during the depression of the 1930s. To cross-promote the merchandise being manufactured with the Disney shorts that were coming on stream, Kamen developed giant window displays that featured first Mickey and Minnie and then when they appeared in 1933, The Three Little Pigs. The first displays appeared in fifty stores and were so popular that the next year over 200 stores across the U.S. used a Disney theme in their window display. Along with a presence in homes and shops Mickey "took to the streets" and became a common site in the window displays of theatres, book stores, department stores and many other shops that sold Mickey merchandise.[4]

By 1935, when the *Cleveland Plain Dealer* published a description of what children might have in their home that depicted their beloved Mickey Mouse, there was little on which his likeness could not be found.

> In his room, bordered with M.M. wallpaper and lighted with M.M. lamps, his M.M. alarm clock awakens him, providing his mother forgets! Jumping from his bed where his pajamas and the bedding are the M.M. brand, to a floor the rugs and linoleum upon which are M.M. sponsored, he puts on his M.M. moccasins and rushes to the bathroom to have the first chance at... no, you're wrong... at the soap made in the Disney manner, as are also his toothbrush, hair-brush and towels.

Through extensive merchandising, Mickey had entered the collective consciousness of the general population over a very short period of time. Because his story was one of cheerfulness and indomitable spirit he became an icon during the difficult period of the 1930s. When *The Three Little Pigs* was brought to the screen, the indomitable spirit the animated story portrayed reinforced the master story Walt was creating of both his characters and the Disney approach to story. Walt was successfully building an image as the creator of stories that were consistently entertaining and made people feel good; as an added bonus they could be enjoyed by the entire family.

### 10.2.2   The Road Show

By 1931 Mickey enjoyed an enthusiastic fan base that demanded to see him and his fellow celebrities in person. Walt and his brother Roy looked for an opportunity to bring a live Mickey to his audience. They found one in the traveling road shows of the producers *Fanchon and Marco*.[5] A part of the vaudeville scene, Fanny (Fanchon)

---

[4] Products depicting Mickey, Minnie and their friends became a part of children's day-to-day activities. Photo of Mickey undies: http://www.kshs.org/p/cool-things-mickey-mouse-undies/10227.

[5] *The Mickey Mouse Treasures*. Enclosure (Tieman 2007, p. 10).

and Mike (Marco) Wolf had traveled the road from being a sister and brother ball-room dance team in the 1920s to being successful producers of their own shows on the West Coast Circuit. They staged their review shows in (among other cities on the west coast) Los Angeles, San Francisco, Portland, Seattle, and Vancouver, BC.

*Fanchon and Marco* introduced acts that featured talented singers and/or danc-ers, many of whom became stars, such as Fred and Adele Astaire, Shirley Temple, and the young Judy Garland (as part of the trio *The Gumm Sisters*). They used the signature term "Idea" in naming their shows—*The Stairways Idea* and *The Jazz Temple Idea* are just two of over seventy shows they produced. Mickey's show became *Mickey Mouse Idea*.

*Mickey Mouse Idea* debuted on March 12, 1931 at the Loew's State Theatre in Los Angeles and played to packed houses throughout 1931. The director of the show, deter-mined to catch "the spirit of the Disney characters and transform them into living, breathing stage entertainers," rehearsed the show for eleven weeks rather than the stan-dard four to ensure the he would attain the quality he wanted (Tieman 10). The show followed the format of all *Fanchon and Marco* reviews and boasted a wide range of acts from dance routines to comedy skits. As in the early animations, one skit/gag followed another and the show offered huge entertainment value. The program for the review as it was presented that year by the Fox Theatre at Gimbel's Auditorium (together with the Will Rogers film *Young as You Feel*) shows the diversity of acts presented. The show at Gimbel's was free and adults were encouraged to bring their children.

Vaudeville entertainer Touts Novelle played Mickey, complete with pointed-nose, black and white head, and long pointy tail. The review began with an animated

---

TODAY! at 2:15 P.M in
## Gimbels Auditorium!
*by courtesy of the FOX THEATRE we present*
Fanchon & Marco's
# MICKEY MOUSE
## *Idea*

1. MICKEY MOUSE – in Per-son!
2. 3 Rolling Stones, International Comedians.
3. Toots Novelle. (*Mickey*)
4. Helen Petch, "Alice in Wonderland."
5. Chrissie Daley Bozo, the Educated Dog
6. Louis and Cherle, Chips of France.
7. Sunkist Beauties, Mickey Mouse Girls
8. William Singly, Golden Voiced Tenor.

*Bring the Children! Come Early! No Admission Charge!*

trailer of Mickey Mouse blowing up a large balloon that read "Mickey Mouse Idea."[6] Touts was blown onto the stage when the balloon burst—and then entertained the audience (as Mickey) in the sketches that followed. In many of the reviews Mickey appeared as an introduction to the skit rather than as a key character. In the comedy skit with Bozo the Educated Dog, for instance, Mickey chats with the entertainer then Bozo chases him off stage and proceeds to show how smart he is by pantomiming answers to the questions.

One feature of the review was a live interpretation of Disney's animations in which Mickey appeared as an orchestra conductor who introduced a *Silly Symphony* ballet. Characters such as skeletons, fish, daisies, and frogs capered their way through humorous dance numbers. The show also featured typical review specialty numbers such as the "3 Rolling Stones" who comedy-acted a slow-motion fight, and the ring-and-trapeze act "Louis and Cheri" who featured as human pinwheels whirling at 120 turns per minute with the "Sunkist Beauties" in the finale. The *Illustrated Daily News* drama editor, Eleanor Barnes, enthused, "There has never been anything finer presented at Loew's State on the stage, in this writer's opinion, than this amusing and delightfully fantastic production." The success of this first show supported the development of a new show for 1932 "Mickey and Minnie Mouse."

There was potential for transmedia storytelling in live theatre performance but as *Mickey Mouse Idea* was a vaudeville review that incorporated a variety of acts rather than focusing on any individual story, it did not extend the Disney "stories," only the Disney Master Narrative. New, cross-media interpretations of Disney stories in live theatre performance would wait until 1994 with the staging of *Beauty and the Beast* by Walt Disney Theatrical Productions.

## 10.3   *The Original* Mickey Mouse Club

Mickey increasingly appealed to children and to their parents as family entertainment. Going to the theatre on a Saturday afternoon to see a new Mickey short became a favorite activity across the country. In the suburban Los Angeles theatre, the Fox Dome, the manager Harry Woodin watched as local children filled the seats and enthusiastically cheered the latest Mickey escapades. He thought it would be a good idea to organize activities around the latest Mickey release and make the theatre a place for the community to gather—and the *Mickey Mouse Club* was born.[7]

Each week children would come to the theatre on Saturday afternoon to celebrate their hero. They said the Mickey Mouse pledge, played in the Mickey Mouse band, and enjoyed one of a number of planned activities before they watched the

[6] Mickey blew onto the stage from an animated trailer as an introduction to the *Mickey Mouse Idea*. Vaudeville Mickey https://disney.fandom.com/wiki/Mickey%27s_Vaudeville_Show

[7] *The Mickey Mouse Club*: an afternoon event. http://santarosahistory.com/wordpress/2018/04/lets-all-yell-at-the-mickey-mouse-matinee/

latest cartoon. Woodin believed that children all across the U.S. would be interested in joining a club like his. When on a visit to the Fox, Walt saw all of the smiling, eager faces, he recognized the appeal to children as well as to the parents who were looking for family activities for their children. Here was an opportunity to boost Mickey's presence in every community across the country. He threw his support behind the project and by January 1930 Woodin was well into a campaign to promote *Mickey Mouse Clubs* across the nation. Theatres could buy a club charter and run special matinees and activities for which they could use *Mickey Mouse Club* products such as membership cards and buttons. There were common formats for advertising and banners to promote the opening of the club as well as ongoing events. Theatre owners soon saw what Woodin had noticed in his suburban Los Angeles theatre, that the clubs were a great way to promote their own theatres as a place for the community to gather; that spring and summer many local chapters were inaugurated.

> **What the Mickey Mouse Club Is And What It Means To Do For the Boys And Girls Who Join It!**
>
> THE MICKEY MOUSE CLUB is an organization for boys and girls with its own officers, creed, and ritual (ceremonies) etc. Regular weekly meetings will be held at 10:00 A. M. every Saturday in the form of matinee meetings at the COLONIAL THEATRE, which is launching and will sponsor the club. In addition to the special, all-different programs to be held each Saturday in the COLONIAL THEATRE, stunts, try-outs and contests will be staged and numerous other events, outings, etc., arranged for members. In short, there will be something doing all the time for Mickey and Minnie Mice as boys and girls who are members of the Mickey Mouse Club are known.

The advertisement for the inauguration of a club described club activities, had space for sponsors, and featured pictures of Mickey and Minnie singing and dancing. Children were encouraged to go to a participating Mickey Mouse store to fill out an application and present it at the free opening matinee. The advertisement, intended both for parents and children, points out the organization will be activity-based and community-oriented.

Much like the Boy Scouts' and Girl Scouts' organizations that were popular at the time, each of the *Mickey Mouse Clubs* established a ritual that was followed weekly. *The Daily Tribune* in Bay City, Texas recorded the events of a typical club meeting: First there was the screening of the latest and greatest Mickey Mouse short together with a chapter of the current adventure serial. This was followed by a formal call to order with all the officials coming to the stage. After this introduction the program included other activities such as accepting new members into the club, carrying the colors to the stage, repeating the oath of allegiance and singing a verse of *America,* giving children with birthdays passes for the next week's show, participating in a cracker-eating contest, singing the Mickey Mouse song, and, as a finale, viewing another cartoon. When they became available, copies of the Bibo & Lang *Mickey Mouse Book* were handed out for free to new members.

Every weekend saw thousands of children giving secret handshakes or special member greetings, singing the special club song, and getting involved in activities that ranged from pie-eating to yo-yo contests, and from playing in the band to rop-ing. The Club Creed emphasized a code of behavior and what were seen as American values; parents saw the clubs as a "safe place that kids could spend the day and enjoy wholesome entertainment."

---

**The Mickey Mouse Creed**

I will be a square shooter in my home, in school, on
the playground, and wherever I may be.
I will be truthful and honorable, and strive always, to
make myself a better and more useful little citizen.
I will respect my elders and help the aged, the
helpless and children smaller than myself.
In short I will be a good American!

---

**The Mickey Mouse Yell**

Handy! Dandy!
Sweet as candy!
Happy kids are we!
Eenie! Ickie!
Minnie! Mickey!
M-O-U-S-E!

---

Within the year, 150 clubs had been established with 200,000 or so members. By 1932 there were over 800 clubs across America with a million members. A typical club was *The Tucson Mickey Mouse Club* that had its first meeting on May 24, 1930 and ran for over 30 years. Until it closed on July 4, 1962, the club upheld the values and provided the type of family entertainment for children Mickey and his friends came to represent. Following are excerpts from an article by Steve Renzi published in May 2005 on the *Downtown Tucsonan* website about those early days. It shows the meaning and wide-reaching effect these clubs had within communities across the nation and the iconic appeal an engaging little mouse had.

Imagine a Tucson youngster walking into the first meeting of the Mickey Mouse Club at the Fox. It begins at noon on Saturday. Today, admission is free, and thereafter for many years the admission price was only ten cents. The Fox Theater just had its grand opening a little more than a month ago, so everything is new, clean, shiny and luxurious. Inside, the theater is big, air-cooled, and jam-packed with over, 1500 noisy kids. There is no assigned seating so everyone moves towards the front....

A typical itinerary of the Mickey Mouse Club was an afternoon of cartoons, movie serials, contests and games. Boys and girls attended. All the Mice had to learn the secret handshake, special member greeting, code of behavior and special club songs.

Over the years, there were roping, yo-yo, and costume contests, rodeo events, parades, and patriotic and citizenship activities.... Celebrities like Kate Smith, Will Rogers and Art Linkletter appeared on the Fox Theater stage. Also appearing was "The Flying Nelsons," an acrobatic troupe and Pinky Gist, a rodeo clown with his two trained burros, Freckles and Peanuts. Also, not to be forgotten was Queen and Semi, two dogs who it was said could understand upto 700 spoken words.

Speaking of dogs, one of the most memorable club meetings ever held had to have been "Dog Day." Held on May 30, 1930...kids were encouraged to bring their dogs.

Over 1,500 kids showed up, along with over 1,000 dogs. Before the meeting, a parade was held outside the Fox and around the block. One-dollar prizes were awarded to the biggest, smallest, best-looking, ugliest and most unusual dogs. At noon, the doors were opened and the kids and all their dogs poured into the theater.

The final meeting of the Tucson Mickey Mouse Club at the Fox was on July 4, 1962. Times had changed. It's been over forty years since that last meeting but the memories of the Mickey Mouse Club still linger in the hearts and minds of many Tucsonans. Important lessons and values were learned. Lifelong friendships started there. The Tucson Mickey Mouse Club was open to all races from day one, thoroughly integrated, unlike the Tucson school system and even the Fox Theater itself.

The children met some wonderful Tucson adults who became important friends and mentors. People like Mabel Weadock, "Aunt Minnie", the head of the Mickey Mouse Club, and Roy Drachman, manager of the Fox, and especially Dooley Bookman, the local merchant with a heart of gold, who organized parades, officiated contests, and handed out prizes. He made kids always feel welcome.

The Tucson Mickey Mouse Club at the Fox was a wonderful place for kids to have fun, learn values, make friends and be thoroughly entertained.

### 10.3.1   Radio? An Advertising But Not Story Medium for Mickey…

During the 1930s and 1940s when radio was King, Walt was a frequent guest on radio programs; his appearances varied from a Public Service Spot for the National Society for the Prevention of Blindness to being a guest on Lux Radio Theatre. Appearances were occasionally in the company of a Disney character, often Mickey, sometimes Donald. Walt saw each appearance as an opportunity to add to the Disney Master Narrative. Lux Radio Theatre, hosted at the time by Cecil B. DeMille, presented one-hour versions of current or upcoming films. During one interview with Walt, DeMille posed the question, "Who is the better actor, Mickey or Donald?" Walt provided an answer that revealed the essential personality of these two characters as he had created them: "Mickey is an actor. Donald is a clown." Walt had thought of and developed Mickey as an actor since his first appearances, slowly building up a personality in the way that the movie studios created their stars, not only through films themselves, but also through appearances, newspaper stories, and endorsements. Walt didn't only appear in interviews; he also made some attempts to use radio to extend stories about Mickey and his friends in a transmedial way. He helped Mickey celebrated his seventh birthday on *Magic Key of RCA* in September 1935 and joined Mickey and Donald in *The Duck Who Didn't Believe in Santa* on the *Electric Hour.*

But Walt didn't want to replicate the animated shorts on radio believing that it wasn't the right medium for them. An exceptional financial commitment from a sponsor, and the upcoming release of *Snow White*, swayed him to take a chance on radio. In1938 Walt took over the Sunday afternoon *Amos 'n'Andy* radio slot with the *Mickey Mouse Theater of the Air*. Produced by the Disney Studios, the program showcased Mickey, Minnie, and a host of friends.

During its 20 week run the show did not engage the radio audience to any extent and was dropped. Walt's closeness to his medium, animation, made him discerning when it came to what was suitable for the stories he told and how he told them. He understood the difference between media and what could and could not be accomplished; he said during the making of the show, "I don't think this show will work. You have to see the characters to fully appreciate them." Aaron Stein, critic for the *New York Post* agreed, "All the strength, the vigor and logic of the Disney films lies in the pictures. The voices, the music, and the sounds are usually funny and effective, but they register only as sound effects which point up the pictures. On the air they offered only disembodied sound effects. Only in so far as the sound calls to mind a vision of one of the Donald Duck frenzies, or of Mickey's dapper contours, is it at all entertaining. Unfortunately, the sound is not very strongly evocative" (Sampson, Mickey Mouse Theatre of the Air 2009).[8] While radio shows which featured scripts with Walt and his characters interacting in events that had immediacy and pertinence for the audience, such as a Christmas show, struck a chord with the audiences, a weekly series, which required the characters to carry the show through their regular antics, did not.

---

[8] https://www.mouseplanet.com/8820/Mickey_Mouse_Theater_of_the_Air

## 10.3.2   *Television*

Walt and Roy were enthusiastic about television (all the executives had TVs in their offices by 1947) and believed that it offered opportunities for developing audiences for their motion picture features. Since his early days of selling Mickey, Walt had believed in going directly to the public with his shows; he felt that television was a way of having direct access to the public without any intermediaries. In addition, as television was a medium supported by corporate sponsors, Walt and Roy saw an opportunity to develop programming that would have the support of someone else's financing. Walt's first appearance on television was in a Coca-Cola sponsored Christmas show he produced for NBC in 1950. In the same way that he had used radio, he used television to promote the Disney films. The Christmas show was a mixture of Disney materials with the addition of other acts that would appeal to a general audience. It featured a preview of Disney's upcoming film *Alice in Wonderland*, a number of other Disney cartoons, and, in addition, the popular ventriloquist Edgar Bergen and his dummy sidekicks Charlie McCarthy and Mortimer Snerd. The show drew a large audience and the *New York Times* said it was "one of the most engaging and charming programs of the year."

Walt and Roy had discussed the possibility of launching a television program that would feature existing Disney shorts in early 1950; although different proposals for programs were developed, none came to fruition. Because Walt felt that television could finance Disneyland and was looking for a 3-year financial commitment that would help him do so, it was difficult to negotiate a contract. ABC, the newest network was interested in increasing its presence, and wanted a series that would appeal to "youthful families." The Walt Disney Company and its family oriented entertainment were a perfect fit. The two companies announced their agreement on April 2, 1954 and the first show debuted six months later on October 27, 1954.[9] According to *The New York Times* this was the "first move by a leading studio into the home entertainment field" (Gabler 2006, p. 509).

For Walt, the purpose of the program was to promote Disney films and Disneyland. The first show was a sampler of Disney fare: a scene from S*ong of the South,* and the shorts *Plane Crazy, Lonesome Ghosts,* and *The Sorcerer's Apprentice* from *Fantasia.* In addition, Walt took the opportunity to present the *Disneyland Story* and talked about his vision for the park and the attractions that visitors would be able to enjoy there. Walt talked directly to the audience in a down-to earth way; in the process he created his own persona of the avuncular, charming gentleman, interested and enthusiastic about many things, who was welcome in people's homes from the first appearance of the show.

In October 1955, a television version of *The Mickey Mouse Club* had its debut. The studio produced the program especially for children and teens; it included short documentaries filmed around the world, live action serials such as *The*

---

[9] *TV Guide* October 1954: https://clickamericana.com/eras/1950s/walt-disney-presents-disneyland-the-tv-show-1954

*Adventures of Spin and Marty,* and a Disney cartoon. The hallmark of the program was the "Mousketeers," young teenagers hired for their talent who did comedy skits, and sang and danced in a themed weekly feature. The program became one of the most popular on television and eventually ran in eighteen countries. The popularity of the program's serials in the first season encouraged the studio to create new titles such as the one based on the popular mystery books for boys, *The Hardy Boys*. While the show only ran until 1959 it was syndicated throughout the sixties and seventies and finally given its own place on The Disney Channel in 1983 where it continued to draw in, entertain, and influence children and younger teens.

Through television programs such as *Disneyland* and *The Mickey Mouse Club* Walt was entering millions of homes each week. Regular appearance on *Disneyland* connected Walt with his star Mickey beyond even the closeness they enjoyed through other media. *The Mickey Mouse Club's* theme and farewell song show very clearly that, even though the television programs included varied types of entertainment, it was Mickey who symbolized and drove the Disney Master Narrative forward.[10]

---

**Theme song:**

Mickey Mouse Club! Mickey Mouse Club!
Who's the leader of the club, That's made for you and me?
M-I-C-K-E-Y M-O-U-S-E!
Hey, there! Hi, there! Ho, there! You're as welcome as can be!
M--I-C-K-E-Y M-O-U-S-E
Mickey Mouse! Donald Duck! Mickey Mouse! Donald Duck!
Forever let us hold our banners high! High! High! High!
Come along and sing a song, And join the jamboree
M-I-C-K-E-Y M-O-U-S-E

**Farewell Song:**

Now's the time to say goodbye, To all our company
Through the years we'll all be friends, Wherever we may be
M-I-C-K-E-Y M-O-U-S-E
Mickey Mouse, Mickey Mouse
Forever let us hold our banner high
M-I-C - See ya real soon! K-E-Y - Why? Because we like you!

---

[10] 26,000 Mickey Mouse ears were sold each week during the show's peak years. Photo of Mouseketeers: http://www.ohiokids.org/tellzall/2004/october.shtml.

# Chapter 11
# Engaging Audiences Across Media

*To all the little friends of Mickey Mouse throughout the world to whom he hopes to bring more happiness by coming into their homes.*

Forward from Walt Disney in the
Mickey Mouse Story Book

## 11.1  Transmedia

Originating different manifestations of Mickey and friends outside of animation and successfully establishing these as a part of the cultural landscape, produced a firm base for the Master Narrative that Walt had conceived of in the first few months of Mickey's success in *Steamboat Willie*. Mickey, Minnie, the Three Little Pigs, and their friends, and then Snow White and her friends the Seven Dwarfs enjoyed a popular, ubiquitous presence in neighborhoods across the country. The name "Walt Disney" became synonymous with these likeable, friendly, and amusing characters, and with the technological innovations that brought them to their admiring public.

In creating a Master Narrative, Walt used individual media for differing purposes. He promoted the animated characters to endear and entrench them in the popular collective conscious through activities such as merchandising, vaudeville reviews, and the *Mickey Mouse Clubs*. He also offered new ways to engage with his stories across different narrative media such as comics and books. Although these transmedia opportunities were seen as objects that could promote the Disney characters, the means for engagement were the stories themselves. Media such as radio and television were initially viewed by Walt and Roy only as promotional opportunities. Over time, stories were created specifically for these media, and, television in particular came to provide the public with a new way to relate to Disney characters. In the 1950s Walt embarked on a transmedia innovation—bringing Mickey and

---

Online photos and graphics provide extra detail and are identified by urls the reader can refer to. This additional reference information will be particularly beneficial as an enhancement for the online version of this book. URLs are current at time of printing.

© Springer Nature Switzerland AG 2020

K. Madej, N. Lee, *Disney Stories*, https://doi.org/10.1007/978-3-030-42738-2_11

friends to life in the real world of a themed entertainment park.[1] It wasn't until the 1980s and 1990s, however, when another new opportunity—console and computer games and stories—would come along for people to engage differently with Disney characters and stories.

## 11.2  Comics

Shortly after *Steamboat Willie's* successful release Walt had set Ub Iwerks to work to develop a comic strip for Mickey. As the strip progressed and Walt and Roy looked for a syndication sponsor, King Features of the Hearst Agency offered them a contract. On January 13, 1930, Mickey appeared in his first comic strip.[2] While the script credits read "Mickey Mouse by Iwerks," it was written by Walt, drawn by Ub, and inked by Win Smith. Ub stopped drawing the strip and Win didn't want the work of both drawing and inking. So Walt assigned Floyd Gottfredson, an animation inbetweener and aspiring new addition to the Disney staff, the task of drawing the strip, telling him he would only need to work on the strip for 2 weeks until they found another artist to do so permanently. Walt wanted to be done with the scripting (and had tried to convince Win to write the gags) so soon Gottfredson was writing the script as well. He continued as artist and writer for the next 47 years.

Comic strips at the time were "continuities"—or a continuing story. They appeared weekly in newspapers across the country. The Mickey Mouse strip was a gag-a-day until it went into story continuities April 1 of that year. The gags for the first 2 months were loosely based on *Plane Crazy* in which Mickey was inspired by Charles Lindbergh's first transatlantic flight. Minnie was the only one of Mickey's friends to join him in his adventures in this strip. Within a couple of weeks into the cartoon, when Mickey loses Minnie, struggles to keep his out of control plane flying, and has to land on a desert island, this angle ends. On the desert island it's one gag after another—Mickey finds skeletons in a chest, accidently bops a gorilla on the head, flees angry monkeys that he's shaken out of a coconut tree—but neither the desert island angle nor a potential pirate angle are explored with the idea of continuing the story. The ending is odd as the palm trees simply give way to ordinary trees for no reason and Mickey walks back home saying "Back to the old farm at last!" where he reunites with Minnie in a few romantic gags. The strips released between January 13 and March 31 were reprinted as a comic book entitled *Lost on a Desert Island*.

This first strip was an effort to quickly produce a comic on a daily basis that was entertaining; it was not well thought out as a continuous sequence of events. As a

---

[1] Mickey and his friends moved across media from books, magazines, and comics and then to the reality of Disneyland. In each medium they engaged and entertained their audience with different attributes. Examples can be found on this site: http://coa.inducks.org/story.php?c=UC+MMW++34

[2] The first Mickey comics were the gag-a-day type; they were inspired by Lindbergh's transatlantic flight. Mickey Mouse daily strip: http://bobcat74.free.fr/mmds/mmdsnotes.htm.

"gag-a-moment" animation its approach was a move backward in Walt's progress in creating a storyline. It no doubt suffered from the uncertainty of who was writing/drawing it during the first 3 months.[3]

The new continuity Walt began April 1 had a storyline that flowed effectively from strip to strip. It was an adventure that helped define Mickey's character from this time on and moved him from a Chaplinesque comedic character to a man (or mouse) of action in the Douglas Fairbanks, swashbuckling hero, mode. Gottfredson took over writing the story on May 17 and completed it on September 20.

More of Mickey's friends joined him in his new adventure—Clarabelle Cow, Horace Horsecollar, Black Pete, the corrupt lawyer Sylvester Shyster, and Mortimer Mouse, Minnie's uncle. In the story, Mickey and Minnie set out to hunt for treasure in the desert. Sylvester tries to foil their plans but Mickey steals back his treasure map and, along with it, Sylvester's roadster. Hair-raising adventures abound after this, including an emotional plea with a cow to let them pass as they race down the rails to get to the treasure. The cow refuses, the roadster gets totaled by a speeding train but Mickey and Minnie survive to go on and find the treasure. The story was later reprinted as the full-length comic book *Mickey Mouse in Death Valley*.

The Mickey Mouse strip became so popular that by January 1932 King Features syndicated color Mickey and *Silly Symphony* comics in their Sunday supplements as well. In 1935 Kay Kamen, together with Disney associate Hal Horne, started to publish the *Mickey Mouse Magazine*, a reprint of the existing comic strip stories in magazine format. When Horne pulled out Kamen went to Western Publishing to have the magazine published. Besides the comics, the magazine included stories, games, and full-page posters. Once comic books that consisted solely of comics proved successful, Western made the magazine into a full-fledged comic book, *Walt Disney's Comics and Stories*.

These new Mickey Mouse stories were a combination of adventure and comedy that was a divergence from the animated cartoons focus on comedy. The stories featured Mickey as a daredevil and adventurer—a winning and gallant character who was the superhero of his day. Throughout the twentieth century Mickey continued to be more adventurous in the comic strips and comic books than he was in the animated shorts.

## 11.3  Books

One of the first merchandise licenses that George Borgfeldt had negotiated was the *Mickey Mouse Book* with the sheet music publisher Bibo and Lang in 1930. This was Walt and Roy's first book title and, together with the merchandising of children's

---

[3] Some of the early comic strips were drawn by Ub Iwerks, others by Walt Disney. By May 17, 1930, Floyd Gottfredson had taken over both drawing and writing. While the new strip was filled with sight gags it also had a continuous story. Mickey Mouse comic strips: https://d23.com/first-mickey-mouse-comic-strip/

products, helped pave the way for Walt to take Mickey from adult entertainment to children's and family entertainment. The first run of the book, which had ads on the inside front and back covers as well as on the bottom edge of the back cover, was advertised to theatre owners in *The Official Bulletin of the Mickey Mouse Club* for distribution as a promotional item to *Mickey Mouse Club* (MMC) members and was distributed almost exclusively by them.[4]

The little book's cover featured a cheerful Mickey waving a greeting to readers. The cover was illustrated by the artist Albert W. Barbelle who was noted for his illustrations of sheet music. Barbelle did a superb rendering of Mickey, catching just the right air of jaunty greeting that would become part of Mickey's signature style. Inside the book there was a four-page story that told how Mickey first came to visit Walt, the new song *Mickey Mouse* (*You Cute Little Feller*), a Mickey Mouse March, and a cutout board game.

The first, rather inventive, history of Mickey was written by the publisher's 11-year old daughter, Bobette Bibo. She told the story of how Mickey, who was at the time Mouse Thirteen, was expelled from Mouse Fairyland because of the pranks he perpetrated. He dropped onto a roof in Hollywood and went down the chimney where he met Walt. They got on famously and after hearing Mouse Thirteen's story, Walt was sure he could make him a picture star. A name change, however, was warranted. As the first thing the mouse had eaten when he'd arrived at Walt's was green cheese, and green was an Irish color, "Mickey" became the chosen moniker. The book showed a caricature of Walt (believed to be the first one ever made of him) shaking hands with Mickey to seal their agreement.

Walt continued to refine Mickey's persona as his star gained popularity. Early shorts were aimed at an adult audience; the *Gallopin' Gaucho*, for instance shows, Mickey smoking and drinking. As cartoons became more popular with parents as children's entertainment, Mickey's character became more moderate. Drinking and smoking stopped and violence was toned down. The *Mickey Mouse Book*, as it went into its second edition, reflected these changes in Mickey's persona; the song lyrics, "When little Minnie's pursued by a big bad villain, we feel so bad, then we're glad when you up and kill him" were removed.

Roy approached many book publishers with the idea that Mickey's humorous adventures would be of interest to boys and girls. But Mickey was untried in the business and there was scant interest until Roy approached the David McKay Publishing Company, who decided to take a chance on the Mouse. In order to offer a Depression public a modestly priced book, the company planned to publish the new book in black and white. Instead, Roy sent the publisher full-color illustrations and a note saying Walt wanted the book printed in color. *The Adventures of Mickey Mouse* was released in 1931 and turned out to be a huge success with Mickey fans. It was reprinted continuously until the Second World War.[5]

---

[4] Mickey's first book was distributed free to *Mickey Mouse Club* members. Mickey Mouse Book: https://disney.fandom.com/wiki/Mickey_Mouse_(comic_book)

[5] Instead of economical black and white, Walt wanted his first book to be published in color. *The Adventures of Mickey Mouse*: https://d23.com/a-to-z/adventures-of-mickey-mouse-the/, https://disney.fandom.com/wiki/The_Adventures_of_Mickey_Mouse

The book showed Mickey in his barnyard roots with many of his vintage friends. The story begins:

> This story is about Mickey Mouse, who lives in a cozy nest under the floor of the old barn… Mickey has many friends in the old barn and the barnyard beside Minnie Mouse. There are Henry Horse and Carolyn Cow and Patricia Pig and Donald Duck, Clara the Hen, Robert the Rooster, all the little Peep-peep Chicks and Turkeys and the Geese, too. But the Hound Dog is hardly a friend, and Claws, the Cat, is no friend at all…

This story is one of the few in which there is ambivalence about Mickey and Minnie's size. In their first cartoon appearances Mickey and Minnie are smaller and more rodent-like in their appearance than they are later in their careers, when they are more anthropomorphized. However, they appear as normal sized rodents/mice only in one early cartoon, *When the Cats Away* (1929) and in this print story.[6] In *When the Cats Away*, when Tom Cat goes off hunting for the day, Mickey pops out of a mouse hole in the floor of the porch and he and his mice friends (including Minnie) proceed to break into Tom's shack. There they have a grand old time playing the piano, saxophone, and record player, and dancing. In *The Adventures of Mickey Mouse*, Mickey and Minnie change size as the story progresses. They are first shown as "mice-sized" creatures living in nests, Minnie in a homey nest hidden somewhere in the chicken house, and Mickey in a nest under the barn floor. The illustrations depict the nests as enclaves of human-type coziness but also depict typical mouse holes cut into the wall; in one view a salivating Claws the Cat is waiting outside Mickey's mouse hole to pounce on him. Soon enough Mickey and Minnie quick-change into their more recognizable selves: pint-sized but not mice-sized.

The story plot in the book is slight and is similar to the one in the cartoon *When the Cats Away* with the larger part of the action being taken up with Mickey and friends partying. Mickey tricks Claws into getting caught in his own trap and then enjoys some musical fun with his barnyard friends. Farmyard pigs, cows, and horses are depicted cavorting both on the inside covers of the book and in the story illustrations.

While *The Adventures of Mickey Mouse* is a single story, the next McKay book, *The Mickey Mouse Story Book*, consists of a number of stories written and illustrated by Disney artists.[7] In addition to the stories, children could enjoy a novel and ingenious flicker feature when they read the book: when the bottom corners are flicked one way Mickey Mouse is seen dancing and when the pages are flicked in the other direction Minnie Mouse is seen dancing.

In the front of the book Walt shares a greeting with his young readers, one that foreshadows his weekly address to audiences on television in the 1950s, in which he

---

[6] Mickey and Minnie appeared rodent-sized in the cartoon *When the Cats Away* and the beginning of Mickey's first book, *The Adventures of Mickey Mouse*. Photo of *When the Cats Away*: https://www.youtube.com/watch?v=aldMRcWAYok.

[7] Mickey reads to his young listeners on the cover of his new "Story Book." Photo of *Mickey Mouse Story Book*: https://disney.fandom.com/wiki/Mickey_Mouse_Story_Book

mentions his hope of coming into their home and bringing happiness to their family life, a goal that he pursues in all media throughout his career.

> To all the little friends of Mickey Mouse throughout the world to whom he hopes to bring more happiness by coming into their homes. WALT DISNEY

Walt had been successful in bringing Mickey's image to homes through a wide range of merchandise and now he was bringing Mickey's stories to children's homes through books. These stories would continue to build Mickey's character and entrench him as family entertainment through a medium that, at the time, had the impact television and computers have today.

The era between the world wars, and in particular the 1930s, was a time of experimentation in children's books. Important changes in lithographic techniques and in particular the use of high-quality photo offset-lithography in large-format volumes such as Jean de Brunhoff's tremendously successful *L'Histoire de Babar le Petit Elephant* (1931), showed the potential of the picture book. Mickey's books benefited from the increasing success of children's books in the market place. Changing technology also encouraged the development of books in new and increasingly popular formats. Two of these in particular are notable: moveable books such as the Mickey "Pop-Up" and "Waddle" books, and the "Big Little Book."

## 11.4   A Little Pop-Up History

Pop-up books had known their first success in the mid-eighteen hundreds. They were "toy books" and were one of different types of moveable books made by publishers to make their stories more interesting and provide greater play value for children by making them interactive. The first of these moveable books was the harlequinade produced by the London publisher Robert Sayer in 1765. Sayers books had cut pages with scenes that turned up new or alternate views of a story. Other moveable's included metamorphoses, books made of one sheet of paper folded in half and cut to reveal hidden pictures, peep-show or tunnel books that had a peephole in the cover for viewing a three dimensional scene inside, and lift-the-flap books. In the 1870s, books such as *Father Tuck's Mechanical Series* were the first to bring stand-up scenes to children. In the U.S., the publisher McLoughlin Brothers took advantage of the new and inexpensive chromolithography process to produce vibrantly illustrated large format moveable books. Also popular at the time were books with cut-out dolls that children could use to create their own stories. All these types of books became a favorite at the turn of the century until the changing fortunes of World War I made them prohibitively expensive. In the late 1920s when less expensive lithography printing processes made them affordable again, they once more became an important genre in publishing. Independent London publisher S. Louis Giraud began publishing "living model" books that featured "pictures that spring up in model form." Inspired by their success, Blue Ribbon Books in the U.S. began publishing what it coined as "Pop-Up" books.

The first Mickey Pop-Up book, published by Blue Ribbon Books in 1933, *The Pop-Up Mickey Mouse*, was a result of the efforts of marketing entrepreneur Sam Gold. At a time when marketing to children was largely unheard of, Gold believed that they were the ideal audience, for once children wanted a product, they would influence their parents to buy it for them. He understood that children had the potential to not only be Mickey's greatest fans, but also his greatest salespersons.

Gold had started his marketing career with the Whitman Publishing Company that had been innovative in introducing children's books to the public at other than seasonal times such as Christmas. When he had left to start his own company, American Advertising and Research Corporation, he included children's books as part of his total marketing packages. These also included "point of purchase displays, posters, direct mail and radio scripts." Gold worked with Kay Kamen to create a product that was appealing to children and maintained the high quality Disney demanded.

*The Pop-Up Mickey Mouse* was another new way to bring Mickey to children. The story and illustrations were created by Disney artists; they told about Mickey's adventures taking care of some circus animals that had been left stranded. The front cover of the book opened to reveal a full-spread pop-up of Mickey and Minnie holding balloons and standing in front of the big top. The broad smiles on their faces show that they are having fun. On the opposite page there is a clown made up as a monkey; he is holding onto a halter worn by a real monkey dressed in a top hat and vest. In the center of the spread are some circus toys from the center ring. The illustration has a dynamic feel and a sense of perspective that gives the impression the reader is a part of the scene. Children could imagine themselves at the circus with Mickey and Minnie as they manipulated the pages to make the pop-up items move.

Twenty-four pages long, the book consisted of text and simple black and white line drawings on most of the pages. In addition to the full-color pop-ups on the inside front and back covers, there was a third that was a center spread. These brightly colored, cheerful scenes brought the animated feel of the motion picture cartoons to children in their own homes.

Minnie was given her very own *Pop-Up Minnie Book* in which she saves some ducklings from a predatory hawk. These two pop-up books were so popular that they were translated into Spanish, Italian, German, and Dutch and were followed up quickly with two new titles: *The Pop-Up Silly Symphonies* which retold two of the *Silly Symphony* stories, *Babes in the Woods* and *King Neptune*, and an entirely new story, *Mickey Mouse in King Arthur's Court*.

Another moveable book format created for Mickey that let children play with "real" figures was the *Mickey Mouse Waddle Book*. Also instigated by Sam Gold and created by Blue Ribbon Books, the waddle book included cardboard cutouts of four characters, Mickey, Minnie, Pluto, and Tanglefoot. These could be detached and assembled as three-dimensional dolls and were designed to waddle, or walk down a slanted surface. The cardboard pathway on which the characters could waddle was included. Unfortunately, this attempt at providing tangible characters with which children could interact did not resonate with the public, and the Waddle books soon passed from public view.

The book format that did prove hugely popular with Mickey fans was the "Big Little Book."[8] Created by Sam Lowe, an executive at Whitman Publishing, the "Big Little Book" promised "a great amount of reading material and pleasure (BIG) within a small and compact (LITTLE) book." The format, approximately 4 inches square with a cardboard cover and 300–400 pages in length, was just right for a pocket or a purse. Each page of text had a captioned picture on the opposite page. Whitman's first book, *Dick Tracy*, was published before Christmas in 1932 and sold over 600,000 copies. When Sam came calling at Disney's door in 1934, these figures impressed Walt and Roy and their first "Little Big Book," (LBB) *Mickey Mouse*, was published before Christmas that year. The books were particularly profitable because they used existing art and stories from the daily comic strips. Disney artists and writers took the text balloon out of the weekly strips artwork and retold the story more descriptively so that it was suitable for a book format.

Like the comic strip, books such as *Mickey Mouse The Mail Pilot* (the second Mickey Little Big Book) and *Mickey Mouse and The Dude Ranch Bandit* (a Better Little Book) showed a character who was dashing, fearless and courageous, and who loved action. These stories, as did the many titles that followed them, brought a hero to children's homes, one that was accessible at the turn of a page. The books were just the right size for the little hands of younger children and parents could enjoy the experience of reading Disney stories with them. The pictures on each facing page made the books good for a "learn to read" experience. For older children Mickey's adventurous stories were now available in inexpensive, handy-sized books they could readily purchase and carry around. By the end of the decade *Walt Disney's Comics and Stories* would replace the Little Big Books and deliver inexpensively published stories for fans to read in comic format.

## 11.5  Disneyland

Throughout the 1940s Walt continued to think about different ways in which he could bring his host of cartoon characters and their stories to the public. It became his goal to provide an environment in which adults and children together as a family could enjoy themselves, and in which adults could find joy in play on their own as well. He said, "The truth of the matter is... We don't aim at children specifically. When does any person stop being part child?" (Jackson 2005).

Walt's intent when he set out to build Disneyland was to create "happy family stories and comedies," that brought joy to all of the American public. Walt had experienced the stories of everyday life on the farm, in the small town, and in the city, first as a youngster and then as a young man. Through his many jobs during those early years he had the opportunity to see people in all walks of life, through his love

---

[8] *The Mickey Mouse Little Big Book* retold the comic strip stories. Photo of *Mickey Mouse The Mail Pilot*. http://www.biglittlebooks.com/newsletters/BLT-May-June2010.pdf.

of entertainment he had learned what made people laugh. He had taken an interest in everything around him and put his experiences to use in his drive to become a cartoonist. As his work matured and he went from drawing to producing shorts to creating feature films these past experience gave him a broad and holistic perspective of the stories he was presenting his audience. The strength of the stories was first their compelling characters and then the sequence of events that created continuity and a compelling storyline. If when he told stories they seemed hokey, they were also honest. "I'm simple and corny at heart and I think the majority of the people are on my side" (Jackson 2005, p. 80). Disneyland gathered together Walt's extensive and varied experience of story, animated film, audience experience, and how these made for good entertainment, into a new medium.

## 11.6   The Disneyland Stories

The stories in Disneyland are many and varied; some add substance to the Disney Master Narrative, others offer transmedial opportunities for the characters and stories that Walt originated in other media over the 25 years prior to Disneyland being built. Walt had talked about finding a way to bring Disney characters to life in their fantasy surroundings throughout the forties. But rather than an amusement park, Walt wanted a "theme" park; the Disney stories were part of his planning from the beginning. A 1948 memo outlines a "Mickey Mouse Park" with a Railroad Station, Town Hall, Fire and Police Stations, Drugstore, Opera House and Theatre, and other attractions that created the atmosphere of an old-fashioned village. A theme park was to surround the village and would act as "headquarters" for the entire enterprise.

One of the projects that was folded into the final version of Disneyland evolved from Walt's interest in miniature trains, an interest that became a consuming hobby of first, collecting, and then, building, miniatures. Walt planned "Disneylandia" as an exhibit that would travel across America as a twenty-one car train and bring to school children and other visitors the story of "Americana" in miniature. The first of the scenes built was *Granny Kincaid's Cabin*. Based on the film *So Dear to My Heart*, the miniature diorama was approximately 8 feet long and showed the interior of Granny's cabin complete with a stone fireplace, handbraided rug, "china washbowl and pitcher, guitar with strings thin as cat whiskers and a small family Bible... . A tiny flintlock rifle hung on the wall and a spinning wheel with flax sat in the corner" (Sampson, 2010). Although Granny did not herself appear in miniature, a recording of her voice described the scene for visitors. Walt showcased the diorama in the *Festival of California Living* in December 1952 to test the public's reaction. "People would watch and watch. They wouldn't go away. They watched the whole show and stayed for the next one. So the show had to be stopped for 25 minutes to clear out the audience. Walt knew it was a success" (Ibid). Walt's earlier interest in wind-up mechanical toys also came to play; he wanted to add movement to the miniatures and had his machine shop analyze a film of Buddy Epson dancing. The result of the experimentation was a 9 inch miniature of a vaudevillian dancing on a frontier music hall stage. This was the beginning of Audio-Animatronics which was to become a main feature of Disneyland's storied characters. From this first scene came the idea for the scene of a singing barbershop quartet. The view of the inside of the barbershop "would include a barber, customer in a chair and two more patrons standing by the chair and waiting." Visitors could see out through the window to the street view. Across the way stood a newspaper office with a view through its front window of the barbershop.

Logistics of moving the train were more complex than Walt had first envisioned and with everybody "planning to make a lot of money, just to let Disney in," the financial cost became prohibitive. Walt shifted his focus closer to home and back to his full-sized *Mickey Mouse Village*. In early 1952 he received tentative approval for developing some property (different sources identify this as 7, 11, and 16 acres) across the road from the studio on Riverside Drive in Burbank. He had one of the Disney illustrators, Harper Goff, draw up sketches for the park that included the main street eventually implemented in Disneyland. But the City of Burbank wasn't interested in a "carny" atmosphere in the area and wouldn't authorize the construction of the park. In any event, Disney's ideas for the park kept expanding and would no longer fit into the confines of the small property.

## 11.7   Preliminary Story Planning

Walt was advised by architect Welton Becket that "no one can design Disneyland for you; you'll have to do it yourself." Walt had hired art director Richard Irvine to help with the original planning. Irvine was joined by Marvin Davis and together they worked with Harper Goff to sketch out Walt's ideas on paper. Key to their planning was studying Disney cartoons and considering how the stories could be made into rides. Walt wanted to bring the cartoons to life. As with the preliminary planning for the cartoons, Walt was involved with developing the story, often describing the story/ride in the same enthusiastic way that he had inspired the shorts and the feature films. The art directors drew storyboards to describe how the story and ride worked together to engage visitors in a "total" story experience. During the first meeting with Stanford Research Institute (who Walt would use to find a location for the park), the consulting group learned Walt was expecting to build something quite different from an amusement park. "Walt's major investment would be committed to creating a storytelling environment. Rides would be subordinate to story and setting. Most shocking, there were no thrill rides, no roller coaster, no super fast fear of falling rides anywhere" (Barrier 260). For Walt, the park offered a never-ending story opportunity. In contrast to films that were complete and could not be changed, Disneyland could change continuously in reaction to input from its audience and to the changing technologies of the day. While today some of the rides are the same as they were on opening day, many older rides have been updated and new rides and environments created. The stories within the park have changed in response to a process of engagement Walt put in place deliberately to get people's reactions. Walt had always watched his audience to gage the effect of his projects: when he stood at the back of the screening room to listen to reaction to *Steamboat Willie*, when he sat with the audience to see how *Snow White* would affect them, when he watched visitors stream by *Granny Kincaid's Cabin*. Once Disneyland was opened, he went on daily walks to see how visitors were reacting to the attractions there.

## 11.8   Mainstreet, U.S.A.

At the entrance of the park—Main Street, U.S.A.—is Walt's "middle America" story based in his experiences living in the farming community of Marceline.[9] From the Railroad Station at one end, the walk down the Main Street, with its the "photographer's shop, ice-cream parlor, bakery, meat market and grocery, bank, music shop, drug store and many others—all operating exactly as they did 50 years ago" was planned to provide the feeling of walking through a turn-of-the-century midwestern town. Marble-topped tables, wire-back chairs, player pianos, and silent movies at the movie house, all contributed to the atmosphere and the illusion being created. In the 1955 Disneyland brochure created for the opening, Walt described Main Street as the "heart-line of America."

Main Street bolstered the Disney Master Narrative and ensured that an environment friendly to families was the first experience visitors had in the park. Walt succeeded in successfully translating the Disney movie experience he had developed into reality a number of ways. The storyboarding approach that had been taken to designing the park provided for a sense of continuity with cinematic-like scenes that visitors entered and passed through to the next scene. Walt wanted a "complete experience" not a disjointed one for his visitors and achieved something similar to a movie "cross-dissolve" by ensuring that the scenes changed in both look and feel as visitors moved from one to another. When ordering trees for the park he required trees planted be native to their environment "maples, sycamores and birches for the Rivers of America; pines and oaks for Frontierland, etc. He sometimes rejected a tree with the comment: 'It's out of character'" (264). When planning for the pavement he required that the texture change when visitors entered the next land, claiming, "You can get information about a changing environment through the soles of your feet."

A crucial way that Walt used to create a comfortable environment was by the manipulation of scale. "Scale meant everything" in maintaining the illusion of story, whether it was on Main Street, Fantasyland, or Frontierland. In the same way that he had Alice enter Adventureland so many years before, Walt now lead visitors into a "real" animated world where he altered the scale of the buildings and attractions to make them more "accessible and inviting." Visitors rode a 5/8th scale railroad and they walked into buildings that were 9/10ths scale on the ground floor and grew

---

[9] Concepts for Disneyland: https://d23.com/five-incredible-early-visions-for-disneyland/

progressively smaller on the second (8/10ths) and third (7/10ths) floors. Throughout the park, visitors encountered attractions of different scale, as for Walt scale had to both be functional and look right. The *Mark Twain Riverboat* had to be both impressive yet fit the scale of the waterway down which it transported visitors. Different parts of the boat were scaled to fit the need; while the boat was scaled at 3/4ths, the railings were left normal size for safety, as well as for look and feel.

It was while walking down Main Street that visitors would have their first experience of engaging with Disney characters—Mickey, Minnie, and their friends were there to greet children, teens, and adults alike, shaking hands, giving hugs, and sharing smiles. At the end of the street, Walt had built a circular park, the hub that sends visitors out to the different story realms: Fantasyland, Frontierland, Adventureland, and Tomorrowland. "Parents can sit in the shade here if they want, while their kids go off into one of the other places. I planned it so each place is right off the hub."[10]

Across the park from Main Street, Sleeping Beauty Castle led to the Fantasyland of Walt's animated stories. Here were found the "cartoon or story book characters that Walt Disney has brought to screen life." The 1955 Disneyland Brochure[11] describes the story experiences of Fantasyland:

> A world of imagination—come to life. You'll cross the drawbridge to enter Fantasyland through the portals of a medieval castle with towers and parapets rising dizzily above you. In Fantasyland you'll take the Peter Pan ride aboard a pirate galleon that soars over moonlit London to Neverland, home of Mermaids, Buccaneers, Indians and Lost Boys, and flit through the Darling home; take the Snow White ride and meet the Seven Dwarfs, the Wicked Witch, who will offer you a poisoned apple, and all the other characters of this immortal classic. Mr. Toad's Wild Ride runs through a series of misadventures in a 1903 vintage automobile, knocking over a cow and crashing into a barn...

Whether visitors were on a ship riding through the sky in *Peter Pan*, in mine cars trundling along a track in *Snow White's Adventures*, or in a vintage car barreling along a country road in *Mr. Toad's Wild Ride*, they experienced a ride that was a short tableau of the original story and that befitted the attraction. In what are known as dark rides, visitors engaged with the characters in an experience that was distinctly different from that of watching them on the screen. Special effects, sound, music, and animated figures were brought to life through the use of special lighting effects. Tight curves and bends added to the excitement of the journey and to the sense of surprise for visitors as new scenes appeared before them. Combined with meeting story characters in the streets of Disneyland, these rides successfully extended Walt's animated creations into reality for visitors. *McCall's* magazine said of the experience, "Walt Disney's cartoon world materializes bigger than life and twice as real."

---

[10] Thomas, Bob. An American Original: Walt Disney. New York: Disney Editions, 1994. p. 13.

[11] 1955 Bank of America Disneyland Guide shows Main Street with the park-like "hub" from which visitors could view and then visit the different lands. Photo of the 1955 Bank of America Disneyland Guide: http://vintagedisneylandtickets.blogspot.com/2008/05/disneyland-1955-bank-of-america.html.

> **DISNEYLAND**
> TO ALL WHO COME TO THIS HAPPY
> PLACE
> ## *Welcome*
> Disneyland is your land. Here age relives
> fond memories of the past … and here
> youth may savor the challenge and
> promise of the future.
> Disneyland is dedicated to the ideas, the
> dreams, and the hard facts that have
> created America … with the hope that it
> will be a source of joy and inspiration to
> all the world
> ## *July 17, 1955*
> *(Official dedication plaque located at flag-pole
> in Town Square on Main Street)*

Disney would continue to add to its repertoire of stories in different media and to the technologies used to present them. When computers opened up the digital environment, the company would innovate and expand, engaging its audiences in ever more creative ways in stories.

# Part III
# From Interacting to Creating and Sharing

*For almost a decade, I kept an office bulletin board showing screenshots of online games and activities that I had designed, engineered, or enhanced... My goals were to inform others what the Disney Online Games Group had been doing and to inspire new ideas...*

Newton Lee

# Chapter 12
# Animated Storybooks and Activity Centers

## 12.1  Arcade Game to Story Game

By 1994 The Walt Disney Company had been producing children's video games for 13 years. Since the release of its first video game, *Mickey Mouse*, for Nintendo's *Game and Watch* handheld game systems in 1981,[1] the company had licensed its characters and established development and publishing alliances with leading inter-active gaming companies, first with Nintendo Entertainment Systems (NES) and then with Sega, Capcom, Square Enix, Sierra On-Line and others. Disney characters featured in platform games, puzzle games, and racing games, among others. Mickey and friends ran, jumped, juggled, collected, raced, got into scraps, danced and taught kids their ABCs and numbers across multiple platforms.

The first of these games were arcade type games that used Disney characters more as a merchandising opportunity than for any particular character trait or potential for story possibilities. In an arcade-type game personality did not affect the game activity. Although the game might consist of an event that had a cause and effect, it would not require a storyline to be successful. Adventure games, on the other hand, different from arcade games are based in story. Originally text-based, these games encourage players to achieve their goals not by repeating arcade-type

---

Online photos and graphics provide extra detail and are identified by urls the reader can refer to. This additional reference information will be particularly beneficial as an enhancement for the online version of this book. URLs are current at time of printing.

---

[1] Mickey Mouse's first game appearance was on Nintendo's *Game and Watch*, a handheld system made between 1980 and 1981. It was released October 9, 1981, featured a single game, and had a clock and an alarm. Mickey's handheld excursion finds him trying to collect eggs from a hen house as they roll down chutes. Mickey normally receives one full miss for every egg he drops, but if Minnie is present in the top left corner of the screen, he only gets a half miss. The game ends when Mickey has three full misses. There is an A and a B game. In Game A, the eggs fall from three chutes. Which three? It's random and changes after each miss. In Game B, the eggs fall from all four chutes, adding more of a challenge.

© Springer Nature Switzerland AG 2020
K. Madej, N. Lee, *Disney Stories*, https://doi.org/10.1007/978-3-030-42738-2_12

actions but by moving through different environments, asking questions of game characters, unlocking secrets, and overcoming obstacles to reach a goal. Some adventure games offer a fully developed story, others are a sequence of activities that are based in or allude to stories that exist in other media or have been presented in previous games. The latter is particularly true of the adventure games produced by Disney. Disney adventure games are based on previously released animated movies and provide a transmedia experience. In the company's first adventure game *Winnie the Pooh in the Hundred-Acre Wood*, published in 1985, the wind has blown objects that belong to the story characters all over the 100 Acre Wood. In similar game play to that in the Sierra On-Line game *Mixed-Up Mother Goose* (mentioned in the introduction), the player's role as Winnie the Pooh is to find the objects, bring them back, and then to match them to their character.[2] All of Pooh's friends, Eeyore, Tigger, Owl, and Piglet have lost things and would like them back; as Pooh can only bring back one thing at a time, and the wind might come back at any time to whisk things away again, time is added as an incentive in the game. Although a simple activity with a minimal storyline, the familiarity of Winnie the Pooh (to most children) brought to the game a sense of continuity within the larger narrative of the child's experience of the character. The A. A. Milne stories of *Winnie-the-Pooh* had been favorites since their publication in 1926. Disney's first Winnie the Pooh featurette, *Winnie the Pooh and the Honey Tree*, a 25 minute animation, was made in 1966. From then until 1985 three more featurettes, a short film, and a feature film, as well as a television series were produced. Winnie the Pooh also appeared in his own stories in Disney books. The popular character quickly became one of the pantheon of personalities in the Disney Master Narrative. Children gravitated to any new activity that featured the friendly, warm hearted, if slightly fuzzy-headed bear and the opportunity to interact with the character, even with the rudimentary representation in the game, was an exciting one. The game play was fun and highly engaging; parents continue to introduce their children to the "virtual hide and seek" that they "love" and "could play for hours."

In 1986 Disney released the first adventure game adaptation (by Sierra On-Line) of one of its full-length movies, *The Black Cauldron*. Game designer Al Lowe followed the action of the original story throughout *The Black Cauldron* game.[3] Taran, the assistant pig-keeper must rescue Hen Wen, a magical pig, so that the Evil Horned King does not find the Cauldron and rule the world. Taran can walk, run, swim, and talk with different characters to get to his goal. To add more interesting game play Lowe created several new plot branches that players could take and that provided for at least six variations on the ending depending on decisions made during play. As such, *The Black Cauldron* was one of the first graphical adventures that gave players true multiple paths through the story. Players who did not rely on the story

---

[2] The 1984 *Winnie the Pooh and the Hundred Acre Woods* used both text and graphics to engage children in the search for lost objects. Screen shots, http://sierrachest.com/index. php?a=games&id=264&title=winnie-the-pooh&fld=screenshots&pid=1.

[3] The *Black Cauldron* graphics were advanced in comparison to games such as the Dark Crystal. Screen shots, https://animationscreencaps.com/the-black-cauldron-1985/

but took the uncommon path most often were rewarded with the most points. The different paths and solutions to puzzles gave players the opportunity to be creative in their play and meant they would return to play again, giving the game excellent replayability.

Disney wanted the game made more accessible for children and so Lowe designed simplified game commands that were easy for children to use. He replaced the text parser normally used to initiate different actions with function keys, an innovation not used again until years later. The game's graphics were also an advancement compared to the very linear and stark graphics of the time. Lowe had access to all the Disney original hand-painted backgrounds, the original animation cells, and the original music score when he created the game. In line with the Sierra On-Line interest at the time in developing better animation and color in their games, there was a new sense of three-dimension created by the backgrounds and by the characters moving about in the virtual space. The graphics were, however, rudimentary in comparison to the animated film and the cover art of the game.

Over subsequent years the release of Disney movies such as *Who Framed Roger Rabbit*, *Ariel the Little Mermaid*, and *Aladdin*, was followed shortly by the release of video games. Game play in each game, which was generally the same for different platforms, always used events from the movie but did not necessarily present the entire plot. In *Roger Rabbit* (NES) the goal of the game is to reach Toontown and destroy Judge Doom; in the *Little Mermaid* (NES and GameBoy) Ursula has taken control of the seas and Ariel goes to the rescue. The *Aladdin* story, however, was developed in different versions. The Super Nintendo version follows the plot of the movie more so than does the Sega Mega Drive/Genesis game in which the player achieves different levels that are based on locations in the movie. Interestingly it is this version that had Disney animators working alongside the game designers. As a result the graphics are closer to the quality of the animated film than are other versions.

## 12.2  "A Story Waiting for You to Make it Happen": The Synergy of Story and Game Technology

In the early 1990s popular children's print stories were successfully adapted as digital storybooks for interactive play and learning on the computer. Different from video games, they presented a complete readable story while including interactive components and so engaged children in both reading and interactive play. Mercer Mayer was one of the first children's authors/illustrators to take advantage of digital technologies to combine his stories with digital play activities. *Just Grandma and Me* is one of the first of the *clickable* children's books. Published as one of Broderbund's *Living Books* series, the screens reproduce the print book pages in exceptional quality with characters that are animated and move the story forward. When the narrator has finished reading the text and the animation sequence for that page is complete, children can "play." They can click to have the text read again or they can find objects to click on and make things happen. Clicking on an object starts a short, site-specific animation: a bird flies out of its nest, a squirrel comes out of a tree knot, a plane flies through a cloud. Different animations appear when the same object is clicked successively. These animations are specific to the item but not necessarily to the story. Unlike the interaction in an adventure video game that can lead the player down new paths in the story, this type of interaction is superficial to the storyline and does not affect it. It adds play opportunity rather than story opportunity.[4] From clickable storybooks such as *Lil Critter*, *The Berenstain Bears*, and *Benjamin Bunny*, publishers moved towards educationally oriented CD-ROMS in which characters from stories such as *Clifford the Big Red Dog*, *Thomas the Tank Engine*, and *Arthur the Aardvark*, among others, were made into frontmen for educational activities. Children could join their favorite personality and work out puzzles, learn math, or do science experiments (Madej, Towards Digital Narrative for Children: From Education to Entertainment 2003).

## 12.3   Along Came Simba

On June 24, 1994 the Disney movie *The Lion King* was released and began achieving worldwide fame and success. It won the Academy Award for *Best Original Score* and the Golden Globe Award for *Best Motion Picture—Musical or Comedy* as well as the Kids' Choice Award for *Favorite Movie*. While the majority of Disney story ideas are adapted from fairytales and myths, or from classic literature, *The Lion King* was an original story written by Disney screenwriters. At the time, it was second in this distinction only to the animated movie *Lady and the Tramp*, made almost 40 years previously. The story expanded Disney's horizons, taking on a mature theme as had the film *Bambi*, Disney's fifth feature animation made in 1942, that was initially criticized for its realistic depiction of the shooting death of Bambi's father.

   An astonishingly short 6 months after the movie's release, just prior to Christmas, *Disney's Animated Storybook: The Lion King* was released.[5] In March 1995 *Multimedia World* described the appeal of the new release to age groups from toddlers to adults:

---

[4] Grandma and Lil Critter leave the house and walk down the road to catch the bus. As they stand there waiting for it, children can "make things happen" by clicking on different objects. Screen shots of *Just Grandma and Me*: http://www.mobygames.com/game/just-grandma-and-me/screenshots.

[5] *The Lion King* was the first of the Disney movies made into an Animated Storybook with a companion Activity Center CD-ROM. Screenshots, https://www.old-games.com/download/10175/disney-s-the-lion-king

"Disney's Animated Storybook: The Lion King" is a winner that everyone can enjoy, from toddlers to adults. The disc tells the now-familiar story of Simba the cub as he grows to adulthood. You can passively listen or click your way along at your own pace. Actor Nathan Lane provides new dialogue as Timon the meerkat, and there are lots of fun games and interesting activities to keep you occupied.

Disney Interactive, the digital media branch of The Walt Disney Company at the time, had been looking for new ways to tap into the growing digital media consumer market. Disney did not have the technology and manpower to make it happen, and as with their media games, they were looking for a group to which they could successfully outsource the work. They approached Media Station Inc., an innovative start-up company noted for their creative approach in developing multimedia software and tools.

Building on the rich material in the movie, Disney brought its ability to tell stories and develop characters to Media Station's expertise in developing multimedia products. Rather than cutting and cropping artwork from the film as a forced fit into a new format, Media Station's animators produced 7000 new frames and Disney's artists added a further 5000. The companies together created over 12,000 new frames of digital animation for the storybook. Media Station also created over 300 music and vocal assets using both traditional orchestration and arrangement and digital composition tools adding to the depth of the auditory component of the storybook.

*Multimedia World* noted in March 1995 that, "the Lion King CD-ROM has the smoothest animation I've seen yet." To achieve this type of quality, Media Station used a number of "proprietary strategic software technologies" that made it easier for the developer to create large animation multimedia and the user to play it back, impossible until that time. These included a playback engine that provided high quality playback from a CD-ROM of large animations, and "WinToon," software that improved performance of playback in Windows by reducing the amount of data that was required. This improved performance was necessary because, unlike other interactive storybook developers who used a palette of 256 colors throughout the entire title, Media Station used 256 colors per screen; this resulted in very large animation files.

As one of the original software engineers at Media Station, Newton Lee had created an object-oriented scripting language in 1994 (similar to the ActionScript in Flash) that enabled the developers to create interactivity for animation quickly and easily. He had also written a cross-platform multimedia compiler to allow the software to run on both the PC Windows and the Macintosh operating system. The new tools and methodology enabled a CD-ROM title to be developed within 3–6 months and were what enabled *The Lion King* animated storybook to be developed so quickly upon the heels of the movie. This quick release was in part responsible for its success in the marketplace.

The other reason for its success was that when Media Station made *The Lion King* an interactive story, they had built on the popularity of both video games with children and learning games with parents by integrating game-like activities within the story. Children could choose what they wanted to do, see, hear, and read on the screen. Eighteen pages long, the story was skillfully edited to both ensure the original continuity and afford interaction. Screen "pages" had text that children could choose to either read or have read to them. To add to the aural experience the story was voice acted. The original movie script was considered from an activity standpoint and clickable features were added to each page so children could make things happen; they could, for instance, turn the Pride Lands from brown to green again. In another reading oriented activity they could ask Rafiki the meaning of words and his "Action Dictionary" would animate the answer. These activities increased engagement with different story scenes/events and created connections with the individual characters, as did other skill building activities that the game developers included. Children could help Simba improve his pouncing skills by following a butterfly. They could collect various bugs for Timon, who was always hungry. Netting eight bugs brought a special award and a move up to the next speed level (three speeds). They could connect stars in the sky to create different pictures; once a constellation was complete, it would fade away and children could create another one. Designed for children three to eight, the game became popular with both children and adults who could enjoy interacting with characters that looked and talked like the ones in their favorite movie.

Although it was eventually chosen as "Pick of the Year" by *Entertainment Weekly*, when it was first released, *Disney's Animated Storybook: The Lion King* got accused of "killing Christmas" for thousands of children that year. In the morning of Christmas Day 1994, Disney's customer service was flooded with phone calls from angry parents with crying children. The parents complained that when they loaded the CD-ROM into their new Compaq Presario computers, they witnessed the infamous "Blue Screen of Death"—an error screen displayed by Microsoft Windows after encountering a critical system error that caused the system to shut down. The problem was that the CD-ROM software title relied on Microsoft's new WinG graphics engine, and the video card drivers had to be hand-tuned to work with WinG. In late 1994, Compaq released a Presario PC whose video drivers had not been tested with WinG. To rush the software to the market before Christmas 1994, the CD-ROM software was not tested on Compaq Presario. A rush to market and the lack of compatibility testing were to blame for the fiasco.

Within days, the video card driver problem was fixed by Media Station Inc., and the second release of *Disney's Animated Storybook: The Lion King* for Microsoft Windows was available for purchase and free exchange. The WinG debacle led Microsoft to develop DirectX, a more stable and powerful graphics engine that was later released in September 1995. Also in 1995, the third version of *Disney's Animated Storybook: The Lion King* that runs on both Windows and Macintosh operating systems was released.

The hard lesson learned from the fiasco/success of Disney's first animated storybook was that the application of technology has tremendous impact on the success of a digital story (as our Disney history shows, on stories in any medium). A piece of software must be thoroughly tested on all supported platforms and system configurations before its release no matter what the marketing department has scheduled or what major holidays are approaching. Disney's trademark attention to detail was as valid when working with new technologies in the 1990s as it had been in the past.

*The Lion King Activity Center*, a companion CD-ROM that focused on educational games and learning activities rather than on the story, was released in 1995. Children could participate in activities that ranged from coloring to making music and had up to three difficulty levels for replayability. Three locations, the Jungle, Rafiki's Tree, and the Shadowlands provided three different games/activities each. In the jungle children could match bugs, learn to spell words, and find hidden animals. In Rafiki's tree they could color, make puzzles, or play Achi, a game similar to tic-tac-toe, against a friend. In Shadowlands, players could take a memory or a maze challenge and play Ed's Xylobones, a musical instrument like a xylophone that makes a water and light show. There are also a number of movie clips from the Magical Pool that could be viewed again and again.

The next animated storybook was *Winnie the Pooh and the Honey Tree* based on the 1966 featurette of the same name.[6] Intended for a younger audience than *The Lion King*, Winnie the Pooh was an ideal character for engaging young children in an interactive medium. A review from *New Media* (April 1996) describes from a parent's point of view why children (and parents) were attracted to this new way of interacting with familiar stories.

> It's hard to resist this honey-loving bear: Hazel pounced on this disc first, and it immediately became her favorite. Pooh, in Spanish and English for ages 3–8, teaches beginning reading and word recognition. Disney took a much-loved story and effectively added more enticements: well-known songs and enjoyable interactive games like finding hidden pots of honey and identifying different colored objects. This disc is a pleasure.

The linear story provides children with the "read it again" opportunities that are for them such an enjoyable part of an early reading experience. In addition hidden animations, mini-games, and sing-along songs were blended into the story and add an exciting level of interaction that is not too complex for a young child to enjoy on his or her own. Even though the story is linear, the interactive components give children the opportunity to make the story their own, as was the goal of the first rudimentary interactive children's story, *Inigo Gets Out*, created only 8 years previously.

As with *The Lion King*, Disney created a CD-ROM *Activity Center* for *Winnie the Pooh and the Honey Tree* that was more oriented towards learning than story. It offered art activities, puzzles, tic-tac-toe, matching activities (including matching music), and mazes that use the scene clips and characters from the animated movie.

In addition to *The Lion King*, some of the best-selling Disney's animated storybooks included *Pocahontas, The Hunchback of Notre Dame, 101 Dalmatians, Toy*

---

[6] Disney movies now had a new avenue for their stories, one that gave children the opportunity to participate in the action. Photos of *Disney's Animated Storybook: Winnie the Pooh and Activity Center:* https://www.mobygames.com/game/windows/disneys-animated-storybook-winnie-the-pooh-and-the-honey-tree/screenshots

*Story*, *Hercules*, and *Mulan*. Each of these gave their audience the experience of reading and of playing simple games in one digital environment. While clicking through the story and its associated activities did not change the story itself, it did change the experience of the story by creating connections with the characters and events and making it more personal. Animated storybooks continued to be very popular until the capabilities of the World Wide Web began to evolve and different story experiences had the chance to evolve in that medium.

# Chapter 13
# Going Online: A Personal Theme Park

*We can't bore the public with these things.... We've got to be entertaining.*

Walt Disney

## 13.1 Taking Disney's World Online

The public recognition and financial success of the Disney CD-ROM story titles prompted The Walt Disney Company to continue their expansion in digital and online environments. Continuing the synergistic strategy that had successfully moved it into new technologies in the past, the company looked to use the graphics capabilities introduced to the World Wide Web in the mid-1990s to expand its transmedia reach and create a virtual environment for its characters and stories. *Disney.com* , the company's official website, was launched February 22, 1996 primarily to promote Disney's theme parks and provide information on such company products as videos, books, and music to adults.[1] Disney developers also took advantage of the site to give children a play space. Children could enjoy a different scavenger hunt each day as well as chat with Disney characters such as Mickey Mouse. The site joined with *Family.com* and through this venue provided parents advice and additional activities for their children.

In 1996, Disney Online, headquartered in North Hollywood , California, was in its infancy with about 100 employees. The online games group was smaller yet; it consisted of two producers, two artists, and four engineers working full-time. In the

---

Online photos and graphics provide extra detail and are identified by urls the reader can refer to. This additional reference information will be particularly beneficial as an enhancement for the online version of this book. URLs are current at time of printing.

---

[1] The 1996 *Disney.com* site brought information about the different Disney entertainment interests to the public in one space. Together with *Family.com* it was designed to provide a comprehensive resource for parents to go to for family-friendly activities. Screen shots for some dates are available at http://web.archive.org/web/*/http://www/disney.com .

© Springer Nature Switzerland AG 2020
K. Madej, N. Lee, *Disney Stories*, https://doi.org/10.1007/978-3-030-42738-2_13

months ahead, the group quickly staffed up with new employees, contractors, and interns. Disney Online worked with other divisions within The Walt Disney Company as well as third party developers to create online content using Flash, Director, and Java. While recent software advancements meant interactive animation could be created for CD-ROMs quickly with high quality results, the web offered new challenges. At the time, most consumers were connecting to the Internet using narrow-band dialup modems. It was a very restrictive environment in which to deliver high quality animation and sounds. Content developers had to time the loading time for each content item to make sure that viewers did not have to wait too long. Clever wait-time animations and activities were created to keep the viewers entertained while the content was being downloaded. As broadband became more popular, broadband versions of online content that used richer graphics and more sound effects were offered. A lot of work was put into maintaining two versions of the online content for the narrow-band and the broadband consumers.

The Disney name was synonymous with family-oriented entertainment programming; taking this premise as its starting point, Disney Online aimed to develop a "one-stop" online entertainment venue that was a counterpart to the real-world Disneyland. It would be suitable for children between the ages of 3 and 12, but also be a place teens and adults could visit to engage with favorite characters. The site was planned with a number of key features: (1) it would be a parent-trusted environment for children, (2) it would be subscription-based with the monthly fee waived for MSN subscribers, (3) it would be predominantly advertising free, and (4) it would feature new programming every week. Producers, engineers, and artists worked together to design this new and quite ambitious idea in digital entertainment. They aimed to make the site creative, engaging, fast changing, and with the widest range of activities available in a virtual environment. The activities would be based predominantly in familiar Disney stories and characters.

On March 31 1997, Disney Online announced the launch of *Disney's Daily Blast*.[2] The site was introduced by a cheerful Mickey Mouse, who welcomed guests to its wide array of activities: tried-and-true arcade style "just fun" games, stories children could read, listen to, or interact with, edutainment games intended not only to entertain but also to develop skills, kids-oriented sports news and highlights from ESPN, and a news report written for children by ABC. Children could match shapes, shoot it out with villains, trade cards, get certificates, and have their names included in the stories they read. While many of the activities were based in Disney's familiar characters and stories, others introduced new characters. Many of the activities were experimental and had not been tried in an online environment before. The site was a virtual Disneyland and in addition to offering entertainment promoted creative thinking and encouraged learning in an animated environment. The subscription route gave its developers the opportunity to create a safe, controlled environment

---

[2] Mickey welcomed children to the new *Disney's Daily Blast* site, and offered them a virtual world of play. *Disney's Blast* had clear menu items and was easy for even very young children to navigate.

with parent-approved email and chat for kids. Long-term goals for the site included offering multiplayer games so that kids could log on and play with their friends.

The site was designed to appeal to a young audience and three major elements were planned to make the interface user/kid-friendly: colorful graphics, simple-to-understand icons, and responsive audio feedback. Site designers used interactivity to engage children from the get go and created entertaining rollovers for the first screens. When a title or a drawing was rolled over with the mouse, an animation appeared or a funny sound was heard. For instance, when the graphic "Mouse House Jr." was rolled over, Mickey's ears popped off. This type of rollover feature had been made popular for children as early as 1991 by CD-ROMs such as Mercer Mayer's *Just Grandma and Me* (Broderbund) in which they were used extensively to encourage active engagement with the print story. Many activities on the *Daily Blast* site included levels of difficulty so that children of different ages between 3 and 12 could enjoy the same activity depending on their abilities, so they could improve their skills, and so they would come back and play the game again. Although the site was large and had the potential to be confusing, the information was well organized and the site was easy to navigate. A menu grouped the contents of the site into categories from which kids could pick activities to go to. As a result, not only were children themselves comfortable on the site but parents, who often make the decision about whether a child has access to a site, could also easily leave their children to play within the site on their own. One of the most exciting aspects of the site (both for the developers and the kids) was that a new game and new activities would be added on a weekly schedule, with newer content being rotated in and older content rotated out. In this way the site would always look fresh and children would less likely be bored if they returned to the site on a regular basis. Sometimes Disney Online received emails from parents and kids who couldn't find their favorite games because they were rotated out. As a result, the most popular games were often kept on the site indefinitely.

Comments by reviewers of children's sites attest to the thoughtfulness that was put into the designing of the site and the wide range of activities it contained. *ZiffNet*, the CBS Webzine, noted at the time that *Disney's Daily Blast* offered "a deep collection of games, animated stories, and articles" while other children's sites such as *Warner Bros. Kids* offered "a mishmash of games, articles and promotions aimed at kids".[3] *Ziffnet* continues, "Even a quick tour through the Daily Blast site reveals why it has gained so many tryouts and full-fledged subscriptions. The home page offers a long menu grouping the service's content into categories such as Games, Story Stuff, Sports, Blast Jr. and such." While not every activity was a hit, and some required improvement to make engagement smoother, the overall experience for children was more positive than on other sites. "It doesn't take long to realize that Warner's isn't yet trying as hard (or, no doubt, spending as much as Disney.)... A 'BBQ Toss' game the site is now promoting invites kids to throw hot dogs into a

---

[3] Unlike *Disney's Daily Blast* which was a complete site dedicated to children, *Warner Bros. Kids* was included as a category on Warner's main menu. Photo of the *Warner Bros* portal: http://web.archive.org/web/19970131181521/www.kids.warnerbros.com/.

moving bun. The game is much clunkier than the best of those on the Disney site."
Not designed to specifically attract children or to meet their age-group needs, the
*Warner Bros Kid's* site was rather an addition to and accessed through the Warner
Bros. main site.

Other children's sites that were noted for their excellent content were of necessity less technically sophisticated and interactive—they did not have the resources a
Disney or Warners had behind them to develop these attributes. *Chateau Meddybemps*
for instance, created for young children by author Jerry Jindrich in 1995, offered a
"playful world… filled with fun and fanciful characters and charming activities"
(*Education World*).[4] This colorful and well-organized site was all about Jelly Beans.
It consisted of activities that ranged from reading stories to learning tasting toasts.
However, all of the stories on the site were text with static illustrations, and the
activities, even those related to music, were organized as printouts of texts/illustrations. This format was common among edutainment sites that were developed by
authors, publishers, and educators whose frame of reference and expertise was print
or who had limited budgets. Disney, on the other hand, had arrived at children's
edutainment from animated media, and, in addition, had the expertise and financial
resources necessary to take full advantage of digital technology. With *Disney's
Daily Blast*, the company continued its tradition of taking innovative approaches to
using new media. Within a few years, other sites would begin to offer a better variety and quality of interactive entertainment for children but none would match the
breadth of the *Daily Blast* site. Organizations such as National Geographic and
PBS[5] would produce sites based on their print or television programming, while
author sites such as Mercer Mayer's *Little Critter* site would feature individual
author's work.

## 13.2   A Range of Engaging Activities Within a Disney World

In *Daily Blast* children were immersed in a Disney environment and engaged with
Disney characters from the portal page onward. Mickey would greet them at the
virtual gate, then, whether they chose to play a game, read a story, or participate in
an activity, more of their Disney friends were there to meet them. The site extended
the engagement children had with Disney characters and stories in non online activities such as reading books, watching television, videos and films, listening to radio
and audiotapes, and playing interactive games. It brought these activities into an
online environment and created a virtual space in which all of these activities were
available at a click of a mouse. When designing Disneyland, Walt Disney had been

---

[4] Sites such as *Chateau Meddybemps* offered content that was limited to text and illustrations.
Facebook page at https://www.facebook.com/pages/category/Education-Website/Chateau-Meddy
bemps-110,414,802,306,984/

[5] PBS's site gave kids access to characters from favorite television programs such as *Arthur, Barney,
Dragon Tales*, and *Teletubies*. Current PBS site has the same charm, https://pbskids.org

concerned that parents and their children would have to walk too much to get to all of the activities and made a concerted effort to plan the parks "lands" so that they were easily accessible from a central hub. In designing this new virtual play world, Disney's designers planned the site with an introductory page as a central hub from which it was easy to navigate via menus that were simple enough for even young children to use on their own.

The menu items on the first *Daily Blast* site included Games, Comics, Stories, Activities, Sports, News, and Blast Jr. for the younger crowd. In addition there was a parent's page that required parents to create usernames and passwords for their children, change profile information, and pay by credit card. Once a child was registered, he or she could use their username and password to login and enter the site, which was simple to do even for a 2 or 3 year old.[6]

The game section of the site featured arcade style games popular since the early 1980s. Children could, for instance, pick the *Hercules* game to play. Featuring the Disney character from the movie and set in ancient Greece, the game was an archery contest in which players could use their mouse to aim and fire arrows at dummies that moved against the background scenery. Or players could choose a *Little Mermaid*, *King of the Sea* game and go on a "Sea Hunt." As Triton, they fired harpoons at eels that swam down the screen in a version of the traditional 1980s centipede game. Other games featured the Disney princesses (Snow White, Cinderella, and others) and the Fab Five (Mickey, Minnie, Donald, Goofy, and Pluto). Characters from *The Lion King* (Simba, Timon, Pumbaa, and others) and *Alice in Wonderland* were also featured in early-on games, as were characters new to the Disney pantheon such as the Penguin, the Grizzly Bear, and the Witch.

A number of the categories encompassed story/reading activities. Comics included stories such as *Duckburg's Day of Peril* that featured the inventor Gyro Gearloose and consisted of cartoon illustrations with the characters speaking in "word bubbles." Children "turned" the pages of the comic to read the story in much the same way they would if they were reading an actual comic book. Gyro appeared again later in Disney's online history as the inventor of the Evil Cogs in Disney's multiplayer online game *Toontown Online*. The text bubble format used in the comics was also used in the Story section of the site. Children could select stories such as *Magical Memories* to read or listen to. Typically these were new short stories based on familiar Disney movies, in this case, *Beauty and the Beast*. Rather than incorporating text as it was used in Disney's animated storybooks, these stories were distinctive in that, like the comics, they were told through speech bubbles.

There were also interactive stories such as *Detective in a Jar*. The main character in this story is a brain inside a jar who, like the classic detective of pulp fiction, wears a fedora and a raincoat (on top of the jar), and is a smooth-talker. Children could follow the brain on his adventures by turning the pages of the comic book and reading or listening to the narration and voice over. In one of the episodes the

---

[6] The *Disney's Daily Blast* site required registration and the creation of a username and password before children could enter and play. Photo of the Disney's Blast registration page: http://web.archive.org/web/20040711034319/register.go.com/disney/login.

detective is at a campground when someone steals a TV from the RV parked close to him. It is the player's job to discover the clues and figure out who the thief is as quickly as possible. This game was developed by a third party developer for Disney and was hugely popular, even generating merchandising spinoffs such as the *Detective in a Jar* t-shirt.

The site also offered play activities such as coloring. If children wanted to color they had access to a program that was screen based. Unlike other sites which offered black and white line drawings that needed to be printed off for coloring, on the Disney site children could pick a line drawing of a favorite character such as Woody from *Toy Story*, color him with the paint program, and print out their handiwork.

In addition to these activities Disney developers introduced an early social networking model in which children could chat with other subscribers by sending pre-written animated messages. To ensure online safety, unrestricted emails and chats were enabled only if children already knew each other in real life, and had agreed to exchange computer-generated passwords over the phone to activate unrestricted emails and chats between the two parties.

The original *Daily Blast* design included a Disney-branded browser (D-Browser) and email (D-mail). The D-Browser was essentially Microsoft's Internet Explorer with added security features such as a restriction on what websites children would be allowed to surf on the Internet. The D-mail was a basic email client with fun features such as Disney background pictures, Disney character stickers, and Disney audio clips to make children's email come alive. However, the time required to keep up with the Microsoft updates for its Internet Explorer, the manpower required to maintain the D-Browser and D-mail, and the servers required to run D-mail were cumulatively becoming too huge an investment and undertaking for Disney Online. In hindsight, D-mail could have become an enormously popular "G-mail for kids." The feature was dropped and instead the team designed and added "trading posts" to the site; children could buy, sell, and exchange digital toys using online currency accumulated by playing the games on the site.

In June 1998, *Disney's Daily Blast* was renamed *Disney's Blast*. At the time, edutainment was a major focus in developing games for children and many of the games on *Disney's Blast* were created with learning in mind. While edutainment games had to be fun, they were intended to engage children in creative thinking and in building such skills as memory. An example of an edutainment game that was prominently featured on *Disney's Blast* and which maintained its popularity throughout the future rebranding of the site was *Stitch: Master of Disguise*.[7] This game exemplified the type of activity that encouraged learning through game play. A memory game, it required a player to use (and improve) his/her recall skills. Players could pick different levels of speed, slow to fast—depending on their skill— at which to play the game. The player was shown pictures of a number of different

---

[7]Favorite games such as *Stitch: Master of Disguise* survived *Disney Blast's* change to *Disney's Game Kingdom Online*, a game-oriented site. Stitch must find the items that will help disguise him from the bounty hunters! Game: http://www.disney%2D%2Dgames.com/stitch_master_of_disguise_31.html

characters. The player then picked one of the characters and was provided with a set amount of time to dress Stitch exactly as the character was dressed in the picture. The player must search Stitch's room to find all four parts of the disguise. If the player could not find all four parts and Stitch was not disguised in time, the alien bounty hunters would find him. If he was disguised in time, he would be safe. Other similar education oriented games on the site included *Donald's Pizza* and *Mickey's Nightshift* that featured Disney characters, and *Car Jam* and *Halloween* that featured new characters.

There were as well plenty of games that were designed to be purely entertaining. Among these, the most popular were *Penguin Bounce*, *Sorcerer's Castle*, and *Bowl-a-Rama*. Disney Online received many inquiries asking if was possible to download games as pay-by-the-minute Internet connection became expensive as kids stayed online longer to play games. So in 1998, downloadable games called *D-Toys* were introduced. An example of a creative and (somewhat) educational D-Toy is *The Rubber Band* which allows the player to make their own tune by placing the notes "DO," "RA," "MI" and so on, on the checkerboard floor; members of a band then play those notes as they traverse across the squares. An example of a purely entertaining and amusing time killer is *Blow 'Em Away!* in which players collect leaves into a pile and can watch animations of the autumn leaves being blown in the air.

In total, the Disney Online games group created over 100 games for *Disney's Blast* and *Disney.com* by 2006. In 2007, *Disney's Blast* was re-branded as *Disney's Game Kingdom Online* to emphasize the shift in focus for this particular website to offering "games" for children. Stories and Comics were no longer part of the line-up as they were replaced by entire online story worlds such as *Pixie Hollow*. Instead of stories, simulation games in which children adopted and cared for pets and decorated homes were added to the site. These new games reflected changes in the types of interactive game activities that had evolved in the gaming world since *Disney's Blast* had first opened. Because of demand, the most popular games, such as *Stitch: Master of Disguise*, continued to be featured on *Disney's Game Kingdom Online*.

Making *Disney's Daily Blast* a subscription site was a daring gambit. While subscription sites did exist on the web, subscription sites for children were unheard of at the time. Disney gambled that parents would be interested enough in providing their children with a safe site for quality online play that they did not need to monitor themselves, to pay a price for it. They were right. Disney succeeded because the site provided a comprehensive entertainment package of diverse activities that appealed to all manner of kids, as well as their parents. "If your kids are going to be spending lots of time online anyway, there isn't much better entertainment to be found" (Thomas 1998).

## 13.3   Reaching Wider Audiences with New Forms

Disney's characters, stories, and games were now reaching a greater number of people than they might have through other media—the number of visitors to *Disney. com* each month jumped from 487,000 in September 1999 to a record 34 million in July 2009. While parents might generally be cautious about their children accessing online sites, as a subscription-based site, *Disney's Daily Blast* gave parents peace of mind. Because parents trusted the contents of the site, children, even quite young children, had a certain amount of autonomy in choosing their own activities. Online media was also providing children with choices in the types of engagement they could have access to at any time—game, traditional story, interactive story—in one virtual space. Each type of activity provided a different experience yet offered it within a comfortable and familiar world. While games like the *Hercules* archery challenge could not be considered stories, they built on stories children knew well and added nuances to the story's schema. Interactive stories such as *Detective in a Jar* let children participate in the action of the story and "figure out the clues;" while with edutainment games such as *Stitch: Master of Disguise*, Disney Online continued the Disney tradition of taking its stories down new avenues, in this case, an educational one. The *Hercules* and *Stitch* activities provided a transmedia experience that extended children's original exposure to the stories into interactive game play. While Disneyland had given guests a place where they could experience a gamut of Disney stories and characters in a real world scenario, Disney's online sites brought these same stories, characters, and opportunities for interaction into people's homes as a virtual Disney world.

# Chapter 14
# Development Cycle: Games

*Whatever we accomplish is due to the combined effort. The
organization must be with you or you don't get it done. In
my organization there is respect for every individual, and we
all have a keen respect for the public.*

Walt Disney

## 14.1 The Disney Online Development Process

The children's audience for *Disney's Blast* (1997–2006) was varied. To appeal to
different interests, Disney Online designed a series of "channels" for players to tune
into.[1] Each of these online channels had their own theme and featured original animation and games. The *Pets and Animals Channel* focused on presenting arcade and
puzzle games to do with animals, like *Penguin Bounce*. *Chat Studio* featured
*Shoutouts* for sharing birthday wishes and other community based events. *Zoog
Disney* featured unique games based on the popular children's TV show. One of the
most popular of these channels was the *Weird and Wacky Channel*. A brainchild of
Michael Bruza, Chris Coye, and Newton Lee, the comical channel featured *Blooper
Market* and *Adopt a Beast*, among others. *Blooper Market* offered printable labels
for spin-off comic products such as Aquaflesh, Macaroni and Fleas, Shampbell, and
Smello. *Adopt a Beast* was a funny take on tamagotchi: the online pet beast was a
crying Baby Beast, a Drooling Beast, or a Hairy Beast. If the crying Baby Beast was

---

Online photos and graphics provide extra detail and are identified by urls the reader can refer to.
This additional reference information will be particularly beneficial as an enhancement for the
online version of this book. URLs are current at time of printing.

---

[1] Players could tune into many channels on *Disney's Blast*. Each channel had a different theme so
that each child would find something that would appeal to him or her. One of these channels was
the *Weird and Wacky* that relied on humorous imitations of products available in the marketplace
(e.g. *Macaroni and Fleas*).

© Springer Nature Switzerland AG 2020
K. Madej, N. Lee, *Disney Stories*, https://doi.org/10.1007/978-3-030-42738-2_14

unattended to, his diaper would fill up; if the Drooling Beast was unhappy he would drown in his own tears; and if the Hairy Creature was left alone for too long, his hair would grow uncontrollably long.

Ideas for online activities and games such as these came from many different sources: the regular games group planning meeting attended by producers, artists, engineers, unofficial "water-cooler" gatherings of a few group members, studio producers of Disney movies and TV shows, lunch discussions with Disney colleagues, and casual conversations about surfing the net. The strategy for developing activities and games was threefold: create a new activity in-house, purchase an existing game and improve or repurpose it, or contract an idea to a third party developer. Because of the limited engineering resources in-house at Disney Online, all three options were used to develop and bring online entertainment to Disney's audience, whom the group called "our guests."

Disney Online activities and games only reached the public after they had gone through an iterative development cycle that was collaborative in nature. Designers and engineers worked in self-organizing teams that adapted to many changing circumstances, either of a product or a company nature, to ensure that new software was delivered continuously. The teams were accountable for delivering products that were current, reflected their customers' interests, and, at their best, were highly innovative. The customer base of *Disney's Blast* included both children and their parents; products were evaluated against a standard developed through focus group feedback and guest feedback such as email, letters, and phone calls. Including feedback in the development process ensured a continuous awareness of the end goal and encouraged frequent inspection and adaptation of software. Overall, the design teams took a business approach that aligned the development of software with customers' needs as well as company goals.

Over time the development process evolved into one that demonstrated many of the traits of what came to be known as agile methodology. As software methods had developed in the industry they had become heavily regulated, regimented, and micromanaged. Reaction against these "heavyweight" methods in the mid 1990s led designers to return to more "lightweight" practices used in the early history of software development. Among other values, agile methodology believed in a close and cooperative working environment, responsiveness to changing consumer needs, and rapid delivery of high-quality products that exhibit technical excellence and good design. The process was formally established in February 2001 when seventeen software developers met to discuss lightweight methods in Snowbird, Utah and published the *Manifesto for Agile Software Development*.

As Disney Online took on more staff and projects, this working methodology helped include new individuals in the process and focus ideas. Unlike the heavyweight methods, which were unidirectional and "waterfall" in nature, the Disney Online Game Development Cycle (See Fig. 14.1) encouraged producers, designers, and engineers to evaluate and react to the market and audience at every instance to ensure a timely and pertinent product. The Agile software development cycle diagram shows the iterative, bidirectional nature of the team's working process and shows the different stages a project would go through to achieve not only

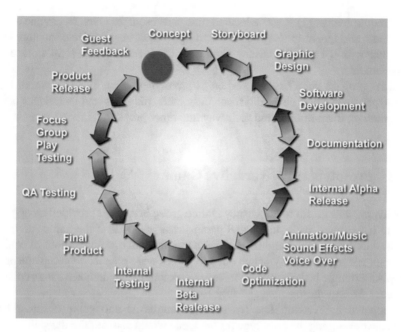

**Fig. 14.1** Disney online game development cycle: agile software development ensures a well-designed, well-tested, pertinent, and timely product

completion, but, as customer satisfaction was key, completion that was satisfactory to Disney's "guests." This process was adhered to whether the team was a small or a large one. The process began with an idea that was conceptualized and storyboarded; at the same time a team was gathered together to work on graphic design and software development. If the project was music-based, musicians were included early in the development. An Alpha version of the game was released for a preliminary internal assessment of its narrative and functionality; the project returned to the team and the different elements revisited to solve issues that were spotted. The background music, sound effects, and voice-overs were then added, and the software code was optimized for online use. The game was then released as a Beta internally for review and testing. Echoing the iterative process in Disney's development of animation, even at this stage the team was prepared to go back to the drawing board, refine the user interface, redo the voice over, or make other software changes based on the internal feedback. The final version of the game was then rigorously tested by QA testers and sent to outside focus groups for play testing. After the game's release to the market, the group paid close attention to guest feedback. Every email sent to Disney customer service was read and, when possible, was replied to by the producers and engineers responsible for the games. Oftentimes, games were enhanced based on the guest feedback.

For all the great ideas that the games group came up with, or which they were sent by aspiring designers and writers, a product could only be made if it satisfied three requirements: (1) It was allocated time and resources (such as graphic artists, engineers, and QA testers). (2) It had funding from Disney Online or another business unit within The Walt Disney Company. (3) It had a green light from upper management.

Many projects were first worked on as prototypes. Even though some of these prototypes themselves never did reach customers, the ideas and techniques developed through them often found their way into other projects.

## 14.2   Prototyping: A Narrative Game

Prototyping was useful to the Disney Online group because it provided an opportunity to experiment with stories and game strategies, even if the game was never released. A small team could be put together quickly to develop a proof of concept in which a storyline was sketched out and games were planned to complement the story. An example is the story and software development undertaken for an episodic game *P.I. Mickey* during June and July 1999.

Instigated by Newton Lee (as software engineer) and game designer Cliff Johnson, developing the prototype for the game would also require the skills of two graphic artists and a website integrator. The first step in the process was to develop a concept from an idea that had been tossed around about a simple private eye story/game. The idea evolved into an edutainment game (see more about edutainment later) in which players search for clues and collect evidence to solve a mystery or a crime through a series of episodes. The game would have both story and game elements that worked together to move players through to a solution. Eventually named *P.I. Mickey* it would be based in the core Disney characters, Mickey and his stalwart cronies, Donald Duck, Goofy, Pluto, and of course Minnie. Personality characteristics that players would already be familiar with, such as Donald's excitable temperament, would set the tone or shape each episode. Playing the game would require basic text literacy skills. As an educational experience the activities and mini-games would provide players with the opportunity to problem solve, they would encouraged players to identify, retrieve, read and use material quickly (or to mobilize information), they would promote pattern recognition and memorization, and they would also improve players visual processing and cognitive and physical response time.

## 14.3   Story Supports Game Activities

Once the idea was given some shape, a prototype episode was storyboarded with sketches, dialogue, and activities/games. The game narrative features Mickey Mouse as a private eye who investigates intriguing situations. Each episode finds Mickey called on a new case by one of his Disney buddies. Mickey is typically to be found in his very traditional detective's office with its well-worn desk and filing cabinet, slowly revolving fan, and trash basket overflowing with paperwork. The beginning scene finds Mickey tossing cards into his hat to pass the time of day. A case is brought to his attention by a frantic telephone call from Donald Duck, who is a guard at the museum. There has been a break in and a valuable jewel has been stolen. Mickey needs to come over immediately to solve the case and retrieve the jewel.

## 14.3.1  P.I. Mickey Storyboards 1–8

*Storyboard 1:* It's another late night for Mickey Mouse, Private Eye.

*Storyboard 2:* The phone rings. It's Mickey's pal Donald, the night shift security guard over at the museum.

*Storyboard 3:* Donald says he was supposed to be guarding the *Sparklee Emerald*, but he fell asleep at his post! The *Sparklee Emerald* has been stolen!

*Storyboard 4:* The exhibit room at the museum—the scene of the crime. Mickey investigates.

When Mickey goes to investigate he finds three clues have been left behind. Detectives normally use a variety of techniques to conduct their investigations. Many of their cases are solved by interrogating suspects and interviewing witnesses. In this detective story, when Mickey returns to his office he finds he has been left a challenge by the thief: there are four photos on his desk; each shows a scene with a different suspect. It is Mickey's job to find out who the real thief is. The three clues he has from the crime scene will help Mickey uncover the truth—the player must complete a series of three brain twisters to solve these for Mickey. When the games are successfully completed, the name of the culprit is revealed and Mickey can apprehend the thief and hand him/her over to the police. The story ends with Mickey receiving a commendation and warm thanks from the police chief.

*Storyboard 5:* Mickey returns to his office. When he arrives, he discovers the thief has left the mouse PI a challenge!

*Storyboard 6:* Four identical photos show a suspect with the *Sparklee Emerald*. The problem is that it's a different suspect in each photo! Mickey has to figure out which one is the real photo, and which ones are fakes!

*Storyboard 7:* Mickey arrives with the clues at his trusty crime lab. He is sure that by solving the clues he can figure out which photos are fake and which one shows the real thief!

*Storyboard 8:* Once again, might triumphs over wrong, brains over brawn, and the *Sparklee Emerald* is back where it belongs!

## *14.3.2   Gameplay*

The three prototype games set different challenges for the players. In the game *Mixed Message*, the player must work out the message by filling in letter blanks similar to the television game *Jeopardy*. The first letter in the secret message appears on the screen. Several letters are highlighted on the keyboard device and the letter blanks can be filled in one by one by clicking on one of these highlighted letters. Every time a highlighted letter is clicked, all the adjacent letters are highlighted and become clickable. The symbol "?" stands for a wildcard that can be any letter from A to Z; and the symbol "??" stands for a wildcard that can be any two letters. To add to the challenge, the last attempt is undone and the letters that were entered previously are erased one at a time whenever time runs out. In the example shown, the player would click on "A" followed by "??," "E," "R," "S," etc. The complete solution to the clue is "The waiter saw the book."

In the game *Jumble Jam*, the reflectors and transformers in the lab are placed on the correct squares when the coins on the bottom right move up and are directed to their shadows on the top left. To add to the challenge, not all the reflectors and transformers need to be used. In addition, multiple transformers can be used for one coin if necessary. Lastly, the coins may not collide with one another as they move. In the example above, the "T" and "O" on the bottom need to be matched up with the "T" and "O" on the top. The third coin on the bottom right needs to be transformed into an "M" before matching up with the "M" on the top. The solution shows the use of two reflectors for "T", two reflectors for "O", and one reflector and two transformers for the third coin.

*Picture Pileup*, is a puzzle/memory game. Players are provided with a pile of nine cards representing nine pieces of a complete picture. Only the top card in the pile and the pieces that are already placed in the squares are visible at any given time. Players can remove the last piece to undo a mistake. To add to the challenge, one of the nine cards may show a "?" instead of a picture, making it difficult to tell where to place that card on the square. In addition, a timer is constantly running, and it removes the last piece and undoes your effort if you do not act quickly enough. Because it was expected that the puzzle game was to be replayed many times, each game had to have a large set of alternative solutions. The game engine was designed in Director Shockwave in such a way that the game designer could simply plug in a solution, and the engine would automatically randomize the game play.

## 14.4   Edutainment

During concept development, *P.I. Mickey* evolved into an edutainment game. Disney Online was at the leading edge of taking the type of edutainment available on CD-ROM and bringing it to an online environment.

Edutainment had evolved from educational computer games.[2] One of the early developers of games to teach skills and concepts such as math, grammar, money, and patterns in educational settings was MECC, the Minnesota Educational Computing Corporation. Their early games included *Lemonade Stand*, a simulation game in which players sell lemonade and depend on different elements such as the weather to make money, *Number Munchers*, an arcade-like game in which players used munchers to eat correct math solutions, and *Reader Rabbit*, a combination of word and memory activities in which children sorted, labeled, and matched letters to learn to read and spell. While these games were first promoted solely to educators, MECC found they became popular with parents as well. One of their most innovative titles was *Oregon Trail*, created in 1971. This was a narrative adventure game in which school children participated in trail blazing across the US. A graphics-based version was made available to schools in 1980 as part of *MECC's Elementary Series* and because of its popularity was packaged as a stand-alone game for the public as well as teachers in 1985.

With the success of these educational games publishers and game developers realized one way to reach parents was to promote their games as educational. Many future edutainment producers took their cue from the games developed by MECC. In 1982 Spinnaker Software Corporation began to promote non-curricular educational software to the public. An early adventure game, *Snooper Troops* (1982) had players searching for clues to solve the puzzle of *The Granite Point Ghost*. *Snooper Troops* was recommended for children 8 years old. One of the first games for toddlers that was created with the intent of mixing stories with education in the video game world rather than the education world was *Mixed-Up Mother Goose*, designed in 1987 by *Sierra On-Line* designer Roberta Williams. Williams had wanted to design a game for her two preschool children that would be both fun to play and provide learning opportunities.

*Mixed-Up Mother Goose* was a retelling of eighteen classic fairy tales and nursery rhymes with a twist.[3] Unlike in stories, in which the outcome cannot be changed, in the land of *Mixed-up Mother Goose* children can make a difference. The rhymes had gotten mixed up and needed help out of their predicament. The players chose an avatar, their representative in the game, from one of eight different characters and went out throughout the land to search for items that story characters were missing. In the rhyme *Mary Had a Little Lamb* they could help find Mary's lamb; in *Humpty Dumpty Sat on a Wall* they could help Humpty find a ladder to get back up the wall. Learning outcomes included beginner reading and problem solving.

The controls for the game were designed to be easy for young children. Cursor keys moved the avatar around the landscape; when it was close to a story character

---

[2] The history of children's educational games, *Children's Games, From Turtle to Squirtle* can be accessed at Springer's Encyclopedia of Computer Graphics and Games (Madej, Children's Games from Turtle to Squirtle 2018).

[3] The player is told to fetch a sixpence in the nursery rhyme *Sing a Song of Sixpence*. Photos of *Mixed-Up Mother Goose* screenshots: http://www.mobygames.com/game/roberta-williams-mixed-up-mother-goose_.

a balloon text would pop up and give simple instructions such as "You there, fetch me a six pence." As the game was intended for pre-readers the object they were to look for was shown visually as well as textually. When found, whether lamb or ladder, the object could be picked up simply by walking through it. It was delivered easily by walking near the character for whom it was intended where it was automatically dropped. There was no particular order to the tasks but they could only be completed one at a time because only one item could be carried at a time. When the found object was delivered, children were rewarded with a short animation sequence.

Although *Snooper Troops* evolved from an educational setting and *Mixed-up Mother Goose* from a video gaming environment, both of these games were essentially the same in their goal, they wanted to entertain and educate at the same time. One can argue that almost all entertainment involves some kind of education, however *edutainment* implies planned learning outcomes.

The term *edutainment* became popular during the late 1980s and early 1990s with the development of CD-ROM technology that made it easier to market software products to parents. Companies such as *Knowledge Adventure* offered grade based and subject based software while children's book publishers such as *Simon and Schuster* published edutainment versions of well-loved children's stories. In this latter iteration of edutainment, stories were presented as digital books with turnable pages that children could read, just as they read print books. Interactive options for children included reading the books by themselves, having these books read to them by a narrator, having sections reread when these were highlighted, and getting an explanation of certain words. Music and sounds were part of the presentation. CD-ROM versions of popular stories such as *The Berenstain Bears* and *Little Critter* also included pop-up and rollover animations.[4] While controversy about children's use of computers was common, parents responded to edutainment software positively and saw it as a way to allow their children to enjoy playing with a new medium but also having a purpose for their play. Soon popular characters such as *Arthur, Clifford, Dr. Suess*, and others were used to teach not only reading but grade and curriculum topics such as math and science as well (Madej, Towards Digital Narrative for Children: From Education to Entertainment 2003).

The transmedia marketing of these stories gave children familiar reference points as they moved from media to media, from subject to subject. Eventually a number of the characters were featured on their own websites that began to offer similar educationally-oriented interaction that CD-ROMs did.

---

[4] *The Berenstain Bears Get in a Fight* CD-ROM screenshots show brother and sister in a tiff:
https://www.mobygames.com/game/berenstain-bears-get-in-a-fight

## 14.5  Disney Edutainment

Disney's entertainment is story based, whether it is an animated film or a ride in one of its theme parks. *Edutainment* had created a symbiotic relationship between stories and learning and was a natural fit with Disney's own focus on using narrative to provide both entertainment and learning to their audience.

Walt Disney had maintained an interest in education as far back as the 1940s when he was contracted to make educational films for the military. He said, "I learned much during the war years when we were making instruction and technological films in which abstract and obscure things had to be made plain and quickly for the boys in military services…. I began, with the return of peace, to plan the informative-entertainment series which now has jelled in the *True-Life Adventures*" (Barrier, The Animated Man, A LIfe of Walt Diseny 2007, p. 208). In the *True-Life Adventures* series, the first of which, *Seal Island*, won the Academy Award for Documentary Short Subject, Walt brought his skill for storytelling to natural events. Walt Disney had extensive footage shot in Alaska by the husband and wife team Alfred and Elma Milotte and then searched it for a story concept. It was extensively edited to provide for a coherent story that could both entertain as well as educate the public. Walt would say, "We can't bore the public with these things…. We've got to be entertaining" (Gabler 2006, p. 444).

Games such as *P.I. Mickey* brought the tradition of combining storytelling and learning into Disney's online environment. The Disney Online team produced many Disney games that included or were based on classic game activities such as puzzles, memory matchup, mastermind, checkers, crossword puzzles, hangman, the Tower of Hanoi, and many others. A prime example of a simple game that encourages kids to think and enjoy themselves with pattern-matching is *Donald's Pizza* in which the player would study each pizza pattern and click on the correct ingredients. The difficulty of the game depends on the level that is chosen for play, Rookie, Pro, and Master.

## 14.6  Hot Shot Business

A much more elaborated and complex edutainment game is *Hot Shot Business* created by Disney Online in collaboration with the Ewing Marion Kauffman Foundation, a nonprofit organization that teaches children about entrepreneurship, and was launched in May 2003. The game was designed for "tweens" between age 9 and 12.

**Hot Shot Business**

**Welcome to Opportunity City:** Introduces the concepts of
entrepreneurship and opportunity recognition, and touches on how
businesses can give back to the community.

**Finance Your Business:** Describes the two most basic methods of
financing a new business.

**Goal:** Challenges player to earn $2,000 in six virtual weeks.

- Game Week 1: The simulation begins, with a focus on responding to
  customer needs.
- Game Week 2: Players see how pricing decisions affect a business.
- Game Week 3: The importance of marketing is illustrated.
- Game Week 4: The difference between marketing a business and
  marketing a product or service is shown.
- Game Week 5: Competition is introduced into the marketplace.
- Game Week 6: Game Weeks 1 through 5 are brought together as
  the player's business matures.
- Game Wrap-Up: Did the player succeed in meeting the challenge?
  Results of the simulation are analyzed.

**The Biz Kit:** Players given access to the Biz Kit if they meet the goal set at
the beginning of the game. Kit includes downloadable tools designed to
encourage continued exploration of entrepreneurship: a guide to
developing a business-plan, a list of business ideas and opportunities, a
business dictionary, and a business card and flyer maker.

*Hot Shot Business* is a real-time, fast-paced simulation game about starting and
maintaining a successful business. It supports the Kauffman Foundation's curriculum on entrepreneurship. Designed to be engaging and highly re-playable, the game
introduces key business concepts and reinforces them through game play to teach
real world lessons in a story format. When tweens arrive at "Opportunity City" they
can use their own money or borrow capital to set up a service business (pet spa), a
manufacturing plant (skateboards), or a retail shop (comics). They are helped by teen
business advisors, Jack, who has a conservative approach, and Kate, who has a more
risk-taking approach. Once the business is financed, they play through a series of
phases that focus on specific aspects of their business such as customer needs, pricing, and marketing the product and the business. At the game's wrap up, successful
players are given a business kit to encourage taking their learning into the real world.

Each phase was carefully mapped out by the development team. The following
chart (See Fig. 14.2) is an example of the planning document from Week 4 that deals
with marketing (Everett 2003).

A complex game such as *Hot Shot Business* required heavy resources and significant time commitment in its design and development. The team wanted to ensure

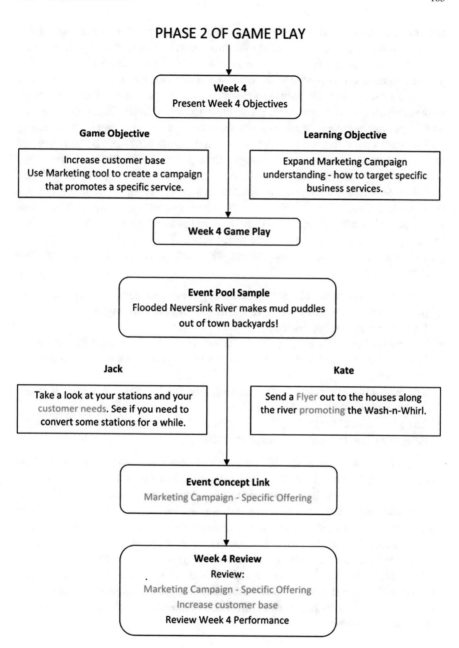

**Fig. 14.2** A planning document

not only that the story and game play were both engaging and intuitive but also that the educational content was clearly communicated. Rather than create realistic products and services, the team chose to develop business scenarios that were fun yet still maintained a balance with business realities. Of paramount importance to the game's success was the focus group play testing that was done during the course of development. During one focus group close to 50 children between the ages of 9 and 12 played *Hot Shot Business* sessions over a period of 6 weeks. The Disney Online team was concerned with issues such as the amount of basic information that had to be presented as text and dialogue during the introductory sequence. This contextual story information had to be presented in an engaging way to maintain attention, as without it players did not have a foundation for the remainder of the business experience. The problem was revisited a number of times before a fun-balanced-with-reality situation was achieved that proved to be very successful during the play-testing with the positive result that kids played sessions for a longer period of time. The focus group taught the development team some invaluable lessons:

- The educational material needs to be clearly communicated in a story via a combination of text, voice-over, and animation in order to engage the children. Brevity and pacing are critical.
- The game play needs to be intuitive. Players respond better with a standard interface but are less confused when there are variations to suit the different types of businesses.
- The products and services in the game must be fun for children, even if it means they are more fanciful and less realistic.
- The game clock and underlying financial models must be adjusted to provide a balance of fun, fairness, and business realities.

*Hot Shot Business* won the 2003 Parent's Choice Gold Award, as well as Best Education Web Site and Best Game Web Site. It became one of Disney's most popular games and was regularly enhanced to keep it fresh and interesting. In the 2004 update, two important aspects of the business environment, risk and opportunity recognition, were added, as were new storylines that included a landscaping business. In keeping with the move towards multiplayer online experiences, a multiplayer environment was also added to give players the opportunity to compete online. Carl Schramm, the President and CEO of the Kauffman Foundation said at the time of the second release "These enhancements offer an even greater real-world experience for kids to learn about the issues associated with entrepreneurship" (Business Wire 2004).

## 14.7  Squeak: An Interview with Alan Kay

Between 1996 and 2001, Alan Kay and his researchgroup were working on Squeak and Etoys at Disney. Squeak-based Etoys is a child-friendly computer environment and object-oriented prototype-based programming language for use in education. Influenced primarily by Seymour Papert, HyperCard, and the Logo programming language, Etoys advances and supports constructionist learning. Etoys offers a media-rich authoring environment with a simple, powerful scripted object model for many kinds of objects created by end-users. It includes 2D and 3D graphics, images, text, particles, presentations, web-pages, videos, sound and MIDI, the ability to share desktops with other Etoys users in real-time and encourages many forms of immersive mentoring and play over the Internet. Etoys runs on more than 20 platforms bit-identically.

Following is an interview with Alan Kay conducted by Newton Lee for Computers in Entertainment magazine on educating children through software such as Squeak conducted on June 4, 2003.

Lee: What do you think about educating children through entertainment?

Kay: Well, I think children should definitely be having a lot of fun when they are learning things, and I think many kinds of learning are fun for children, particularly sports learning, many kinds of music learning, and for those who find what's fun about math and science, they think that's fun when they are learning as well. But I think there's a difference between hard fun and soft fun. So a lot of our entertainment today is kind of soft fun where you're in a kind of vehicle and you're taken around, so you're watching a movie fairly passively or you're in an amusement park ride or something like that; you're watching baseball on television. Hard fun would be learning to hit the baseball or learning to play the musical instrument, actually doing the drawing and the painting and so forth. I think the balance between hard fun and soft fun has changed; I don't think it's changed for the better. So I think one of the things that we need to do is to understand what Montessori was saying, which was that children are set up by nature to learn things by play; play is a natural form for them. Her idea was if we'd like them to grow up in the twentieth century, now the twenty-first century, that we should give them twenty-first century environments and twenty-first century toys and still let them play. She didn't think that taking a university classroom, which is not clear is that good for university students, and trying to put six and seven year olds into a setting like that wasn't a very good idea. So I think that we have both a moral obligation and also a pleasure in helping young people learn. We want them to learn some really difficult things, particularly a lot of the ideas in the last 400 years, and so we should put quite a bit of effort into showing the kids why if you ask a mathematician what they're doing they'll say "I'm playing" and if you ask a scientist what they're doing, they'll say "I'm playing." I think most students who take math and science can't imagine what that might mean; so we have to show them what that might mean, and I think they can find the fun in it as well.

Lee:  In the 90's, at Apple and Disney, you developed Squeak based on your invention Smalltalk. Can you tell us what Squeak is in relation to education?

Kay:  Well Squeak is sort of a big alternative to personal computing that came out the ideas we had at Xerox PARC in the 70's. So, you can think of it as kind of a meta system for trying out many kinds of ideas. Inside of Squeak is an authoring environment that we made for children and for people interested in media. We've tested the children's environment out on many thousands of children and it's worked out very, very well all over the world: many different countries are using it now. It's based on ideas of Piaget, Jerome Bruner, and Montessori to give children a set of authoring tools for allowing them to draw things and make things and give them dynamic behaviors through scripting. Side effects are to learn the kind of mathematics that is used to describe science and to learn a little bit of real science along their journey. From their standpoint, they're thinking up kinds of play that they're interested in. They're exploring things and making models of these things, and so it's a kind of a deep extension of the kind of exploratory activities and construction activities that children do without computers. There are certain very important things about computers that have to do with describing dynamic behavior in terms of programs that bring very complicated math that is used by adults and not understood by many down to children in a very simple way. One of the big influences on this was Seymour Papert and one of his insights was that a form of vector differential calculus, differential geometry, could be made into children's toys using the computer. We've used his ideas and many other ideas to make this environment.

Although Squeak Etoys did not materialize as commercial products at Disney, The Company was interested in tapping Kay's expertise in applying new technologies to educational entertainment (edutainment) benefiting children.

## 14.8  Purchased Games

While games such as *Hot Shot Business* were created in-house, and those such as *Lion King* were contracted out, Disney Online also purchased games which were promising and which could fit into their goals for the Disney sites. Although Disney does not accept any unsolicited games or ideas from outsiders, the Online Group actively surfed the Internet to look for interesting games and contacted the authors to negotiate a deal. Two games that caught the attention of the group were *3D Blox* and *Car Jam*. The group had discovered the games online, found them very engaging, and played them incessantly. Developed by the successful Java game programmer Karl Hörnell, *3D Blox* was an action maze game while *Car Jam* was a brain twister thinking game. Both fit into Daily Blast's line-up; Disney Online producer Peter Levin negotiated a purchase for them from Hörnell in 1997.

In *3D Blox* the basic idea is to help Pixel Pete, an endearing penguin, get through many challenging levels to get to the golden treasure. Pixel Pete must collect golden coins and find the key to unlock the door to each of the levels within a given amount of time, or he ends up dead and has to start again. Besides coins, the playing field also has a number of keyholes from which a special crystal block appears when the correct key is inserted; Pixel Pete can step on the block to reach new places. After collecting all the coins and keys, the penguin has to find the door to advance to the next level. The golden treasure is guarded by the Evil Eye—a free-floating eye appears out of nowhere, patrols the space, and shoots at Pete when he gets close.[5]

Newton Lee worked with Hornell to fix a number of bugs in the games and to create graphical level editors for designing new scenarios for the games. This was necessary for replayability to keep the games fresh for audiences returning to the Disney site.

The interface of the game, which originally used the G, N, M, and L keys, was improved by enabling the use of the arrow keys for navigation. Inspired by Escher's Stairway, Sleeping Beauty Castle, and Disneyland rides, Lee created many novel game scenarios to give players more choices and greater challenges. To further heighten the excitement of game play, each game level was accompanied by original background music written by Stephanie Wukovitz, Jeff Essex, and Eric Huff.

The enhanced *3D Blox* debuted in May 1997 on *Disney.com* and it became an instant hit. The fast-paced action, stunning visuals, and background music in the game kept the adrenaline flowing and the players engaged. Its huge popularity prompted a sequel, *3D Castle*, in July 1997, in which new exciting levels were created and the free-floating orb was replaced by the Sorcerer's hat.

In the brain twister game *Car Jam*, the player must get their car out of a jam-packed parking lot using as few moves as possible. *Car Jam* is a version of the classic sliding-block puzzle *Rush Hour* developed by the Japanese puzzle inventor Nobuyuki Yoshigahara (Nob) in the 1970s. First marketed in the US in 1996, it became a popular "edutainment" game for children. The goal is to get a red car blocked by cars and trucks to the exit by moving the vehicles on the six by six grid. Vehicles can only be moved back and forth in the direction they are facing; they cannot be lifted to face a different direction. Solutions range in difficulty from Beginner to Grand Master. In *Car Jam*, the player's vehicle is in a parking lot and blocked by other vehicles such that it can't be driven out.[6] The action for moving the vehicles is the same, the player rolls the other vehicles back or forth, a little bit at a time, until the player's car reaches exit. An added difficulty is that only a limited maximum number of moves can be made in each level. Occasionally the game

---

[5] Pixel Pete, the penguin, must get through many challenging levels to reach the golden treasure. http://www.javaonthebrain.com/java/3dblox/.

[6] *Car Jam* offered many different levels of play from Beginner to Grand Master. https://www.old-games.com/screenshot/6160-3-smart-games-stratajams.jpg

awards the player a "car bomb" that facilitates the removal of an unwanted car in the parking lot.

Karl Hörnell originally wrote *Car Jam* for a software company that unfortunately went bankrupt and he was never paid for the game. Then, in July 1997, Disney Online bought the game from Karl. It was later renamed *Autocrazy*. In keeping with repurposing games for release with Disney movies, the company released a version entitled *The Love Bug Game* soon after the release of the movie remake of *The Love Bug* in 1997.

Before the public release of *Car Jam*, facts and statistics were added to the game to increase its educational value. However, the statistics about accidents and death caused by drunk driving were not considered suitable by the producer Pamela Bonnell. She said, "You are scaring the kids from riding in their parent's cars!" Subsequently it was decided to exclude all facts and statistics from the game. Even without these, because it was a problem solving game, it fit into the edutainment goals of the group.

## 14.9   *Kingdom Hearts*

*Kingdom Hearts* is a single-player, action role-playing game that is a crossover between two companies and their universes.[7] The two companies are Square Enix (originally known as just Square) and Disney Interactive. Square Enix and Disney Interactive Studios were the major developers and publishers, but the series itself has also had help from other companies to compile the game together.

*Kingdom Hearts* resides within its own series (*Kingdom Hearts*) and spans over nine main games. *Kingdom Hearts* was first created on its own in-house engine, Luminous Engine, but with the release of *Kingdom Hearts* 3, the game was switched over to Unreal Engine 4. *Kingdom Hearts* was a PlayStation 2 exclusive, released on March 28, 2002. The player takes on the role of the main protagonist, Sora. *Kingdom Hearts* is rated as E, but as the series progressed, the ESRB rating has change to E 10+.

*Kingdom Hearts* follows the story of a boy, Sora, who sets off on an adventure after his home, Destiny Islands, is consumed by Darkness. Throughout the series of the games the player gets to watch Sora grow as a hero. In the original game he arrives in Traverse Town and meets a new set of friends, Donald and Goofy, and then sets off to find Riku, Kairi, and King Mickey. His relationship with every friend he meets enables his growth to flourish throughout the story. The trio meets many heroes and villains spanning across both the Disney and Final Fantasy universes. Since *Kingdom Hearts* consists of both Disney and Square Enix characters, they wanted to attract both hardcore and casual players. They were able to create a game that could bring together people from all ages, young or old, to enjoy this series of

---

[7] An analysis of *Kingdom Hearts* by Michael Phillips and Newton Lee.

games. *Kingdom Hearts* managed to secure the spot for the tenth best-selling Playstation 2 game of all time as well.

*Kingdom Hearts* took much influence from Square's Final Fantasy franchise and it consists of a hack-n-slash approach to its gameplay. The main objective was to travel around defeating bosses to advance to different worlds. The player controls Sora with the ability to use basic attacks, special attacks, magic, and in some cases: dodges. Meanwhile, Donald, Goofy and/or another character who can replace the two will assist Sora within battles. The player can also control the behavior of the assisting characters to a certain extent. Sora's stats are based around his level, and the game in its entirety is set around an experience point system. Defeating enemies is the only way to earn experience points which in turn increases Sora's level (capping at 100). *Kingdom Hearts* is relatively linear; the player moves from world to world defeating Heartless, bosses, etc., but the player also has the chance to run into short side-quests to secure items, experience, etc. Among all these systems set in place, the combat interface seems to be the simplest. There is a command bar consisting of: Attack, Magic, Items, and Specials. Lastly, there is a health bar and magic bar, as well as both of the assisting character's health and magic bars.

*Kingdom Hearts* was a one of kind collaboration, which was perceived rather impactfully in the public's eyes. Due to its massive success, *Kingdom Hearts* never had any controversies surrounding the series. At first, no one thought Disney and Final Fantasy would be a good combination but were proven wrong. The original characters, especially Sora, were unique because the player could witness how their personalities grew and altered throughout the stories of each of the nine games.

*Kingdom Hearts* made the 22nd spot on IGN's top 25 PS2 games of all time. IGN had this to say, "The premise behind the game was completely absurd: Disney cartoon characters like Mickey Mouse thrown in with Square Enix characters to make a new kind of action RPG. However, as strange as it sounds, these two dissimilar franchises came together incredibly well." The characters—original, Disney, and Final Fantasy—helped develop the game into such a hit as it is still today. *Kingdom Hearts* suffers from linear progression but not in an unplayable manor. *Kingdom Hearts* hasn't really changed up its graphical capabilities over the years, but here is a YouTube video showcasing the evolution of the series.[8]

As stated earlier, *Kingdom Hearts* managed to secure the spot for the tenth best-selling Playstation 2 game of all time as well. *Kingdom Hearts* had such a unique way of going about its gameplay, but it could be comparable to games like the "Tales of" series, the "Persona" series, and of course the "Final Fantasy" series.

---

[8] Evolution of *Kingdom Hearts* Games 2002–2019. https://www.youtube.com/watch?v=Wu-QQgWeCi4

# Chapter 15
# Development Cycle: Quality and Feedback

> When we consider a new project, we really study it—not just
> the surface idea, but everything about it. And when we go
> into that new project, we believe in it all the way. We have
> confidence in our ability to do it right. And we work hard to
> do the best possible job.
>
> Walt Disney

## 15.1    Developing a Community-Based Musical Activity

The advantage to having an abundance of well-loved (or even hated) characters
from established stories is that there is an opportunity to use what's special about
them to create innovative activities and games. Children are often already familiar
with Disney characters through the animated films the company releases and then
regularly re-releases, the print and digital books that retell the story, and the dolls,
toys, and other products that are merchandising spinoffs. Peculiarities of character
and nuances of environment are generally already established by the time a character reaches Disney's online environment. Take for instance the game mentioned in
an earlier chapter, *Hercules*, in which players shoot arrows at a target in ancient
Greece. The game is based in the character Hercules from the animated film of the
same name. For children who have watched the film, possibly read the animated
storybook or the print book, and played with the Hercules and Megara dolls, this
legacy of experience with the character adds the extra dimension of a larger, all-
embracing story within which they engage with the character's activities in the
game. This past experience also gives younger children the sense of familiarity and
inclusion that makes a new game enjoyable rather than stressful. Disney relies on
building schema and providing a sense of continuity to ensure that reiterations of its

---

Online photos and graphics provide extra detail and are identified by urls the reader can refer to.
This additional reference information will be particularly beneficial as an enhancement for the
online version of this book. URLs are current at time of printing.

© Springer Nature Switzerland AG 2020                                              173
K. Madej, N. Lee, *Disney Stories*, https://doi.org/10.1007/978-3-030-42738-2_15

characters in both new stories and new media are successfully embraced by audiences.[1]

Disney characters come with a family and cultural pedigree; their character quirks, their relationships, their circumstances, their surroundings, all of these can be used to advantage when new ways of engaging children in interactive online activities are being conceived. *Mushu*, the diminutive fire-breathing dragon from the Disney animated movie *Mulan* (1998), proved an excellent match for an idea that developed into *Mushu's Music Maker*. Mulan, the movie's heroin has disguised herself as her father and joined an all male army called together by the emperor to fight invading Mongolian hoards. Mushu, who is a hilarious mischief-maker who cannot sit still, goes along as Mulan's guardian.

The original concept for the musical activity was that it be simple and funny and take advantage of Mushu's dragon property of breathing fire: when a player pulled (clicked on) one of Mushu's fingers, a musical note would be played and Mushu's mouth would open and breath fire. Each finger would represent a different note in an octave and trigger a fire of various shapes and sizes. In the final version three timpani drums were added to create a more orchestrated sound behind the display of fire "works." The interactivity was designed to be straightforward so that children would be able to create music and images quickly and easily. Furthermore, children could compose and submit a composition to the music gallery. *Mushu's Music Maker* debuted on *Disney.com* in July 1998 after one week of development by a team that consisted only of a software engineer and a graphic designer. A more complex game would require more than one engineer and one artist. The dynamic and scalable team size at Disney Online allows for efficient development of online games and activities of different scales ranging from one week to several months and multiple years of development.

With the completion of *Mushu's Music Maker*, senior software engineer Newton Lee, who instigated the project, started the ball rolling on discussions with producer and musician Andrew Rapo about a more ambitious music activity game. These discussions synchronized with the November release of the Disney/Pixar movie *A Bug's Life*, which had a musical score composed by Randy Newman that would win numerous awards in the coming spring. In November 1998, Vickie Ocheltree, director of the business unit websites, approached Disney Online about creating a music composer activity game based on the movie. The project was given the necessary funding, resources, and upper management support so that development could begin in earnest.

In planning *Music Room Composer* the team wanted to bring a range of musical activities to children to experiment with. In addition to creating music they wanted kids to be able to share their music by jamming together, publish their music to the site so that others could hear it, and comment on each other's music. In the final format *Music Room Composer* children were able to:

- Play the virtual piano with the mouse and keyboard.
- Load various music themes along with new instrument sounds and animation.
- Compose, record, edit, and playback music.
- Adjust the playback speed using the tempo controller.

---

[1] Disney's characters brought a complete backstory from their animated films to their appearance in Animated Storybooks, Activity Centers, and online games and activities. Screenshots of *Hercules*: https://rawg.io/games/disneys-animated-storybook/screenshots

- Enter the Jam session.
- Submit a music composition to the gallery.
- Listen to and vote on others' music compositions.

The program was developed using Macromedia Director and required a team that included a senior producer, a website integrator, graphic artists, engineering resources for the back-end DDL support for the game, and in-house audio/video engineer support to craft the virtual piano sounds and many other sound effects in the game. The producers kept track of the spending and obtained the legal rights to use some of the songs from *A Bug's Life*.

Apart from the game play, graphic design is a big part of the game's appeal. If a game is based on a Disney or Pixar animated film (Disney acquired Pixar in 2006), there is a comprehensive style guide and digital assets are available for all the animated characters in the film. The digital assets include the standard poses of each animated character in 2-D, as in *The Lion King*, or 3-D, as in *A Bug's Life*. In-house graphic artists manipulate these assets to give Disney games the same high quality look as the movies. To facilitate the process of creating new assets for the *Music Room Composer* specific guidelines were written for the graphic artists that ensured the authenticity of the look and feel of the characters. As an artist creates new animation sequences for a character, the character is always expected to behave according to the personality that was developed for it on-screen—it should never act out of character. Sometimes artists might take the liberty to expand on a character's personality in order to create a new storyline as a spin-off of a movie. Producers are ultimately responsible for making sure that the characters are never too far out of line from the original concept.

## 15.2  Quality Assurance and Software Testing

Following through on the well-established tradition of quality developed over the years, quality assurance (QA) is an important part of the game development cycle. Before it is released to the public, a game must be rigorously tested according to a written test plan detailing the functionality of the software and the test procedures.

---

**MUSIC ROOM COMPOSER TEST PLAN**

**/DisneyRecords/composer/composer.html**

**Goal:** Test all the functionality of the Music Room Composer application.

**Functionality:**

> Play the virtual piano with the mouse and keyboard.
> Load various music themes along with new instrument sounds and animation.
> Compose, record, edit, and playback music.
> Adjust the playback speed using the tempo controller.
> Enter the Jam session.
> Submit music composition to the gallery.
> Listen to and vote on others' music compositions.

A test plan must be precise and it ought to pay attention to all possible details such that it leaves no room for misinterpretation. Bug reports are tracked in a database accessible by the QA testers, producers, artists, and engineers. The relentless and meticulous QA testers spent many days and nights testing the game to make sure that there was no bug in the software to affect player engagement. The following test plan for *Music Room Composer* provides an example of what a tester (and by default, a player) would do once they entered the game.

---

**Procedure:**          Initialization

Before running the Music Room Composer for the very first time, you must have already installed "almanac.di!" in /cgi-bin/apps1.dll/global/ on the server. Now issue the following two commands from Netscape or IE browser once and only once:

http://apps.disney.go.com/global/almanae.dll?AddEvent&event=MusicPrehistoric
http://apps.disney.go.com/global/almanac.dll?AddEvent&event=MusicBugslife

Each of these urls should return a success message. For example:

    Almanac Version: 1,2,0,1
    Function: Add Event
    Event = MusicPrehistoric
    Size = 100
    Persist = 1
    Result: Success

**Procedure:**          Log on to get a cookie

Before you run the program every time you open the browser, you must log on to Disney go.com to get a cookie.

**Procedure:**          Startup

    Go to /DisneyRecords/composer/composer.html to start up the Music
        Room Composer. You should see:
    A piano with a computer keyboard layout.
    Your user name in the text message "Welcome <your user name>"
    The miniature picture of the Prehistoric theme.
    At this point, you can play the piano using the mouse or the keys.
        Notice that the last note played is in red on the music score and
        the corresponding musical letter (e.g. C#, A, E) is shown on the
        piano. Moving the mouse around different keys also shows the
        corresponding musical letter.
    If you click on the arrow buttons, you can choose from various
        themes including Prehistoric and A Bugs Life.
    To continue, click on the "Prehistoric" theme. You can still play the
        piano while it loads the theme that you have selected.

---

**Procedure:**      Prehistoric theme

When a theme comes up, it loads the composer's last submitted song. The red bar on the right shows the length of the song. If this is your first time, the bar remains black. If not, you can click on the "play" button on the right to playback your submitted song.

Play the piano using the mouse and the keyboard. Click on the "record" button on the right to start recording. Click on the "erase" button to delete the last recorded note. Click on the "play" button to playback the recorded song. Each note makes the conductor move and activate a particular animation.

Click and drag the wooden musical note on the left bottom of the screen to change the tempo. Click on the play button to listen to the song in the new tempo. The conductor and the animation also move with the new tempo.

The eggs on the right bottom represent pieces of pre-composed music. You can add them to your composition at any time.

Click on the "jam" button on the right activates a pre-recorded song or music.

Click on the "gallery" button brings up a new panel of "top ten" and "new" composers and their submitted music. You can submit your own song by clicking on the "submit" button on the new panel. You can refresh the rankings by clicking on the "update" button on the panel. To listen to other composers' songs, move the cursor to the name you want, and then click. At the end of the selected song, a scroll will appear and you choose whether you liked the song or hated it. Liking the song adds a vote count of 1 to the composer (except yourself - you are not allowed to vote for yourself). Hating the song does nothing.

The gallery is automatically updated only once when you first enter the gallery. On subsequent visits to the gallery, you must click on the "update" button in the gallery panel to see the latest results. To quit the gallery, click on the "close gallery" button.

To return to the main piano and select other themes, simply click on the conductor "return home" button.

---

**Procedure:**      A Bug's Life

A Bug's Life is very similar to the Prehistoric theme. The graphics and animation are now different so as to fit A Bug's Life theme, but the application's functionality is identical.

**Procedure:**      Multi composers' tests on "top ten" and "new" composer listings in gallery

Multiple composers should log on to Disney, run the Music Room Composer application, submit their songs to the gallery, listen to and vote for each other's songs, and verify that the "top ten" and "new" composer lists show the correct results:

The "top ten" list should show the user name with the highest vote first. The "new" list should show the composer who submitted a song most recently first.

Clicking on a song plays the correct song that was submitted by a particular composer.

You can vote on any song from both of the lists after you have listened to the entire song.

Clicking on the "update" button in the gallery displays the updated lists and the new vote counts.

Voting for or against your own song has no effect.

---

Once all the known bugs were fixed and QA approved the game, it went into a queue for the final approval by the producer. As soon as the producer gave the go-ahead, the game was deployed at the designated Disney Online website.

The entire iterative process of submitting, testing, fixing, and approving a game was tracked and annotated with *TeamSite*—a *Web Content Management Platform* from *Interwoven* that encompasses content authoring, workflow, versioning, and security. With the proper use of *TeamSite*, which helps optimize and analyze content across both internal and external applications, it was theoretically impossible to upload any erroneous or untested web pages and games to the Disney websites. Even so, there were a few mishaps had occurred due to human error!

The final release of the game was the culmination of a process that began in conceptualization, and went through extensive collaboration between software engineers, animators, graphic designers, sound effects engineers, and other creative and technical talents. The *Music Room Composer* game was so appealing and well received that before it was completed it was quickly expanded to include a prehistoric theme in addition to the *Bug's Life* movie theme. The final version of *Music Room Composer* debuted in February 1999 on the *Disney.com* website. A localized Spanish version was created, but unfortunately, edición espanola was never officially released.

## 15.3   Focus Groups and Guest Feedback

Depending on the project size and budget, Disney Online might conduct Focus Groups for feedback on individual games and to gage their success before they were released to the general public. *Usability Lab* was an interchangeable name for focus group workshop. Each workshop housed about 20 kids separated into age and gender groups whose behavior was studied to measure responses and generate statistics. In February 1997, Disney Consumer Products conducted one of their largest focus group workshops to kid-test some of *Daily Blast's* online games. While overall the feedback indicated games on the site engaged children successfully, it also provided valuable direction to the development team for improvement.

Guest feedback became an invaluable part of the group's analysis of the activities and games on Disney sites, in particular because it was unsolicited and pointed to what was most important to the different audiences who used the site regularly. Guests commented on the site as a whole, on individual games, and on music; they offered compliments, complaints, and suggestions for improvements to the games or the site. Every email that was sent to Disney Customer Service was read—Disney Online listened to every voice, took pride in every compliment, and worked to resolve every problem identified. Following are some of the comments and the different aspects of the site or game for which they provided feedback.

---

**Guest Feedback**

*Site comment, audience group – child and parent, child age - 5, game preference*

"My son loves the site…He liked the painting and the bowling game.  It was simple but interesting for a smart five year old." April 12, 1997

*Site comment – interactivity*

 "I think that this is one of the best sites to visit and having been a beta tester for many programs and sites, I find it fun and refreshing.  It is this kind of interactivity that I have been looking for in online services and I think I have found it. Not only am I a former Disney Cast Member, stockholder and frequent visitor to the parks, I am now a true Disney's Blast user. Thanks for working so hard to bring us the best in interactive sites." April 30, 1997

*Site comment – quality of games*

"We love your games on Disney's Blast!!! They give irrefutable proof that murder, destruction, and general violence aren't mandatory elements to make games enjoyable. Your games are obviously designed by creative, clever individuals who should be quite proud. Thank you for helping me

raise kids for whom violence is neither acceptable nor a daily part of life."
May 24,1997.

*Site comment - safe family entertainment, audience group - child,*
*adults/parents, child age - 7, frequency of use - daily, game preference*

"This is truly a FANTASTIC site! All three of us use it regularly, our 7-yr old
girl, my wife and I. Although Disney has taken some criticism recently,
NOBODY else provides safe FAMILY entertainment like Disney. We love
Daily Blast, Disney.com, and family.com. We visit all three almost daily.
Other games we really like besides Penguin Bounce are: Sea Hunt, Bowl-
A-Rama, Hit the Heckler, Alice's Maze, ESPN's Break-out. Finally, THANK
YOU for a spectacular web-site at a fair price." July 7, 1997

*Site comment - fun/enjoyment, audience group - child, grandparent/senior,*
*child age - 16 months, senior -63, frequency of use - regular individual use*
*plus family visits*

"Iam a 63 years old granny and I have been playing the games and
generally having fun enjoying myself with all the Disney Blast offs comics
etc. My grandson is only 16 months old but when he comes visiting we
have a lot offun... We here in Australia enjoy all Disney's World... One day
we hope to visit ... thank you for letting me enjoy being a kid again..."
August 13, 1997

*Site comment - encourages concentration, audience group - adult,*
*handicapped child, game preference*

"You have a fantastic site! Your bowling game is wonderful. I have a son
who is handicapped and has a very limited attention span, your bowling
game however has encouraged him to concentrate and really pay
attention to what he is doing instead of haphazardly pushing buttons. We
have been working for years to enhance his eye-hand coordination and I
think your bowling game has helped us to make huge strides. Thank you!"
October 26, 1997

*Site comment - enjoyment, game comment - replayability/change*

"My 3 year old really likes the Disney Blast Jr. He has several computer
CD's, but with as often as the games change, it's like buying all new games
every week. Thanks for a site we don't need to worry about. "June 3, 1997.

*Game comment -replayability/change*

"I would like to see the puzzles change more often. My 3 year old son
loves them butgets bored with them quickly." June 3, 1997

*Game comment - change*

"Why did you get rid of bowling? That was my favorite game that you had." May 26, 1997

*Game comment - change*

"Signed on when Bowling was offered. This was a great game. Now you replaced with basketball, Not so great. It would be nice if you could archive games, and members could choose. Maybe this is not practical or possible. If not, maybe you can alternate games or bring back popular games periodically."

*NOTE: The popular bowling game was brought back, and an archive of all the games was created for Disney's Blast members.*

*Site comment, game comment - downloadability, support group comment, audience group - children/grandparents*

"I found your offer on the Earthlink home page and signed up. I contacted your support group regarding frustrating problems. Iam so,so, so pleased with your timely response. 'Ed' called me the following morning and gave very easy to follow instructions which rectified my problem. I have a question regarding the games. I wanted this "site" for my granddaughters, now they are lucky if grandma will let them have a turn.A few of the games have held me hostage, I can't leave them alone. Will these games, such as the bowling and Minnie's marbles (not the correct names) remain on the site? Can they be downloaded? Please advise. Thank you, Donna" October 22, 1997

*NOTE: When the feedback was about a technical problem with a game, the group would contact the sender when the problem wasfixed or if additional information was required from the sender.*

*Site comment, game comment - downloadability*

"Your site is great, but I want to know if it is possible to download any of the games or stories. My kids just loved to play with Little Mermaid matching game and the 101 story of today. But, I cannot afford to be online too much, my phone service is very expensive to do this." May 11, 1997

*NOTE: In response to numerous requests, in 1998, o-toys - downloadable games - were introduced to the site.*

Guest feedback clarified for the development team the characteristics that were necessary to create a good game, no matter what the genre of the game, or how simple it was. These included:

- A distinctive idea, concept, or storyline.
- Engaging user interface and interactivity.
- Appealing graphics and stirring music and sound effects.
- Good value in entertainment and/or education.
- Highly re-playable.

The game design might include advanced physics, artificial intelligence, 3D graphics, digitized sound, an original musical score, and complex strategy. It might use several input devices such as the mouse, keyboard, gamepad, and joysticks. The game might be playable against other people on the Internet. However, complexity and fancy graphics do not necessarily improve the gameplay; characteristics must be balanced to successfully reach and appeal to an audience.

Paying close attention to guest feedback and responding to customer needs in a timely manner earned *Disney's Blast* reviews from the journalists that acknowledged the "high standard" of the games and their wide reach across ages.

> The newest Web site from this children's entertainment Goliath is a zany, hyperactive place, crammed with Disney characters, stories, comics, and games. Amid the wild and wacky, there are also ESPN sports updates, kid-size daily news reports, and a weekly magazine with entertainment bulletins. But the games beat all—even advanced age provides no immunity to Penguin Bounce, a race to slide a green springboard under falling penguins before they splash into a frigid stream. Other kids' Web sites pale in comparison to Blast. (Parenting, October 1997)

> Simply put, Daily Blast is so technically astonishing that it instantly rewrites the rules for online entertainment.... The whole site feels alive. (Entertainment Weekly, May 16, 1997)

## 15.4   New Directions

When *Disney's Daily Blast* debuted to the public in April 1997 it was a transmedia experiment in bringing Disney content to children through a new medium. The idea for a comprehensive site dedicated to a range of content that included games, stories, and edutainment was supported at Disney by leading-edge thinking, technology, and sufficient financial resources to bring the project to fruition. Despite the subscription model of the site, a possible deterrent, it met with great success. The site fulfilled its mandate and delivered on its promise to be a trusted environment for children (of all ages) for fun and challenging, as well as continuously changing, content. It added to the extensive list of media already in the Disney Master Narrative that carried the company's stories, characters, and comprehensive approach to entertainment to people of all ages.

In June 1998, *Disney's Daily Blast* was renamed to *Disney's Blast Online* (or *Disney's Blast* for short). Many new games were created for the site—in total, the Disney Online games group created over 100 games for *Disney's Blast* and *Disney. com*. Nine years later in 2007, *Disney's Blast* was re-branded as *Disney's Game Kingdom Online* to emphasize the focus on games for children; a number of the original games proved so popular they continued to be included as part of the line-up. The story components of the site were given new venues as role-playing games became increasingly popular. Multiplayer games and the communities they build would be the next direction for Disney Online.

# Chapter 16
# MMORPGs: Player-to-Player Interaction

*The only problem with anything of tomorrow is that at the
pace we're going right now, tomorrow would catch up with
us before we got it built.*

Walt Disney

## 16.1 Initial Steps

The majority of games, activities, and stories developed for Disney sites in the first
few years of online development were for the single player. Early on however, the
first steps in the type of community building that had been created in the early days
of Disney by the *Mickey Mouse Clubs* had already appeared on the horizon. One of
the simplest community building ideas in gaming is sharing high scores among the
players, a feature of arcade style games. In its original line-up, *Disney's Daily Blast*
included a bowling game that was designed so scores could be posted and children
could compare their performance with others. The top scores were updated daily on
one of the ESPN pages. Many other Disney online games kept the daily top 100
scores and the all-time top 10 scores. If a player scored high enough to be listed in
the all-time top 10 or daily top 100 list, the player would be allowed to enter his or
her nickname in the hall of fame.

Two other types of community involvement that were simple to instigate and
became common were paint contests and game shows.[1] In a paint contest a player
could submit a painting using the Disney branded paint application on Disney

---

Online photos and graphics provide extra detail and are identified by urls the reader can refer to.
This additional reference information will be particularly beneficial as an enhancement for the
online version of this book. URLs are current at time of printing.

---

[1] Even in the early Internet years Disney games incorporated community interaction. In the
*Halloween Painting* contest players paintings were posted in a gallery display space; a winner was
featured each week. In the *Game Show* contest, players answered trivia questions to score top
points and get included in the high score gallery.

websites. The Disney producers would handpick the winners and display them in an online gallery where all Disney online users could view them. Many contests were themed for special holidays such as Christmas, Halloween, and Valentine's Day.

In the game show, contestants were paired up to answer trivial questions. A writer came up with interesting questions for children, these included ones about the size of the world's largest bagel, the distance of smell for a polar bear, and random facts about music, movies, food, countries, and celebrities. When players achieved higher scores than others, their usernames were posted in the high-score gallery.

The level of player-to-player interaction increased in complexity with the release of *Music Room Composer* in 1999. In addition to being able to submit their compositions to a gallery that other players viewed, where they were listened to and voted on, players could also enter jam sessions with other players. The initiative was part of an ongoing interest on Newton Lee's part in community building and user participation in interactive online environments.

In June 1996, Lee had developed the concept *Virtual Community Interactive* (*VCI*), a new genre of community-based interactive games and entertainment. Moving beyond repetitive arcade-type games and limited educational software, *VCI* was envisioned as a virtual world with digitized cinematic footage and strong storylines. The main components of *VCI* were stories, role-playing games, and expert systems working synergistically with the communication interface of the Internet. Stories would provide the paradigm for the experience, role-playing would offer engagement through creative involvement in a virtual environment, expert systems would provide the knowledge base for being able to create specific or specialized identities and situations, and the Internet would provide the connection between players for chatting, sharing information, and acting/playing cooperatively to create their community.

While many of the titles on the Disney sites included characters from such stories as *Winnie the Pooh* and *Toy Story,* and catered to a younger audience, the target audience for *VCI* stories would be kids 10+ who would find more complex interaction exciting to be engaged in. Storylines envisioned for *VCI* included roles such as "Virtual Lawyer," "Virtual FBI Agent," and "Virtual Doctor." To build this virtual community in which players could interact both with the game and with each other, the *VCI* software would integrate a number of technologies. These included A.I. personalities, expert systems, full-motion video, 3-D animation, multimedia database, search engine, downloadable music, player's feedback, multi-player compatibility, Internet phone, proactive/reactive user interaction, and multi-title story interaction.

## 16.2   Chat Studio: The First Disney Virtual Community

Although *Virtual Online Community* (*VCI*) remained a dream product, the idea of developing a virtual online community for Disney continued as a real goal for Lee and in April 2000, with the creative support of Leslie Wilson, and the executive support of Scott Wessler and John Clarke, the community-based dream product *Chat*

*Studio* became a reality. Similar to *VCI, Chat Studio* had a downtown theme with places to go and things to do, fostering a sense of virtual community. It included the following features:

- Shoutouts: A banner across the city sky displayed public messages left by online users to express love, birthday wishes, anniversaries, congratulations, etc. A kid-friendly application *Shoutouts* was created to write public messages. A player could select one of the predefined icons and type a message. All messages had to be prescreened by Disney producers before they could be displayed.
- You've Got Friends: An online chat area where players built their own avatar and met other friends. To ensure online safety for children, only canned messages could be exchanged in any one of the themed chat areas such as Slumber Party, Lava Lounge, and Weird Planet.
- NetNotes: A message board on various topics of interest to kids, a place to share ideas on trendy and interesting topics. All messages were prescreened by Disney producers to ensure kids' online safety.
- Bogus Boards: A painted message board where kids could display their artistic talent with a message. All paintings were prescreened by Disney producers before they were publicly displayed.
- Other places of interest included Person, Place, Animal, Things, DJ Dome, X-Games, and a number of billboards that highlighted popular games and other places of interests.

## 16.3   Multiplayer Jabber Flash Games

Over the years Disney Online gradually introduced multiplayer turn-based games to their young audience. However, software complexity and high maintenance costs hindered the development and deployment of multiplayer games. The team found a solution by integrating *Flash* and *Jabber* to take advantage of superior streaming animation and reliable, scalable, real-time communication.

Disney Online had supported *Future Splash*, the ancestor of *Flash Player* built by Jonathan Gay, when it used the program to create its initial online animation and user interface in 1996. Purchased by Macromedia in December 1996, *Future Splash Animator* became *Macromedia Flash 1.0*. Best known for its efficient streaming animation on the Web, *Flash* conveniently provides an XML socket object for client-server applications that allows the client application to communicate with a server identified by an IP address or a domain name.

*Jabber*, an open standard communication protocol that is XML-based and allows near real-time extensible messaging and presence, was developed by Jeremie Miller in 1998 and first released in 1999. *Jabber* provides presence management, transparent interoperability, and real-time routing of structured information among cross-platform applications. As the traditional use of *Jabber* is instant messaging, the challenge for Disney Online was to integrate *Flash* and *Jabber* into a reliable, high-performance, scalable, and viable multiplayer gaming solution that would make it easy for their software developers to create multiplayer games.

Spearheading this effort, Lee worked with Jeremie Miller, Joshua Baguss (creator of *Flabber*), Todd Olson (*jabber.com*), and the engineering teams at Disney (John Clarke, John Barnhart, Adam Fritz, Robert Temple, Paul Ruiz, Mark Budos, Markus Ries, and Thomas Streeck) to solve a number of integration problems between the two programs (see the article *Jabber for Multiplayer Flash Games by Newton Lee*, ACM CiE October 2004, for more information). Fixes were applied to the *Jabber* software and as a result, within a matter of weeks, the Online Group built three prototypes:

1. Two-player tic-tac-toe
2. Three-player tip-toe-race
3. Two player handball

The test results for the turn-based tic-tac-toe and the tip-toe-race games, where three players simultaneously guess a unique number within a given time limit in order to advance the corresponding number of steps, were excellent. But the results for the twitch game, handball, were less than they team hoped for. In twitch games players' reaction time and precision is tested and rapid feedback keeps them engaged, while in turn-based games players must wait for an outcome to their actions before they can continue. A sudden burst of XML messages from a single *Flash* client sometimes caused server error. When using *Jabber* with *Flash*, the team found that turn-based games were much more reliable than twitch games.

Doug Parrish, chief technology officer at the Walt Disney Internet Group commented, "As a platform to instantly distribute relevant and personalized notifications, media, and content directly to visitors to our Web site, *Jabber* will provide an excellent user enhancement."[2]

In January 2002, Lee worked with game engineer Kevin O'Sullivan, intern Laura Knight from Woodbury University, and graphic artists Kathleen Bruno, Tom Neely, and Andrew Wiener to design Disney's first multiplayer *Flash/Jabber* game, *Pooh Bear's Meadow Trails*. The game is based on the classic *Hex* strategy game. In it two players team up with Pooh or Rabbit to create a connected trail, or line, of chips from one end of the meadow game board to the other. The team who first completes a trail of chips connecting the sides of the meadow game board, wins. During the game, players may get extra chips or some stones may stand in the way. The players may trade a chip with the opponents one time at each level of difficulty.

The development team chose not to allow free form chats for child safety. Instead, a built-in chat feature offered canned phrases, each of which was represented by a special code transmitted to and from the *Jabber* server. It also implemented a notification agent that sent the player an alert if he or she wished to be notified when

---

[2] Tonight Live: Jabber Moves Forward plus Microsoft, Linux and the Fat Lady. https://www.linux.com/news/tonight-live-doc-searls-jabbercon/

someone wanted to play the *Meadow Trails* game. An invitation panel popped up and the player could select to join the game or to reject the invite.

Using *Flash/Jabber*, *Pooh Bear's Meadow Trails* was developed in less than a month. This was a considerably shorter time than it took to develop multiplayer games in Java and Shockwave, the standard at Disney until that time. The performance of the *Jabber* server was also outstanding. A single server could handle more than 2000 simultaneous players at a fraction of the cost of other commercial multiplayer server solutions. Again at the leading edge of technology, Disney launched the game in February 2002, 2 years before its competitor Nickelodeon launched their first *Flash/Jabber* multiplayer game in 2004.

## 16.4   Massive Multiplayer Online Games (MMOGs)

In 1998, the Virtual Reality Group at Walt Disney Imagineering were exploring the viability of creating a massively multiplayer online game (MMOG) as an addition to Disney's online presence. An MMOG is a computer game played by thousands of players simultaneously on the Internet. MMOGs evolved from the text adventure games and MUDs (Multi-User Dungeons) of the 1970s and 1980s. Unlike arcade games, these early computer games were narrative and text-based.

The earliest text adventure game, *Colossal Cave Adventure*, was developed by Will Crowther in 1975. Crowther's real-life adventures spelunking in Kentucky caves dovetailed with his interest in interacting in the fantasy world of *Dungeons and Dragons*, a fantasy role-playing board game popular at the time. At the same time he wanted to find a way to share his interests with his two daughters. He said of the game, "I decided I would fool around and write a program that was a re-creation in fantasy of my caving, and also would be a game for the kids, and perhaps some aspects of the *Dungeons and Dragons* that I had been playing." Parts of the game were re-creations of cave systems Crowther knew; players progressed through the caves by exploring, asking questions, and giving commands concerning the area in which they were located. Crowther used a natural-language parser, which was a leap above the computer directions of other games. He said, "My idea was that it would be a computer game that would not be intimidating to non-computer people, and that was one of the reasons why I made it so that the player directs the game with natural language input, instead of more standardized commands." The program spread quickly through ARPANET, the predecessor to today's Internet, in part because of the natural language commands.[3]

In 1976 Don Woods, working at Stanford University's Stanford Artificial Intelligence Lab at the time, found *Colossal Cave Adventure* on ARPANET and contacted Crowther to ask if he could expand the program. At the time, J.R.R. Tolkien's

---

[3] The first adventure games from the 1970s were text only. Players provided instructions such as: turn right. Screenshot of Colossal Cave Adventure and similar games. http://faculty.cbu.ca/jgerrie/Home/jgames_TextAdventures.html

*The Hobbit* and *Lord of the Rings* were very popular and influenced Woods to add elves, trolls, a volcano, and other fantasy elements. He made the mazes more complex, and added more puzzles, traps, and treasure to the front end of the adventure (Crowther had more of these at the end of the adventure), and changed the game from one of exploration to one of "intriguing puzzles and challenges" (Rick Adams). Written in Fortran and useable on many different computer systems, the program, now called *Adventure*, was passed around on ARPANET and became very popular.

*Adventure* inspired other computer programmers and game lovers to write their own text adventures. In 1977 a group of MIT students wrote the game *Zork*, a variant of which became known as *Dungeon*. The story takes place in a magical underground empire, a place of trolls, unicorns, and grues, where spells are thrown, and monsters vanquished. The player is an adventurer who looks for treasures hidden in the caves of this fantasy realm. When he returns alive with his treasure, he becomes the Dungeon Master. The game was noted for the richness of its storytelling and its parser, which wasn't limited to simple-verb-noun commands as was that of *Colossal Cave Adventure* and *Adventure*. It improved the narrative quality of player engagement by introducing prepositions and conjunctions, going, for instance, from "hit grue" to "hit the grue with the Elvish sword."

Dave Lebling, one of *Zork's* designers comments, "Where [journalists and historians] tend to go wrong is to overemphasize the importance of our parser. You can't blame them for that, because we pushed it hard as a 'unique feature' as well. What was a least as important was coming up with good writing, good stories and rich environments." About the writing and story David Stone of *Computer Gaming World* said in March–April 1983, "*Zork* is all text—that means no graphics. None are needed. The authors have not skimmed on the vividly detailed descriptions of each location; descriptions to which not even Atari graphics could do complete justice." Nick Montfort in his book on interactive fiction, *Twisty Little Passages*, discusses the narrative features of the game, "*Zork* introduced an actual villain, the thief, who opposed the player character during the initial exploration of the dungeon, who could be exploited to solve a puzzle, and who had to be confronted and defeated. This was a real character with the functions of a character as seen in literature, not the mere anthropomorphic obstacle that was seen in Adventure."

Not intended as a commercial product, the game nevertheless became the first text adventure sold to the public. It was published as *Zork I* (the name *Dungeon* was already taken and could not be used) by *Infocom* the company formed by the students who had created it (*Infocom* was purchased by *Activision* in 1986). Matt Barton situates *Zork:* "What *Zork* seemed to contribute more than anything was the idea that the computer could simulate a rich virtual environment much, much larger and nuanced than the playing fields seen in games like *Spacewar!* or *Pac-Man*. Furthermore, the game demonstrated the literary potential of the computer." It was however, still a single player game.

It was possible in the late 1970s for a number of people to be connected to each other at the same time via a common server. In university and other research settings, students and researchers took an interest in exploring adventures like *Dungeons and Dragons* together and in interacting in chat rooms in these games. In

1979 at the University of Illinois, students developed a text adventure game called *Oubliette* (an oubliette is a dungeon reached only by a hatch up in a high ceiling). People worked together to solve clues for getting around the different dungeon levels. Jim Schwaiger, one of the designers tells us of the language used in the game, "One of the more purist players of the game, David Emigh, was a graduate physics student and also an amateur linguist. He created a language just for the game, including deriving word roots so the spells have a consistency and poetry you would not expect if you simply made up a name." In 1980 at Essex University in the U.K., Roy Trubshaw, a final year student, also began work on a text adventure game in which multiple users worked together. He called it *MUD* for *Multi-User Dungeon* (after the game *Dungeon* which Trubshaw enjoyed playing); the name became a soubriquet by which all such games became known. When he graduated the next year he passed the game on to fellow student Richard Bartle The two students wanted to create a realistic virtual world in which players would become immersed. Bartle "... wanted people to be able to escape the confines of the real world, to try on new identities, to be... not so much new people, but to try to find out the people they really were." He developed the game further to include more players with more options for action. The game was played on the Essex University intranet and then when the university connected its network to ARPANET, it became the first multi-player online game.

As technology improved, graphics became a standard feature of games. In the first graphical adventure *Mystery House* (*1979*) these were simple line drawings. Graphics soon progressed to animation and began to replace text, as in the game *King's Quest* (*1980*) in which players would point and click rather than enter text to journey through the land and obtain items to help with their quest. Interactive text adventures and role playing games took two different paths: text adventures involved exploring spaces, finding objects, and using them in the quest to get to new locations and locate treasure; role-playing games used statistics building and battling to move their players through the game.[4]

In 1988 in the U.S., Lucasfilm had developed a technologically advanced story oriented online game *Habitat*, but it was not released past the beta stage. In 1992 *Sierra On-Line's* game *Yserbius*, was released as the first graphical online MUD in which a traditional text box was supported by point and click graphics. Early multiplayer online games were accessed through proprietary servers for amounts that ranged from five to twenty dollars (U.S.) an hour, depending on the server and the time of day. The audience was still small and select. In 1996 the first commercial 3-D online massively multiplayer role-playing game *Meridian 59* was released by 3DO. It was also the first real-time online game. The beta game, which opened April 1996 and closed September 27, 1996, had a community of over 25,000 players. While initially *Meridian 59* was called a graphical MUD, in 1997 this "genre name"

---

[4]Graphics improved significantly from *Mystery House* to *King's Quest*. Text adventures became point and click graphical adventures. Photo of *Mystery House* http://en.wikipedia.org/wiki/Mystery_House. Photo of *King's Quest* http://www.mobygames.com/game/pc-booter/kings-quest.

was supplanted by the now commonly used Massively Multiplayer Online Role-Playing Game or MMORPG.

Massive multiplayer games differ from other computer games in a number of ways. Massive multiplayer games have hundreds of thousands of players and now some have millions. The world created in MMOGs is persistent, that is, the game continues whether or not any individual continues to play. Since the purpose of the game is multiplayer gameplay, for the most part the games do not have any significant individual player attributes and typically players do not usually finish the game as they would in a single player game. Because they host a large number of players they have very large-scale game worlds that players traverse by different methods (such as teleporting). Each of the thousands of players can interact with another player at any given time. The game states rarely reset, that means the level reached by a player will be available when he/she returns to the game.

Massively multiplayer games were played predominantly by adults. Then in 1996 *Castle Infinity* was developed as on online game for kids between the ages of 8 and 14. Players could join friends in saving the dinosaurs and their castle from the evil monsters who were invading their home. Graphics and audio were provided in a purchased CD-ROM; players could then log on online at no cost. Players needed a password and a unique name to get started. They could then create their avatar from different pieces of animals, plants, or machines that would make up the head, the body, or the legs. Starting in his or her bedroom, a player went to join other players in a common area to chat and then traveled on to other areas of the game. Players navigated over pits, around fires, through water, under moving elevators, and, in addition, battled randomly appearing monsters to move through the castle's rooms and levels. Their chat appears in cartoon bubbles as they play and talk (or type).[5]

The philosophy of the company *Starwave* was to invest in building online communities and through its *ESPNet SportsZone* it offered statistics, sports scores, and chatrooms for sports fans to share information. The company saw *Castle Infinity* as a way to help establish multiplayer games and develop an online playing community. Disney purchased an equity stake in *Starwave* in April 3, 1997 shortly after announcing it was launching their new children's online site *Disney's Daily Blast*, and purchased the company a year later.

### 16.4.1   Toontown Online

When the Virtual Reality Group at Disney began working on developing a multiplayer game they had to overcome some perceptual difficulties concerning multiplayer games for the mass market: multiplayer games were played by adults, the content of such games was violent and unsuitable for kids, playing online games

---

[5] *Castle Infinity*, launched in 1996, was designed as a multiplayer game for children between the ages of 8 and 14. Photo of *Castle Infinity:* http://en.wikipedia.org/wiki/Castle_Infinity.

cost money. In their preliminary discussions the VR Group made a number of design choices that would differentiate their game from existing ones and position it solidly within the Disney pantheon of safe, quality, children's entertainment. These include using positive stories and themes, keeping kids safe through menu-driven or password protected chat systems, encouraging social behavior through cooperative game play, making the environment friendly, and providing simple game mechanics yet with interesting role-playing game (RPG) qualities.

Named *Toontown Online*, the game is based not in the traditional quest, fantasy, or science fiction themes of most MMORPGs. Instead, *Toontown* is a whimsical virtual world in which *Toons*, cartoon characters of the 1940s variety, inhabit six neighborhoods. The neighborhoods are happy, colorful places and each is associated with a classic Disney character. As an element of conflict in the game, mean *Cogs*, out-of-control business robots, have come to town and are ruining this happy environment by making it a black and white city of skyscrapers and businesses. The game enlists players to become *Toons* to save the town. *Toons* talk with each other through word balloons and take their world back by using traditional cartoon practical jokes and slapstick comedy such as cream pies, seltzer bottles, and whistle blowers against the Cogs, who have no sense of humor and can't take a joke. The VR Group created the game for children over seven, but found that adults also enjoyed *Toontown's* nostalgic elements, humor, and game play.

## 16.5  *Toontown's* Backstory

*Toontown's* story begins on the outskirts of the place cartoon characters call "home." On this day, world-famous billionaire Scrooge McDuck decides to pay a visit to his favorite employee, eccentric inventor Gyro Gearloose.

Gyro has posted a warning sign on his laboratory door that says "KEEP OUT." Scrooge ignores it, opens the door, and calls out "Gyro?" He walks pass a vast array of laboratory equipment, test tubes, and microscopes. Gyro is nowhere to be found.

"I wonder where Gyro could be?" thinks Scrooge. In the back of Gyro's laboratory, Scrooge is stunned by what he sees and cries out, "Sufferin' catfish! A g-g-giant robot!"

Scrooge then thinks to himself, "Hmm... A giant robot... Perfect... Why, a thing like this could be a really big help to the citizens of Toontown... And make me a big pile of money!"

However, Gyro has left a huge note on the robot that says "DO NOT TOUCH!" Scrooge is upset. "Do not touch?" he thinks, "Phooey! That can't mean me! After all, I paid for it…. Let's get my investment up and running!"

Scrooge proceeds to connect the broken wires—the blue one to the red one. The giant robot instantly comes to life!

"All systems ready!" says the giant robot in a deep voice. Scrooge begins to worry, "Great heavens to Betsy! What have I done?"

His fears are fulfilled as the giant robot stomps towards the control panel, pushes the red buttons, pulls the lever, and manufactures hundreds upon hundreds of evil robots called Cogs. They come in various sizes, shapes, and abilities to inflict evils in *Toontown*. Scrooge panics, "Oh my heavenly days! This can't be good…".

The story ends with Gyro's invention running amok. Scrooge has placed himself and all of *Toontown* in danger. Can anyone stop this army of robots? "*Toontown* needs your help now!"

## 16.6  Becoming a *Toon*

To save *Toontown* from the evil *Cogs*, the player has to become a *Toon*. Each account holder can create up to six *Toons* in the virtual world. A menu of characteristics such as height, weight, color, and fashion style are available to make each *Toon* an individual character that reflects a player's preferences.

Naming characters in games has often been abused and in Beta testing the VR Group found it impossible to create a filter that would prevent players from using inappropriate names that might be offensive to some of the audience. Instead of relying on an automated "naughty list" filter such as the one being used by *Disney Online* for game high scores, the VR group created a name generator that gives a player millions of possible combinations based on a choice of title, first name, and last name from a suggested list. The generated list provides names that are in keeping with the humorous nature of *Toontown*. To avoid the problem of inappropriate names, players are offered a list of titles and first and last names from which to choose their avatar's name. If the player chooses, they may enter their own name, which goes through client and server side filters and is reviewed by a Disney customer representative before acceptance.

Once a player has made and named her/his own *Toon*, they are ready to enter *Toontown* and meet and play with other *Toons*. In keeping with the positive, upbeat tone of the site, if *Toons* join on a special day such as New Year's Day, they are greeted in the playground with a display of fireworks.

## 16.7  Safe and Friendly Socializing

*Toontown* encourages socializing and incorporated in the game are features that facilitate socialization that is friendly, safe, and fun. Communicating through chat is a necessity in a multiplayer game; in most MMORPGs it is unrestricted. To protect kid's privacy and ensure online safety, the VR group developed *SpeedChat*, a menu based chat system that provided safe player-to-player text interaction. Kids choose what they want to say from an extensive set of pre-selected context-sensitive words and phrases that automatically adapt to the player's objectives and status in the game. The set menus eliminate game jargon that may not be understandable by new players and helps novice typists who may have difficulty with grammar and spelling. A particular feature is that the phrases are friendly and encourage engagement and cooperation between players.

The VR Group had initial concerns that menus of words would be "overly restrictive" but these were allayed during focus group testing. Feedback indicated that *SpeedChat* is sufficient to convey a player's feelings (e.g. happy or sad) and simple thoughts (e.g. follow me, let's play a game) that are enough to play the *Toontown* game without hindrance. In addition the focus group found that the friendly nature of the word sets "helped to overcome shy players' inhibitions." Overall, the lack of open chat helped the players focus more on the gaming tasks at hand rather than spending time on chitchatting and digression.

Open chat *is* available in *Toontown* between "true friends." True Friends are those who are friends in actual life and may want to chat more extensively when playing online. To activate open chat between two *Toons*, a randomly generated secret password that is valid for only 48 hours is given to each of them. Friends share their secret password over the phone, via email, or instant messaging; each friend must then enter the correct password in *Toontown* before it expires. True Friend chat is filtered for inappropriate language and the chat is incomprehensible to other *Toons*.

In addition to making chatting safe as well as friendly and engaging, *Toontown* offers many shared activities to help with making friends and becoming a part of the community: there are mini games to play, opportunities to go fishing, and ongoing *Cog* battles to join. Socializing is encouraged by the simple way in which *newbie's* (newer players) can join play: they could hop on a trolley car and meet other players going to a game or simply walk up to a battle that may be in progress and be instantly included without any chat. *Elders* (more experienced players) are rewarded when they help out a newbie in battle against the cogs; because the rewards received in a game are proportional to the contribution made, elders are not penalized in battle when a newbie joins. This positive approach facilitates newer players inclusion in the gaming community.

Other features were included to make *Toontown* a friendly environment: portable holes allowed players to teleport immediately to wherever their friends are located, there is no player-to-player battling or any opportunity to steal or hoard items, and, instead of getting hurt or dying, *Toons* become sad and go back to the playground to become happy again.

The VR Group created a causal relationship between the different activities of *Toontown* making them interdependent.

> Our goal was to divide a player's time into roughly three equal parts: battles, minigames, and social/playground activities. The activities were designed to be interdependent. To fight Cogs, Toons need gags. To buy gags, Toons need jellybeans. To earn jellybeans, Toons play minigames. To play minigames, Toons need friends. To meet friends, Toons head to the playground. In the playground, Toons heal up for battle, and the cycle continues. (Mine 2003)

## 16.8   Collecting and Cooperating to Save *Toontown*

*Toontown Online* offers many mini games for the players to win the "jelly beans" necessary to make purchases of cartoon weapons to fight the evil robots. Jellybeans are the main component in the game's system of barter.

Some of the popular mini games are maze, tag, memory, treasure dive, slingshot, ring, cannon, jungle vine, and tug-o-war. Most of these games are action adventure in nature to keep the adrenaline flowing and maintain a quicker pace in the overall mood of *Toontown*. Although most of the mini games are competitive, there is no "winner takes all" mentality. If the player exerts some amount of effort, chances are she will win some jellybeans, although perhaps not as many as the winner. For newbies there is a series of training tasks to follow to learn how to win jellybeans, explore the virtual world, and destroy the evil robots. *Toons* battled *Cogs* with cooperation and comic rather than violent action.

*Cogs* have different names such as Pencil Pusher, or Tightwad, according to their different abilities, and they are classified into different levels according to their power. Regardless of their abilities, high-level *Cogs* are more dangerous than low-level robots. It often takes simultaneous actions from a team of *Toons* to destroy a high-level cog. When fighting against the evil robots or *Cogs*, *Toons* need to cooperate with each other.

Once all the *Cogs* have been evicted from a building and eliminated, the ugly grey building is magically transformed into a happy place with bright vibrant colors. The team of *Toons* that accomplished this task is rewarded by having each player's *Toon* name displayed on the wall of fame inside the building. In addition, the top *Toons* and their accomplishments are announced in *The Toontown Online Times* daily newspaper.

## 16.9   Panda: The Little Engine that Could

In considering the requirements of running a successful MMORPG the VR group decided it would be best to develop their own rendering and storytelling system rather than to use a commercially available graphics engine. The group had created a number of real-time engines previously and building an engine "from the ground up" provided answers to a number of problems. The most important of these was the issue of longevity. Massive multiplayer games are intended for long-term online life and with Disney's commitment to quality upkeep and continuous new features, third party involvement was risky. Another issue was the desire to create a "unique feel and look" for the game. Making their own system would provide the opportunity to create a completely new feature set different from what was available through commercial systems. In addition, the VR group wanted to have full access to the source code in order to avoid any issues around licensing. A final concern was the VR group's work with Disney Imagineering. In order to support other R&D projects it would be more useful for the VR group to develop their own system that they could then use without the concern of licensing and paying for a proprietary commercial system.

To be successful in the online marketplace, the engine the VR group built would have to be capable of operating across different platforms. The resulting system, *Panda-3D*, took its name from just this feature: Platform Agnostic Networked Display Architecture, or more briefly Panda, provided the portability and flexibility for *Toontown* to run on any operating system. Initially only offered for Windows, Linux, and IRIX, it soon became available for Macintosh and console ports as well.

Built on an efficient low-level C++ engine, Panda-3D expressive scene graph architecture gave designers tools for creating diverse and dynamic worlds for *Toons* to inhabit while its interpreted scripting language gave programmers flexibility to prototype software rapidly and debug game logic quickly.

*Toontown's* download architecture allowed players to enter almost immediately into a full-featured game that was completely downloadable. To provide time for the complete download without a boring waiting period, players were occupied with introductory activities: watching the *Toontown* back-story via a 2D Flash movie, creating their own cartoon avatar, and a *Toontorial* to provide directions for playing the game. The game servers were designed to be low-cost, scalable, and robust as well as flexible. As guest testing showed players had a better time when they found their friends in the game, programmers made districts an attribute of the *Toon* rather than the server and so allowed players to both chat and teleport to their friends without being restricted by the district they were in.

Panda-3D is open source. Its many features are described by Mark Mine, Joe Shochet, and Roger Hughston in their article *Building a Massively Multiplayer Game for the Millions: Disney's Toontown Online*

> When we began development of Toontown Online, we did not fully appreciate the challenges associated with building a persistent online world for the mass market. Much is required to build a safe, social, simple yet nontrivial experience, especially for children. We owe a great deal of our success to the fact that we were building our game on top of such a powerful and flexible foundation. Panda's platform agnostic, expressive, scene-graph architecture, combined with facile interpreted scripting layer tools, was the key to our success.[6]
> (Mine 2003)

## 16.10  *Toontown Online*: A Work in Progress

*Toontown Online* was designed as "a safe social game that was simple to learn yet challenging to master" (Mine 2003). When released, *Toontown* proved to be innovative in many ways:

---

[6]The first of Disney's MMORPGs, *Toontown Online*, created an interactive mass market experience. *Toontown Online* screenshots: http://www.mobygames.com/game/toontown-online.

- It provided a safe online environment for children thanks to the *Toon* name generator, *SpeedChat*, and *True Friends*.
- It encouraged both competitiveness (in the mini games) and cooperation (in fighting against evil). There is no "winner takes all" mentality even in a competitive mini game.
- It minimized violence in the gameplay through the use of cartoon slapstick weapons such as cream pies and seltzer bottles instead of guns and swords, and by using robots that are mechanical rather than humans. Because *Toons* never die, but rather become sad, issues of physical pain, blood, and death didn't arise as they do in adult MMORPGs.

Work on web integration for the beta launch of *Toontown Online* had begun in June 2001. The game was extensively tested and feedback was provided on gameplay and performance to the Virtual Reality group. The project was cancelled during the continuing downsizing of Walt Disney Imagineering. Fortunately in September 2002 Disney Online absorbed the Virtual Reality group from Walt Disney Imagineering, and the entire team moved into the Disney Online office building in North Hollywood. *Toontown Online* was soon resurrected and was released in "sneak peak" mode in October 2002. When the game finally debuted to the general public in June 2003, Mike Goslin, Disney's Virtual Reality Studio head said, "Our background at Imagineering developing theme park attractions has taught us a lot about creating mass market, interactive experiences. We've learned so much from the many guests who have played Toontown in its various pre-release versions, and we're very excited about the new directions we already envision to build out this online world."[7]

Although *Toontown Online* was designed as a non-violent game alternative for kids aged seven to twelve, adults enjoyed the game as much as kids did, making *Toontown Online* family entertainment similar to a Disney theme park where kids and parents have fun together. The monthly subscription model with reduced rates for longer memberships, proved acceptable to the audience and profitable for the company. A basic level of play is available free on the site so anyone interested can make a *Toon* avatar, enjoy walking about, and play a mini game or two to see if they like the environment. In addition to the online subscription plans, prepaid subscription cards (one or more months) were made available at retail outlets to allow sampling of premium content.

*Toontown Online* quickly gained enormous popularity with a high retention rate after the initial free three-day trial. In mid-2005, Mike Goslin stated "we have nearly 10,000 people playing simultaneously during our busiest times." In May 2007, independent Internet research firm Comscore estimated *Toontown Online* had nearly 1.2

---

[7] Disney's Toontown Online to Launch June 2003; After Successful Preview, Toontown to Be Launched Widely with New Gameplay Features and Broad Marketing Support. http://www.businesswire.com/news/home/20030505005247/en/Disneys-Toontown-Online-Launch-June-2003-Successful

million users. Disney also produced versions of *Toontown Online* for the United Kingdom, France, Spain, Japan, Southeast Asia, and Brazil.

A massive multiplayer online game is more than a game, it is an ongoing world that requires constant attention to keep the experience interesting for players. As with the *Disney's Daily Blast* and *Disney's Game Kingdom Online* sites' continuous flow of new materials for users, the plan for *Toontown Online* included continuously improving and expanding the game play features to make the story interesting and the games replayable.

# Chapter 17
# Online Worlds and Cross-Media Engagement

*It's kind of fun to do the impossible.*
Walt Disney

## 17.1 Online Theme Park: *Pirates of the Caribbean*

While MMORPGs were instrumental in connecting gamers and building gaming communities around stories, the Internet was evolving into a social environment that stimulated exchanges of information and conversations between users of every age and interest. The online virtual world that Disney's Virtual Reality Studio had created in *Toontown Online* was part role-playing game and part social interaction. In keeping with the company's history of taking a comprehensive approach to engaging audience in any new medium, whether film, book, radio, television, or theme park, The Walt Disney Company was creating a network of virtual story worlds on the internet that would attract and engage audiences in social interaction as well as in game-like activities. In particular, it would continue to grow the children's web playground it had started with *Disney's Daily Blast*.

Following the *Toontown Online* success, the VR group began work on their second MMORPG, *Pirates of the Caribbean Online*. Based on the very successful 2003 movie, the release date was planned to coincide with the film's 2006 sequel. The original movie had been based on a very successful ride that opened at Disneyland in 1967.

The *Pirates of the Caribbean* ride was originally planned as a guided walking tour of famous pirates *The Rogues Gallery* at the time Walt Disney was designing

Online photos and graphics provide extra detail and are identified by urls the reader can refer to. This additional reference information will be particularly beneficial as an enhancement for the online version of this book. URLs are current at time of printing.

© Springer Nature Switzerland AG 2020
K. Madej, N. Lee, *Disney Stories*, https://doi.org/10.1007/978-3-030-42738-2_17

Disneyland in the 1950s.[1] Walt had been fascinated by the potential for creating movement or animating figures since he had purchased a mechanical bird that moved in New Orleans in the 1940s. In 1952, he started Walt Disney Imagineering (imagination + engineering), the "blue sky" design group that would be responsible for developing animatronic attractions at Disneyland. Audio-Animatronics, a robotics technology that uses audio sounds to trigger actions in animated figures, was the group's first major technological breakthrough. With it the group created *The Enchanted Tiki Room* for Disneyland, an attraction that featured singing and moving birds. For the1964 World's Fair, they created their first Audio-Animatronic human figure, a crowd pleasing Abraham Lincoln reading a part of the Gettysburg Address.

The advances in developing human characters were soon adopted for *The Rogues Gallery,* which took on a completely new story. A transportation system invented that took guests through a boat ride attraction was also adapted for *The Rogues Gallery.* With an expanded storyline, the ride became *Pirates of the Caribbean* and opened at the theme park in March 1967. Disney guests set sail into the Caribbean Sea from the dungeons of an old Spanish Fort only to find themselves between the fire of the pirate's galleon and the defending fire of the fortress. The excitement of gunshots, cannon blasts, burning buildings, together with the carousing and plundering of the life-like pirates proved exceptionally popular and the ride became the park's biggest hit. It was replicated at Disneyworld in Florida in1973 after complaints from guests that it had been excluded in the original design. It became part of Tokyo Disneyland in1983 and Paris Disneyland in 1992.

In 2001, the Virtual Reality Studio took the pirate's story to the next level of entertainment: *Pirates of the Caribbean*: *Battle for the Buccaneer Gold* opened at DisneyQuest, an entertainment centre that featured virtual reality attractions.[2] Audiences wore head-mounted display (HMD) gear that made them feel they were in the midst of a three-dimensional fantasy world where they enjoyed the combined thrill of a ride and the exceptional graphics of a video-computer game. In *Pirates,* guests set sail on a pirate ship into a virtual sea where they encountered enemy ships and sea monsters and searched for treasure. An epic cannon battle and a flying skeleton added to the excitement. "People absolutely loved it" (Goslin 2007) and the attraction won a Thea Award for the best new theme park attraction in 2001.[3]

---

[1] "Your adventure begins in the swampy bayous of New Orleans Square…" reads the promotional brochure for the *Pirates of the Caribbean* ride at Disneyland in 1967. This adventure, the last Walt Disney was personally involved in designing, has traveled across media to bring its story through books, movies, virtual reality, all manner of merchandise, and, finally, a virtual online world. Photo of the ride brochure for the *Pirates of the Caribbean*: http://matterhorn1959.blogspot.ca/2010/09/things-from-gate-pirates-of-caribbean.html

[2] Audiences were made part of the action in *Pirates of the Caribbean* at *DisneyQuest*. Wiki and game play: https://lostmediawiki.com/Pirates_of_the_Caribbean:_Battle_for_Buccaneer_Gold_(lost_DisneyQuest_arcade_game;_2000–2017)

[3] Disney Quest closed in July 2017 after 19 years at the Walt Disney World Resort in Florida.

MMORPGs had grown as an entertainment genre in gaming since the first graphical MUD *Yerbius* had been released in the early 1990s and had steadily acquired a large and dedicated audience of gamers. The VR Studio saw MMORPGs as a way to bring the excitement of the virtual reality attractions they had developed for Disneyland and DisneyQuest into people's homes, echoing Walt Disney's decision in the 1950s to bring his films into people's homes through television. As early as 1999 the VR Studio was proposing an online virtual world featuring pirates, one in which players would not only chase and interact with pirates, but also "BE pirates" (Sklar). The group believed that the pirate environment created for the VR ride could be successfully translated into an engaging online world that would attract a large audience because of its very entertaining story. In 2000, they pitched the idea of an online theme park that would consist of different virtual worlds, including *Toontown* and *Pirates of the Caribbean,* in much the same way Disney theme parks consisted of a number of different story worlds.

Unlike VR attractions that are a five-minute experience for guests, games require that hours, sometimes hundreds of hours, of gameplay be available for a player. In this the developers were fortunate to have "the richest, most compelling film, television, attraction, and character properties in the world" to draw on. Developing *Toontown* was the group's first introduction into the very different process of creating sustainable gameplay in a story environment. Although *Toontown Online* was based in Disney characters, the storyline was new, simple, and created specifically for the MMORPG as a vehicle for engaging in fun action with friends.

The *Pirates of the Caribbean* franchise, on the other hand, was an intricately built-up world of Caribbean and pirate history (albeit fictional), complex environments, characters, and fantastic storylines that had been created over 50 years—the VR Studio took this established and successful story franchise and ported it to a new media. Martin Sklar, president of Walt Disney Imagineering expressed the importance of story in Disney's cross media approach to entertainment, "We believe the same world-building and story skills we have used to become the leading creator of theme parks in the 'real' world will allow us to become a successful developer of entertainment spaces in the 'digital' world."

There was, in addition to an existing story, a large audience that marketers could tap into for interest in the proposed new entertainment product: in addition to the Disney theme park audience, the first movie, *Pirates of the Caribbean: The Curse of the Black Pearl*, was released in 2003 to great success. The movie established a broad-based audience for the upcoming online game. In a press release issued April, 2005 Ken Goldstein, EVP and Managing Director of Disney Online, announced the new MMORPG, "We've learned through our experience with *Toontown* that the market for massively multiplayer online role-playing games can indeed reach beyond traditional gamers." The potential audience for *Pirates* included existing Disney online users, fans of the movie and the theme park attractions, as well as online gamers. While the movie was based on the theme park attraction, it was the movie that defined the imagery in the online game and delivered a broad-based and extensive audience.

While *Pirates* and *Toontown* had a lot in common, including sharing the same 3D engine and programming paradigm, they were very different games. Planned for an older audience (10+) *Pirates* was more ambitious and designed to offer an increasingly authentic experience, one that provided a richly textured and detailed world similar to those available at the time at DisneyQuest. One of the concerns with the MMORPGs, however, was the need for the expensive hardware necessary to run the graphically realistic games smoothly. This was a drawback as far as Disney's younger and family audience was concerned. The development team opted to provide simpler graphics for the site that could be supported with lower and more affordable PC and Mac system requirements while still maintaining exciting and engaging storylines and rewarding immersive gameplay. Although announced for April, release delays kept the game in Beta (still fun to play) until October of that year.

## 17.2   *Pirates* Story and Gameplay

*Pirates of the Caribbean Online* took players into an era of swashbuckling pirates where they join the quest for treasure and battle to become the most legendary pirates in the Caribbean. Much of the early story in the online game was orchestrated; the action was quick and uncomplicated and led the player through introductory scenes that set up the pirate environment and introduced some of the players. Several scenes into the story, once the player began to gather a crew, there were more battles, quests, and activities, and the game became more complex and individualized. A simple tutorial for playing the game was offered to the novice pirate/player. Directions and storyline were provided by text shown at the bottom of the playing screen and were augmented by the characters' commentary, while hints for acquiring skills were provided by text balloons that popped up as the player moved through the game.

The online *Pirates* referenced graphics and characters from the movie but introduced new adventures. The game was intended as a kid and family-friendly (grandparents included) adventure and the action was designed to be intuitive; there was not as much of the type of character and asset building that existed in more complex MMORPGs. Everyone started from a level playing field as a common pirate. The player created a male or female avatar (or two or three) that could be customized with different body shapes, facial features, hair, and clothes and then joined in the fray! Pirates walked, ran, and jumped their way across the landscape. When they met adversaries, battling was uncomplicated: click, click, and click again. The attacks were timed and if done right, they could be chained together to create bigger damage. With wins the player gained Notoriety and went up a level where there were new moves. In quests, a player fought anyone and anything from navies to crabs in the search for buried treasure (gold and precious gems). Pirates could put together a crew of friends (or strangers) and acquire a ship to take to the sea for some exciting battles. While the captain could order firing of cannons for ship battles, players could also aim and fire their own individual cannons to broadside other ships. There was a touch of reality when they headed for a visit to the tavern for a game of poker or blackjack: they could cheat, but when caught they got thrown into jail. Notoriety could be used to purchase combat abilities, gain shot bonuses, or fix a damaged ship or ships.

The first of two beta releases was showcased at the Electronic Entertainment Expo (E3) in May 2006. The "first images" of the game showed that it reflects the imagery of the movie and the "playable version" allowed players to engage with the likes of movie characters Jack Sparrow, Elizabeth Swann, and Will Turner in an exciting quest for "treasure and notoriety" (WD Press Release May 10, 2006).

On the game's release, Paul Yanover, Executive Vice-President and Managing Director of *Disney Online* commented, "We believe the game's focus on action and adventure, combined with many customization options will appeal to a broad audience of both gamers and fans of the *Pirates of the Caribbean* Franchise as they set out on their own course to live the legend" (WD Press Release).

## 17.3  Making the Story "Their Own"

As with previous Disney CD-ROM activities and online games such as *The Lion King Storybook* and *A Bug's Life Music Room Composer*, the assets and storyline of the associated movie, in this case *Pirates of the Caribbean: The Curse of the Black Pearl*, were available to the VR Studio for use in developing the MMORPG. The new *Pirates* online virtual experience, however, did not slavishly follow the movie, instead, it turned the player loose in a unique-to-the-player adventure, a mix of on-foot exploration, fighting with guns and swords, and hunting for treasure, into which themes, storylines, characters, and creatures from the movie were intricately woven. Dick Cook, chairman of The Walt Disney Studios pointed out, "This game captures the same swashbuckling sense of humor, spirit and action that moviegoers loved in the first 'Pirates of the Caribbean' film... ." (Business Wire 2005).

The *Pirates of the Caribbean* online game included players in the action from the first scene:[4]

---

[4] First-hand game-playing experience described from the author's perspective.

Entering the *Pirates of the Caribbean* website you find yourself on the floor of a jail on the island of Rambleshack. A lively pirate theme plays in the background as someone looks down at you.

It's Jack Sparrow! He's there to greet you and hauls you up with a helping hand, setting the tone for a "rollicking, good-fun" adventure when he suggests you "pull yourself together," i.e. create your own pirate avatar. Once you are Constance Stormwalker or Chris Darkwalker, you are ready for adventure.

Jack breaks you out of jail; you escape only to discover the island is under cannon attack and you must flee!

You run towards a warehouse where inside Will Turner confronts you. He recognizes you as one of Jack's friends and teaches you to use a cutlass. As Will is attacked by pirate skeletons, you head out the back door with the cutlass in hand.

Pirate skeletons block your way as you head towards a ship in the harbor and you battle them using your new skills, collecting some skill points on the way. At the ship the captain, Bo Beck entreats you to hurry on board and orders you to man a cannon and sink an "undead" warship.

Success! The ship sinks but Jolly Roger himself appears on deck in a frightful state. He learns that Beck double-crossed him by helping Jack Sparrow (he let you on board!). As a warning to Sparrow he turns Beck into a skeleton and spares you; but you must walk the plank and brave the dangerous waters to swim to Port Royal.

You make it to Port Royal and there you meet with the Voodoo Mistress Tia Dalma. She reveals that dark forces are gathering against the pirates and the *Black Pearl* is needed to "keep piracy alive" but the *Pearl* has been captured by the Royal Navy.

You approach Elizabeth Swan for help and she gives you a light sloop to go after the *Pearl*. Captain Barbossa arms you with a pistol when you arrive at his Grotto in the Devil's Anvil and you get a list of the crew you must recruit for the *Pearl* from Jack who you meet at the *Faithful Bride*, the bawdiest tavern on Tortuga. From here on there are Poker and Blackjack games, Voodoo enchantments, treasure digs, and battling both Navy soldiers and monsters in the quest to become the most legendary swashbuckling pirate in the Caribbean!

Players could create new stories each time they played by changing their character, by creating additional characters, or by asking different players to join their crew. While initially the story had a linear path, as players entered deeper into the pirate world of the Caribbean of the past there was more opportunity to create new events. Along the way, their companions were characters who had full and lively personalities in other media such as the movie versions with which the players were familiar. The events players were creating echoed previously seen scenarios yet they were constructing their own story within them. Each story became a personal journey, unique to the player, reflecting their cumulative experience of the characters and events as they had come to know them across media.

The game proved very popular but there were issues with the free/play model. Once Level Eight was reached players were reminded often that they need to pay to get access to more levels. In addition Disney acquired *Club Penguin* in August 2007 and began to put resources into that game; with only so many gamer developers and engineers on staff, every new addition was at a cost to existing games and players began to feel the lack of development. Updates slowed even more as *Club Penguin* became a hub for new TV shows, books, and toys. When Disney added *Pixie Hollow* as another online game, fans felt that the company was no longer interested in *Pirates* as updates and fixes slowed to a trickle. Fans were not surprised when Disney closed *Pirates, Toontown* and *Pixie Hollow* in 2013 and concentrated on *Club Penguin* and its new online Sand Box, *Infinity*, released in August 2013. *Pirates of the Caribbean* however, was not *just* a game. Fans had taken the story to heart and played it as an active community of people who felt like a family. After the closing, fans created their own version of the game that merged it with *The Legend of Pirates Online* and can still be found on the web. *Infinity* was also closed in 2016 as it was not as successful as anticipated and Disney decided they would from then on only look at games as a licensing opportunity.

The *Pirates of the Caribbean* that began life as an adventure ride showcasing audio-animatronics in 1967 achieved immense reach across storytelling media. It is an exemplar of the magnitude of the Disney Master Narrative: it is represented in all of the Disney theme parks around the world, in books, movies, virtual reality, all manner of merchandise including both real and virtual Lego, video games, and, finally, a virtual online world. The popularity of the original ride inspired the movie, the movie in turn inspired new additions to the theme park attraction extending the original voyage for "guests" to include images from the movie. It's a swashbuckling good tale, humorous and spirited, embodying the qualities of entertainment that endear a story to its audience, and representing how Disney makes advantage rather than takes advantage of story across media.

Change was a constant in Walt Disney's commitment to tell a story well, to bring it to an audience through the technology of the day, and to push that technology so that rather than controlling the story, it enhanced the story and gave it an opportunity to touch people, to speak to each of them individually, to make it believable. To make a story compelling and believable the characters had to be empathetic—the people in the audience had to identify with them. Walt had achieved this goal in his successful features, television programs, and with the theme park. The company has continued this commitment to story and with interactive online media has taken the story a step further into interactive immersion. As part of the *Pirates of the Caribbean* online world, a player could walk hand in hand with the characters virtually and not only be a part of the story online but help create it. The next example brings story back into the real world.

## 17.4   *Star Wars* Cross-Media

With its expansion in the 2000s Disney has shown it can take a story at any stage and be inventive about enlarging its presence. Disney acquired Marvel Entertainment in August 2009, Lucasfilm in October 2012, and Fox Entertainment in March 2019. This gave the studio access to some of the most successful and well-established stories and characters in moviedom, as well as most of the superheroes on the planet. *Star Wars* (Lucasfilm) is one of the best loved in their panoply of story properties. Since it was folded into the family, Disney has expanded the cross-media presence that had developed over the years.

As with the Disney's *Pirates of the Caribbean* franchise, Lucasfilm had, over the 40 years since the first *Star Wars* movie been released in 1977, built intricate alien worlds, complex characters, and fantastic storylines that were targeted at fans across many media including books, video games, toys, action figures, and Lego, among others. Disney inherited these. It continues book publishing with a "new unified storytelling approach" that will connect the novels to films in development (StarWars 2014), continues making video games with Electronic Arts (EA) (Fogel 2019), has renewed its license with Lego for building sets, both real and as video games, and is adding its own expertise to the mix.

Story characters and story lands are a feature of Disney theme parks. In 2015 Disney announced *Galaxy's Edge* for its parks, a themed attraction that would tell the *Star Wars* story through a completely immersive and interactive world and "redefine" the theme park experience (Glover, 2015). And so it has. *Galaxy's Edge* was planned to be a completely believable place—as if you'd stepped into the movie. The original movie changed space adventure from existing in a clean and sterile world into the messy, worn, often broken, real world of Hans Solo. *Galaxy's Edge* creates the same beat-up, rough reality look: the sand floor has embedded droid tracks, wires hang outside buildings, futuristic vehicles have seen better days, as have the restrooms with their simulated pipes and dirty lights (Sylt 2019). Not intended to imitate any existing place from the movies, the 14 acres have been meticulously designed by Walt Disney Imagineering and the Lucasfilm Story Group (Hewitt 2019) to provide an authentic *Star Wars* feel for Batuu, a remote outpost that houses a busy spaceport and some very notorious characters. Guests create memories based on immersing themselves in new experiences situated in familiar, often well-loved, places: just being there is as interesting as the rides.

Guests can visit the Resistance forest, the First Order territory, and the spaceport, where a number of spaceships, including the Millenium Falcon, "the fastest hunk of junk in the galaxy," have landed. These can be boarded… and flown. The Falcon sits at the entrance of the hanger which is carved into a set of rocky spires. The ship is the entrance to a simulator; the queue is through the same cargo hold of the ship seen in the movies and ends in the cockpit where luck plays in which role, including the most coveted—pilot, is assigned to the guest. There are two pilots, two gunners, and two engineers for each mission; each pilot operates different controls, one operates the up and down movements, the other the right and left. The right hand pilot gets to use a silver lever for the jump to hyperspace. Piloting the ship can be very rocky as the pilots learn to work together. If they get it right, the mission is successful and makes a profit, if not, the boss has to be paid credits for the repairs (Thompson 2019).

The boss is Hondo Ohnaka, who has assigned the mission in a pre-game show. Honda is an animatronic character so realistic people mistake him for an actor. He's head of smuggling operations on Batuu and has been loaned the Millenium Falcon (by Chewie) to steal the hyperfuel coaxium from the First Order (Thompson 2019). Unlike the hydraulic-based animatronics in operation at the park since the 1980s, today's animatronics use electric motors which gives them more precise and realist movements (Corless 2019).[5] Hondo is just one of the realistic robots at *Galaxy's Edge*. Others include, Dok-Ondar, an Ithorian trader, and Niem Numb, a Sullustun pilot, who appeared in Return of the Jedi, as the co-pilot of the Millenium Falcon who helped destroy the second Death Star (Corless 2019).

The immersive environment is key in creating equally immersive interactivity. An app provides guests engagement through their phones: they can make droids beeb and ship engines whirr, they can complete tasks, like solving puzzles to lock doors and keep the evil order out, and they can listen in to conversations as the app translates the different languages being spoken by characters around them (Sylt 2019).

*Galaxy's Edge* has been brought to life from past and current stories: from both the classic six films and those made after the Disney acquisition, from children's and adult's books, from video games, and from the new live action series *The Mandalorian* created for Disney Plus.[6] Following in the footsteps of both Walt Disney and his hope for Disneyland, and George Lucas and his vision of a "Galaxy Far Far Away," *Galaxy's Edge* embodies their "quality, innovation and bold creativity" and "is an opportunity to play and engage with your friends and family in a shared experience that will forge lifelong memories" (Walt Disney 2019).

The *Star Wars* themed land, within itself, is a cross-media storytelling experience. Guests are able create their own stories through technology that gives them access to apps with which they can make things happen, brings Hondo as a "real" character to them, and lets them fly the Falcon (and give it a few dings) in a land that

---

[5] Animatronics, operated with electric motors, were first used in 2009 and include figures from *Enchanted Tales*, *Frozen Ever After* and *Guardians of the Galaxy* (Rocket Raccoon) (Corless 2019).

[6] Disney Plus is a video on-demand streaming service launched by the company on November 12, 2019.

encourages exploration of new story events, not only a replay of old ones. The breadth of media the *Pirates of the Caribbean* story crossed has been stretched by a jump into hyperspace with *Galaxy's Edge.*

Walt's credo continues to guide the designers of Disney's new world across the many media it encompasses and the many technologies used to create it:

*I honestly feel that the heart of our organization is the Story Department.*

Walt Disney

# Correction to: Disney Stories

**Correction to:**
**K. Madej, N. Lee,** *Disney Stories,*
**https://doi.org/10.1007/978-3-030-42738-2**

This book was inadvertently published without updating the below corrections. These have now been updated throughout the book.

Page 76, Dora "Lux" has been changed to Dora "Luz".

Page 87, 1st paragraph under 9.3, the date May, "2006" has been changed to May "1986".

Index page 237: "Lux", Dora has been changed to "Luz," Dora.

---

The updated online versions of these chapters can be found at
https://doi.org/10.1007/978-3-030-42738-2_8
https://doi.org/10.1007/978-3-030-42738-2_9
https://doi.org/10.1007/978-3-030-42738-2

# Addendum I

Newton Lee interviews Roy E. Disney for ACM Computers in Entertainment magazine on May 28, 2003

## An Interview with Roy E. Disney

In October 2003 the inaugural issue of *ACM Computers in Entertainment* was published with the theme "Educating Kids through Entertainment." Newton Lee, the editor for the fifteen years of the magazine's tenure, interviewed Roy E. Disney, Vice Chairman of The Walt Disney Company, for the magazines issue. The following is the transcript of the video interview held on May 28, 2003 in Disney's office at the Walt Disney Studios in Burbank.

Newton Lee: Congratulations on your 50 years of achievements in entertainment.

Roy E. Disney: Thank you. It doesn't seem like 50 years, I promise.

Lee: Based on your half a century of experience, what do you think about educating children.

© Springer Nature Switzerland AG 2020

K. Madej, N. Lee, *Disney Stories*, https://doi.org/10.1007/978-3-030-42738-2

Disney:       Well, certainly it's one of the functions of entertainment, I think, is education. But I think you have to be very careful not to pose as an educator when you're an entertainer. I think you have to entertain first, but you have to understand that no matter what you do, there's a subtext. And it can be for good or bad, but it's always there, there's always some lesson to be learned by storytelling. And, so, keeping that at the back of your mind is a good idea.

Lee:       Given there is a wonderful children story to tell, how do you decide whether it should be told using traditional animation, like *Lilo & Stitch*, CGI animation, like *Finding Nemo*, or live action movie, like *Spy Kids*?

Disney:       That's a really hard question and I think it really is answered by the particular filmmaker as much as anything. I think different artists see things differently, and one artist may envision the look of a film in a different way from another. We have such an enormous choice now of looks and styles that it really becomes a particular artist's choice, or a producer's choice maybe, as opposed to being generated by the story itself. Sometimes I think *Lilo & Stitch* wouldn't have been as good a movie in 3D as it was in 2D because there was a cartooniness about it, but I'm not sure in the hands of another filmmaker if that would still be true. It's a matter of choice and the choices get wider and wider as time goes by.

Lee:       Speaking of computers in entertainment, does a CGI film that strives towards more realistic animation add to the magic and power of animated storytelling?

Disney:       We had a sequence in *Fantasia 2000* that involved whales that flew, and it was done in a semi-photorealistic style, but it was about magic. And I think the realistic style actually contributed a great deal because the whales, since they looked so real, appeared to have weight and volume and all of the things that whales have, so the magic when they flew was especially clear. Again, it's a question of style. It's a question of what does the story calls for and how realism plays off against fantasy. All the *Matrix* and *X-Men* kind of films that are out right now, for instance, play on that very same thing: they look real, but of course they're not real at all, they're almost completely animated films, in one way of looking at it. You could go back to *Titanic*. You could almost consider *Titanic* an animated film because so much of it was unreal or not filmed in the real world at any rate. So it contributes tremendously, there's such a blurred line right now. I keep wondering why the Academy decided that they needed a separate category for animated films just at a moment when there are a lot of people who couldn't tell you whether a film is animated or not.

Lee:       Is there a tradeoff between traditional animation and CGI animation?

Disney:        Yes, there are definite tradeoffs; certainly one of the, at least tradi-
               tionally, looks of a *Toy Story* or a *Finding Nemo* is a kind of a
               plasticized look. That doesn't have to be what CG films look like,
               but it's, I think, the public conception of what a CG film looks like.
               Everything we've done since *Beauty and the Beast*, at Disney, has
               passed through the computer, so you could probably say that every-
               thing we've done for the last twelve or fourteen years is, in a sense,
               computer graphics. All that means is that we have these wonderful
               tools at hand and we can make a movie look like anything we
               choose it to look like. Every time we make a decision about the
               look of a film, we've got this hugely broad palate to choose from.
               So I get back to where I started, which is it's an artistic choice that
               artists need to make. It's not a business decision, I think, unless that
               one is outrageously expensive and one is very cheap which will
               never be true for the same kind of quality.

Newton Lee would like to posthumously thank Roy E. Disney for his support of ACM Computers in Entertainment which has published more than 500 peer-reviewed papers with over 2,500-citation count and 500,000 downloads. Roy is truly missed by all of us.

# Addendum II

Newton Lee worked at Disney as a software engineer, game designer and finally as a senior producer between 1996 and 2006. This is his story with the company.

## Newton Lee: Ten Years at Disney

In 1994, Disney Interactive, the digital media branch of The Walt Disney Company, was looking for an entry into the growing digital media consumer market. Without internal resources they needed to outsource for the technology and manpower to

© Springer Nature Switzerland AG 2020
K. Madej, N. Lee, *Disney Stories*, https://doi.org/10.1007/978-3-030-42738-2

make it happen. At the time the blockbuster Disney movie *The Lion King* was achieving worldwide fame and success and a CD-ROM project was planned. It was outsourced to Media Station Inc. and I became one of the lead software and title engineers for *Disney's Animated Storybook: The Lion King*.

I had been hired in 1992 by Henry Flurry, Hal Brokaw, and David Gregory to develop multimedia software and tools at Media Station Inc., a creative software engineering start-up located in Ann Arbor, Michigan. While working for them I created an object-oriented scripting language in 1994 (similar to the ActionScript in Flash) that enabled the developers to create interactivity for animation quickly and easily. I also wrote a cross-platform multimedia compiler to allow the software to run on both the PC Windows and the Macintosh operating system. The new tools and methodology enabled development of a CD-ROM title within three to six months.

Following the success of *Disney's Animated Storybook: The Lion King*, Media Station Inc. received many more contracts from Disney, Hasbro, Mattel, Scholastic, Crayola, IBM, and Harper Collins. During the development of Disney's *Winnie the Pooh and the Honey Tree* CD-ROM, however, several key engineers threatened to quit Media Station Inc. I stepped in to co-manage the engineering team and successfully uplifted the employee's morale and we were able to deliver the CD-ROM to Disney Interactive on schedule. Both *The Lion King* and the *Winnie the Pooh* titles received outstanding reviews.

In 1994 my colleagues and I received the 1995 Michigan's Leading Edge Technologies Award for the inventions and the applications that the company developed using them. These included the CD-ROMs *Disney's Animated Storybook: The Lion King, Winnie the Pooh and the Honey Tree, The Hunchback of Notre Dame, 101 Dalmatians, Lamp Chop Loves Music, If You Give a Mouse a Cookie, Haunted House, The Frog Prince, Barbie as Rapunzel*, and *Puzzle Castle*.

After working at Media Station Inc. for four years, I received a phone call from Disney Interactive in Los Angeles, California to discuss the direction of the media work and ask if I was interested in working with the group. I ended up joining Disney Online, the interactive online division of The Walt Disney Company, in 1996 as a game designer and engineer.

At the Disney employee orientation, we were shown a short film about the history of Walt Disney and the company that he and his brother Roy O. Disney had created. We were asked to name our favorite Disney characters. On July 16, 1999, I put on an Eeyore costume at Disneyland in Anaheim, California, during an employee training camp "Disney Way One," a four-day program to familiarize selected Disney employees (aka cast members) with the major business entities at Disney (See Fig. 16.1). I learned how to sign the name "Eeyore" using a glove with no fingers and then was taken into the theme park area where very soon I was surrounded by kids of all ages. My acting time was over in 20 minutes but, in spite of the hot summer sun and profuse sweating, I did not want to leave. Being a real-life Disney character at Disneyland was an experience of a lifetime.

The first Disney online domain, *disney.com*, was registered on March 21, 1990 but it was not until February 1995 that Disney Online was formally created by entrepreneur Jake Winebaum as a separate entity from Disney Interactive and February 1996 that the website *www.disney.com* was launched. Disney Online had only about 100 employees when in November of that year I was hired by Art Holland, vice president of software at Disney Online, to join the games group in designing and programming Java based games for the Disney websites.

Headquartered in North Hollywood, California, the core games group consisted of two producers (Pamela Bonnell and Jung Suh), two artists (Carrie Pittman and Kenneth Ng), and four engineers (Johnny Gibson, Andrew Forslund, Mark Andrade, and myself) working full-time. In the months ahead, we quickly staffed up with new employees, contractors, and interns. We lost Johnny Gibson to Digital Domain for the postproduction of the blockbuster film *Titanic* (1997), but we added Lorin Wiener, Kevin O'Sullivan, and Jon Humphreys. We also worked with many other groups within Disney Online and third party developers to create online games. The work environment was dynamic with many ideas on the go, either being discussed, prototyped or in production.

*Disney's Daily Blast* debuted to the public in April 1997. One of the earliest adopters of the subscription model on the Internet, the site was designed a safe and parent trusted entertainment environment offering games, stories, activities, comics, and news suitable for children of all ages. To celebrate the first anniversary of *Disney's Daily Blast,* the Disney Online "Love Crew"[1] (See Fig. 16.2) wrote and performed the song *Keep the Love Online* and its remixes during our spare time.[2] (See Figs. 16.3 and 16.4).

In June 1998, *Disney's Daily Blast* was renamed as *Disney's Blast Online* (or *Disney's Blast* for short). Many new games were created for what had become the leading online club for kids. Nine years later in 2007, *Disney's Blast* was rebranded as *Disney's Game Kingdom Online* to emphasize the new focus on "games."

In total, I had led the games group in creating over 100 games for *Disney's Blast* and *Disney.com*. We had also launched many popular online "channels" including my favorite *Weird and Wacky Channel*. One of my games developed with graphic artists Chad Woods and Christopher Cooper, *Stitch: Master of Disguise*, was prominently featured on *Disney's Blast* and *MSN Gaming Zone* in June 2002. The game was so popular that it was again featured in *Disney's Game Kingdom Online* in December 2007.

Popular games, attractive user interface, and family-oriented content helped propel *Disney.com* into the Number 1 website for families and children. The number of unique visitors per month jumped from 487,000 in September 1999 to 23.03 million in August 2007.

In April 1998, Disney Online acquired Starwave from Paul Allen and the search engine company Infoseek. The idea was to create an Internet powerhouse by integrating Disney's portfolio of rich content, brands and promotion, Starwave's leading Web design, production and technological expertise, and Infoseek's in-depth understanding of the Internet portal consumer and business.

Disney Online became a part of the newly formed Buena Vista Internet Group (BVIG) and practically everyone at Disney Online received stock options competitive to other Internet startups. In 1999, BVIG was renamed GO.com, which was heavily promoted on television and movie screens. The infamous traffic light logo for GO.com cost Disney US$ 21.5 million to settle the legal dispute with GoTo.com in May 2000.

In mid-2000, I led the development of the enhanced-TV (interactive television) program "Number 1 Fan" for ABC's "Summer Jam Concert" featuring Christina Aguilera and Enrique Iglesias (on June 23, 2000) as well as Disney Channel's "In Concert" featuring Jessica Simpson and Jason Raize (on June 24, 2000). It was the first two-screen interactive TV experience offered by Disney Online.

The number of Disney Online employees alone grew from about 100 in 1996, around 250, above 300 in 1998, over 400 in 1999, more than 700 in 2000, to the peak of over 800 in 2001. Disney's top executives Michael Eisner and Bob Iger frequently visited Disney Online to test drive new products and brainstorm new ideas. But then the Internet bubble burst. On January 29, 2001, Disney announced it was shutting down its struggling Internet portal GO.com and laying off about 400 employees across the board. The tracking stock for GO.com was dissolved and the shares converted into Disney common stock. The hope of Disney employees for becoming millionaires at GO.com vanished. GO.com was renamed The Walt Disney Internet Group (WDIG) in 2001.

In spite of the industry setback and stock market crash, the remaining 500 some Disney Online employees were encouraged by winning numerous top awards from International Web Page Awards, Modalis Research Technologies, FamilyPC, WebCriteria, Internet Crisis Volunteer Award, Web100, Webaward, Adding Wisdom Award, WiredKids.org, Parent's Choice Award, Gaming World, Children's Software Service, Webby Awards, and Internet Advertising Competition.

In March 2001, I pioneered the use of open-source XML-based Jabber for multiplayer games at Disney Online. I spearheaded the successful integration of Flash and Jabber to enhance online user experience and reduce software development time and deployment cost for multiplayer games. In February 2002, my team at Disney Online launched the world's first commercial multiplayer Flash/Jabber game. In comparison, Nickelodeon launched their first Flash/Jabber multiplayer game in 2004.

In June 2001, I started working on the web integration for the beta launch of the MMORPG *Toontown Online*, where the guests assume a Disney character in a fantasy world and take back the town occupied by the evil robots. I offered extensive testing and feedback on game-play and performance to the Virtual Reality (VR) group at Walt Disney Imagineering (WDI).

In August 2001, I created the Disney Online Technology Forum. It was partly inspired by my colleague and Virginia Tech alumnus Bob Lambert, corporate senior vice president of new media and new technology at The Walt Disney Company, who organized a quarterly technology forum for the Disney executives (mostly directors and vice presidents).

The Disney Online Technology Forum was a monthly brown bag meeting for all Disney employees (regardless of rank) to exchange ideas, foster team spirit, promote synergy, and push the envelope of technological innovation. For the following three years from 2001–2004, guest speakers from Disney, Microsoft, Intel, Sun

Microsystems, UCLA, USC and other companies were invited to give presentations each month. The topics mainly focused on computer games, user interface, interactive television, and digital media. Among the notable speakers were Lanny Smoot and Eric Haseltine from Walt Disney Imagineering R&D. Smoot, formerly with Bell Laboratories, demonstrated his experimental interactive hologram—a *Star Trek* and *Star Wars* like technology that will enhance Disney's storytelling in the future. Haseltine, co-founder of Disney's Virtual Reality Studio, lectured on how a human brain reacts neurologically to stories. Haseltine left Disney in 2002 to join the National Security Agency as Director of Research.

In July 2002, I ported 10 Flash games from *Disney's Blast* to a cable television set-top box as part of an experiment with interactive television (iTV). A company known as ICTV (aka ActiveVideo Networks in 2006) offered a platform called "HeadendWare." The system pushes complex, IP-based iTV applications, encoded as MPEG-2 streams. In 2002, ICTV called the iTV-based *Disney's Blast* the "the most advanced iTV gaming application developed for the Motorola platform to date." The application was showcased at the E3 Expo in May 2003.

The *Toontown Online* project was cancelled during the continuing downsizing of Walt Disney Imagineering in 2002. Fortunately the project was resurrected not long after its cancellation. In September 2002, Disney Online absorbed the VR group responsible for *Toontown Online*, and the entire team moved into our office building in North Hollywood. The game was debuted to the general public in June 2003 and it quickly gained an enormous popularity.

From 2003–2004, I served as the technical architect for *Disney.com* Motion, *Disney.com* 3D homepage, Disney Mobile (domestic wireless), El Capitan online ticketing, *Movies.com/Amazon.com* e-commerce integration, *FamilyFun.com* TV, Radio Disney database publishing, Disney Pin Trading, Disney TriTeam, high scores Java servlet, multimedia search, and other interesting projects such as Disney Corporate greeting e-cards for exclusive use by Disney's senior executives.[3]

In 2003, I started the nonprofit magazine ACM Computers in Entertainment and in May of that year I had the opportunity to interview Roy E. Disney for the inaugural issue. The topic was "Educating Kids through Entertainment" and Disney commented, "there's a subtext [in a film]. And it can be for good or bad, but it's always there, there's always some lesson to be learned by storytelling." The magazine was fortunate to have his support on its board.

In that same year, I was invited by Shelly Palmer and Marty Yudkovitz to be a juror for the first-ever 2003 Advanced Media Technology Emmy Awards given by the National Academy of Television Arts and Sciences. Rick Mandler, General Manager of ABC Enhanced TV, and I were the two industry jurors from The Walt Disney Company. Disney's ABC did not win that year, and the Emmy Awards went to *NASCAR.com's* PITCOMMAND and iO Interactive Optimum Digital Cable Service from Cablevision.

In 2004 full-motion video playback on the *Disney.com, ABC.com* and *ESPN.com* homepages was facilitated by *DigStream*, an executable that downloaded streaming videos as a background process on Windows PC. I worked with *DigStream's* creator Eric Freeman, Elisabeth Freeman (Robson), and the Disney engineering group in

Seattle to ensure smooth integration with the Disney websites. By 2005, however, *DigStream* was replaced by Flash Video Streaming that works on both PC and Macintosh.

Between 2004 and 2006, I served as the senior producer of search engine optimization and Internet domains management in an effect to improve guest experience and company revenues in web search. I worked closely with strategic partners such as Google, Yahoo!, and WebSideStory (Atomz). The internal search redesign of *FamilyFun.com* in October 2005 resulted in doubling the search traffic and page views. I also created software to block online advertisements for illegal download of pirated music and movies.

In July 2005, Disney Online announced plans for a mobile virtual network operator (MVNO) deal with Sprint PCS. Disney Mobile, launched in June 2006, is targeted at kids and families and it offers cell phones with GPS, parental control, and exclusive Disney content. However, Disney Mobile ceased its wireless operations in December 2007, after just one year of operation. Disney also dropped the ax on the unprofitable MobileESPN.

In January 2006, one of my early predictions came true: Disney announced the acquisition of Pixar, the animated studio headed by Steve Jobs. Disney had released all of Pixar's films since 1995, and all of them had been box-office smashes. Disney CEO Bob Iger wrote, "The addition of Pixar significantly enhances Disney animation, which is a critical creative engine for driving growth across our businesses."[5]

For a decade between 1996 and 2006, I had experienced a roller coaster ride at Disney Online as a part of Disney Consumer Products (DCP), Buena Vista Internet Group (BVIG), GO.com, and finally Walt Disney Internet Group (WDIG) before it was renamed Disney Interactive Media Group (DIMG) in 2008. By the time I left Disney Online in 2006, most of the online games were being outsourced to third party developers—a business model similar to the early days of Disney Interactive contracting out the development of *Disney's Animated Storybook: The Lion King* and other CD-ROM titles in the 90's. Life indeed goes full circle!

Working for Disney was more than just doing my paying job. A wonderful lifetime experience was working with the Disney VoluntEARS in community services such as Christmas toys distribution at Fred Jordan Mission, tennis coaching for the Special Olympics, 5 k Revlon Run/Walk for breast and ovarian cancer research, and back-to-school shopping with the Boys and Girls Club. The Disney VoluntEARS also helped with the silent auction at the American Film Institute (AFI) for the 2006 *Computers in Entertainment* Scholarship Awards co-sponsored by the AFI, the Institute for Education, Research, and Scholarships, and the National University of Singapore Mixed Reality Lab. With special guest speakers Quincy Jones and Alan Kay, the silent auction offered one-hour brainstorming sessions with Alan Kay (Viewpoints Research Institute), Seamus Blackley (Creative Artists Agency, formerly Microsoft Xbox), and Seymour Papert (MIT Media Lab).

In 1995, Michael Eisner, Chairman and CEO of The Walt Disney Company at the time, said, "I know Disney shareholders everywhere will be proud of the following figures: During fiscal 1995, a total of 27,435 Disney cast members worldwide, working through the Disney VoluntEARS Program, donated 227,102 hours of community service in 361 separate projects involving charities and agencies ranging from the American Cancer Society to Pediatric AIDS. Much of the volunteer work involves helping children, which is only appropriate for a company named Disney."

I had been awarded along with my fellow colleagues the Disney VoluntEARS Project Leader Awards for outstanding leadership in volunteer service. On March 9, 2005, I was selected to serve on the Disney VoluntEARS Leadership Council and Steering Committee whose members came from all divisions of The Walt Disney Company in an effort to serve the nonprofits in Los Angeles County. Led by community relations managers Andrea Nwokedi Gibson, Jamie Keyser and Jen Marie Manship, the 25-member committee evaluates project proposals, assigns project leaders, recruits VoluntEARS, and guides the overall volunteer activities at Disney.

I left Disney Online in 2006 as a senior producer, after a decade of working for the mouse. Apart from a 20-minute stunt as Eeyore at Disneyland for "Disney Way One" and countless joyful hours of volunteering with my fellow colleagues, my job at Disney Online was mainly to make children happy by creating entertaining and educational games.

Newton Lee
January 2012

# Bibliography

*Focus On: 100 Most Popular United States National Film Registry Films.* 2019 Wikipedia.

*Black Friday/Toy Story/ Disney-Pixar*. Retrieved from Pixar: https://www.pixar.com/feature-films/toy-story.

*Luxo Jr.* 1986. Retrieved from History of Computer Animation: https://computeranimationhistorycgi.jimdofree.com/luxo-jr-1986/.

*Step inside Disney's first virtual-reality animated short, Cycles.* 2018. Retrieved from Entertainment Weekly: https://ew.com/movies/2018/09/12/disney-virtual-reality-cycles/.

*Walt Disney and Live Action Films.* 2011. Retrieved September 2019, from The Walt Disney Family Museum Blog: https://www.waltdisney.org/blog/walt-disney-and-live-action-films.

Alexander, J. 2015. The history of compositing. In *The VES Handbook of Visual Effects: Industry Standard VFX Practices and Procedures*, ed. S.Z. Okun and S.Z. Okun. Burlington, MA: Focul Press.

Anderson, S. 2013. The computer wore tennis shoes. *American Literature* 85 (4) Retrieved from Chaos and Control: http://scalar.usc.edu/anvc/chaosandcontrol/humanist-critique-the-computer-wore-tennis-shoes-1969.

Apgar, G. 2015. *Mickey Mouse: Emblem of the American Spirit*. San Francisco: The Walt Disney Family Foundation Press.

Arndt, T. 2012. *Evolution of the Acme Peg Registration System.* Retrieved November 2010, from The Animation School Daily: https://animationschooldaily.com/evolution-of-a-peg/.

The explosion of online sources in all areas of study provides an almost inexhaustible reservoir of information that a researcher can access easily, at any time of the day or night, with little restriction. Such an avenue encourages sharing of knowledge and expertise, and when travel to sites is not possible or access to private archives is unavailable, supports general and scholarly exploration. We would like to acknowledge the many individuals who have added to the store of online information on every aspect of The Walt Disney Company and its stories. This bibliography barely skims what is available in print and, particularly, online. Divided into three sections, literature, websites, and videos, it is intended to provide an entry point into the history of Disney stories that will encourage further inquiry. Facts used in this book that can be found commonly in sources such as encyclopedias are not referenced. Some general information sites, nuanced by special interests, are included.

© Springer Nature Switzerland AG 2020

K. Madej, N. Lee, *Disney Stories*, https://doi.org/10.1007/978-3-030-42738-2

Aarseth, Espen. (2004). "Genre Trouble: Narrativism and the Art of Simulation." *First Person*. Eds Noah Wardrip-Fruin and Pat Harrigan. Cambridge: The MIT Press.

Bailey, A. 1982. *Walt Disney's World of Fantasy*. New York, NY: Everest House Publishers.

Baktin, J. 2017. *A Journey Into Self Differences, Culture, and the Body*. Abingdon, UK: Routledge.

*Bambi World Premiere in London*. 1942. Retrieved from D23, The Official Disney Fan Club: https://d23.com/this-day/bambi-world-premiere-in-london-2/.

Barret, M. 2016. *Classic No. 29. The Rescuers Down Under (1990)*. Retrieved from The Disney Odyssey: https://thedisneyodyssey.wordpress.com/2016/03/02/classic-no-29-the-rescuers-down-under-1990/.

Barrier, M. 2007. *The Animated Man, A Life of Walt Diseny*. Berkley, CA: University of California Press.

Barton, Martin. 2006. *The History of Computer Role-Playing Games Part 1: The Early Years (1980–1983)*. 2006. Armchair Arcade: Videogames and Computers. http://armchairarcade.com/neo/node/1081.

Boone, A. R. 1938. *Modern Mechanix, Yesterday's Tomorrow Today*. Retrieved from The Making of Snow White and the Seven Dwarfs: http://blog.modernmechanix.com/the-making-of-snow-white-and-the-seven-dwarfs/#mmGal.

Buhl, C. 2019. *Pete's Dragon*. (Advisor: Jonathan Furner) Retrieved from AFI Catalogue of Feature Films: https://catalog.afi.com/Catalog/MovieDetails/56314.

Business Wire. 2004. *Disney Online and Kauffman Foundation's "Hot Shot Business" Teaches Excitement and Challenge of Entrepreneurship*. Business Wire. June 23, 2004. https://www.businesswire.com/news/home/20040623005540/en/Disney-Online-Kauffman-Foundations-Hot-Shot-Business.

———. 2005. *Disney Online Developing "Pirates of the Caribbean" Massively Multiplayer Internet Game*. Business Wire. April 26, 2005. https://www.businesswire.com/news/home/20050426005253/en/Disney-Online-Developing-Pirates-Caribbean-Massively-Multiplayer.

Carlson, W.E. 2017. *Computer Graphics and Computer Animation: A Retrospective Overview*. Columbus: Ohio State Press.

Cho, S. 2018. *A Laugh Can Be a Very Powerful Thing: Who Framed Roger Rabbit, 30 Years Later*. Retrieved from RogerEbert.com: https://www.rogerebert.com/far-flung-correspondents/a-laugh-can-be-a-very-powerful-thing-who-framed-roger-rabbit-30-years-later.

Cohen, K.F. 2004. *Forbidden Animation*. Jefferson, NC: McFarland & Company.

*Computer Animation History—CGI*. 2018. Retrieved from The Great Mouse Detective: https://computeranimationhistory-cgi.jimdofree.com/the-great-mouse-detective-1986/.

Cotter, Bill. 1997. *The Wonderful World of Disney Television*. New York: Hyperion Press.

DeMaria, Rusel, and Johnny L. Wilson. 2002. *High Score: The Illustrated History of Electronic Games*. Berkley: McGraw-Hill/Osborne.

Deja, A. 2016. *The Nine Old Men*. Boca Raton, FL: CRC Press.

Disney, M. 2012. *Snow White and the Seven Dwarfs: The Creation of a Classic*. Retrieved from Walt Disney Family Museum: https://www.waltdisney.org/exhibitions/snow-white-and-seven-dwarfs-creation-classic.

Douglas, J. Yellowlees, and Andrew Hargadon. 2001. The pleasures of immersion and engagement: schemas, scripts and the fifth business. *Digital Creativity* 12 (3): 153–166.

Ebert, R. 1982. *TRON*. Retrieved from rogerebert.com.

Ebiri, B. 2019. *The Story of the 1991 Beauty and the Beast Screening that Changed Everything*. Retrieved from Vulture, The New York Magazine: https://www.vulture.com/2019/11/the-beauty-and-the-beast-screening-that-changed-everything.html.

Eisner, Michael. 1998. *Work in Progress*. New York: Random House.

Estrella, M. 2014. Big Hero 6. *Fort Worth Star-Telegram*.

Failes, I. 2016. *25 Years Ago: The CG Secrets of the Ballroom Sequence in "Beauty and the Beast"*. Retrieved from Cartoon Brew: https://www.cartoonbrew.com/feature-film/25-years-ago-cg-secrets-ballroom-sequence-beauty-beast-145174.html.

———. 2019. *Before You See the New CG "Lion King"*. Retrieved from Befores and Afters: https://beforesandafters.com/2019/07/17/before-you-see-the-new-cg-lion-king-re-visit-the-cg-of-1994s-lion-king/.

Feild, Robert D. 1942. *The Art of Walt Disney*. New York: The MacMillan Company.

Finch, C. 1975. *The Art of Walt Disney, From Mickey Mouse to the Magic Kingdom*. New York, NY: Harry N. Abrams, Inc.

———. 1994. *The Art of The Lion King*. New York: Hyperion.

Fromme, Johannes. 2003. Computer games as a part of children's culture. *Game Stud* 3: 1.

Gabler, N. 2006. *Walt Disney*. New York: Alfred A. Knopf.

Goslin, Mike 2007. Developer Diary #1—The Virtual Reality Studio. https://www.ignboards.com/threads/pirates-of-the-caribbean-online.122019305/.

Gordon, Bruce, and Tim O'Day. 2005. *Disneyland: Then, Now, and Forever*. New York: Disney Editions.

Greene, Katherine, and Richard. 2001. *Inside the Dream: The Personal Story of Walt Disney, 2001*. New York: Disney Editions.

Groff, David, and Kevin Steele. 2004. *A Biased History of Interactive Media*. http://www.smackerel.net/.

Hellenk, Stan. 2006. "Interview with Stan Hellenk." *Walt Disney: Conversations*. Ed. Kathy Merlock Jackson. Jackson, MS: University Press of Mississippi.

Henne, M. 1996. The Making of Toy Story. *Proceedings of COMPCON '96*, 463–468.

Higgins, B. 2017. *Oscars Flashback: 1988's 'Roger Rabbit' Won 4 Awards the Hard Way*. Retrieved from HollywoodReporter.com: https://www.hollywoodreporter.com/news/oscars-flashback-1988s-roger-rabbit-won-4-awards-hard-way-1065675.

Hill, J. 2017. *How "Pinoccio" beat "Bambi" to become Disney's second feature-length animated film after "Snow White"*. Retrieved September 2018, from HuffPost: https://www.huffpost.com/entry/how-pinocchio-beat-bambi-to-become-disneys-second_b_58758edfe4b0f8a725448376.

Hoyenski, Edward. 2002. A Brief History of Early Movable Books. University of Northern Texas. http://www.library.unt.edu/rarebooks/exhibits/popup2/introduction.htm.

IEEE. 2008. *Edwin Catmull, Awards Recipient*. Retrieved from The Computer Society, IEEE: https://www.computer.org/profiles/edwin-catmull.

Imagineers, The. 1966. *Walt Disney Imagineering: A Behind the Dreams Look At Making the Magic Real*. New York: Hyperion.

Iwerks, Leslie, and John Kenworthy. 2001. *The Hand Behind the Mouse: An Intimate Biography of Ub Iwerks*. New York: Disney Editions.

Jackson, Kathy Merlock, ed. 2006. "The Wide World of Walt Disney." Newsweek. *Walt Disney: Conversations*. Jackson, MS: University Press of Mississippi.

Jenkins, Henry. 2006. *Convergence Culture: Where Old and New Media Collide*. New York: New York University Press.

———. 2004. "Game Design as Narrative Architecture." *First Person*. Eds. Noah Wardrip-Fruin and Pat Harrigan. The MIT Press, Cambridge, 2004.

———. 2003. Transmedia Storytelling. *MIT Technology Review*. https://www.technologyreview.com/2003/01/15/234540/transmedia-storytelling/.

Johnston, S. F. 1995. *Computer Graphics Imagery, Scott F. Johnston*. Retrieved from YouTube: https://www.youtube.com/watch?v=HLmAT6t5kL0.

Kindy, D. 2019. *The Original 'Dumbo' Story*. Retrieved from Smithsonian.com: https://www.smithsonianmag.com/innovation/in-its-intended-format-original-dumbo-story-would-have-had-more-twists-and-turns-180971785/.

King, S. 2017. *'Tron' at 35: Star Jeff Bridges, Creators Detail the Uphill Battle of Making the CGI Classic*. Retrieved from Variety.com: https://variety.com/2017/film/news/tron-jeff-bridges-cgi-1982-disney-anniversary-1202486941/.

Kois, D. 2010. *The Balck Cauldron*. Retrieved from Slate.com: http://www.slate.com/articles/arts/dvdextras/2010/10/the_black_cauldron.html.

Konow, D. 2015. *Putting the Original Tron's Special Effects Together*. Retrieved from Tested.com: https://www.tested.com/art/movies/520562-putting-original-trons-special-effects-together/.

Korkis, J. 2016. *The Story Behind "Pete's Dragon" (1977)*. Retrieved from Cartoon Research: https://cartoonresearch.com/index.php/the-story-behind-petes-dragon/.

Kroyer, B. 2012. *Development of the Digital Animator*. (Oscars) Retrieved from Oscars: The Adventures of André and Wally B. Lucasfilm's computer animation division creates an all-CGI-animated short. https://www.youtube.com/watch?v=A42aqazyhGs.

Kurtti, Jeff. 2006. *Disney Dossiers: Files of Characters from the Walt Disney Studios*. New York: Disney Editions.

Lasseter, J. 1987. Principles of traditional animation applied to 3D computer animation. *ACM Siggraph Computer Graphics 21* (4): 35–44. https://www.cs.cmu.edu/afs/cs/academic/class/15462-f09/www/lec/Lesseter.pdf.

———. 2009. The Making of Tron—Birth of Computer Animation https://www.youtube.com/watch?v=ZGQUvKtTZdg.

Lingan, J. 2013. *Bristling Dixie*. Retrieved from The Slate Book Review: https://slate.com/culture/2013/01/song-of-the-south-disneys-most-notorious-film-by-jason-sperb-reviewed.html.

Lister, Martin, Jon Dovey, Seth Giddings, and Iain Grant Kieran Kelly. 2009. *New Media: A Critical Introduction*. London: Routledge.

Lutz, E.G. 1998. *Animated Cartoons*. Bedford: Applewood Books.

Maltin, L. 2010. *Song of the South, Notes*. Retrieved 2019, from Turner Classic Movies: http://www.tcm.com/tcmdb/title/90871/Song-of-the-South/notes.html.

Madej, Krystina. 2003. Towards digital narrative for children: from education to entertainment, a historical perspective. *Computers in Entertainment (CiE)* 1 (1) (2003): 12–12.

Markle, Fletcher. 2006. "Interview with Fletcher Markle." *Walt Disney: Conversations*. Ed. Kathy Merlock Jackson. Jackson, MS: University Press of Mississippi.

Martens, T. 2019. *The original 'Dumbo' arguably was Disney's most important blockbuster*. Retrieved from Los Angeles Times: https://www.latimes.com/entertainment/movies/la-et-mn-dumbo-animation-20190329-story.html.

Mason, T. 2007. *CG 101: A Computer Graphics Indsutry Reference, 2nd ed*. Digital Fauxtography. Retrieved from http://www.cs.cmu.edu/~ph/nyit//masson/nyit.html.

Merritt, Russell, and J.B. Kaufman. 2000. *Walt in Wonderland: The Silent Films of Walt Disney*. Baltimore: Johns Hopkins University Press.

Miller, Carolyn Handler. 2004. *Digital Storytelling: a creator's guide to interactive entertainment*. Oxford: Focal Press.

Miller, D. D. 1956. Disney's Folly. *Saturday Evening Post*.

Mine, Mark R., Joe Shocket, and Roger Hughston. 2003. Building a massively multiplayer game for the millions: Disney's Toontown online. *ACM Computers in Entertainment (CiE)* 1 (1).

Montfort, Nick. 2005. *Twisty Little Passages: An Approach to Interactive Fiction*. Cambridge: The MIT Press.

Neupert, Richard. 2016. *John Lasseter*. Chicago, IL: University of Illinois Press.

———. 1994. Painting a plausible world: Disney's color prototypes. In *Disney Discourse*, 106–117. New York: Routledge.

Norman, F. 2016. *MRFUN'S JOURNAL*. Retrieved from The Amazing Disney Peg System: http://floydnormancom.squarespace.com/blog/2016/11/22/the-amazing-disney-peg-system.

Novak, M. 2011. *Boxing Robots of the 1930s*. Retrieved from Smithsonion.com: https://www.smithsonianmag.com/history/boxing-robots-of-the-1930s-5235014/.

Noyer, J. 2009. *Richard M. Sherman on Bedknobs and Broomsticks: a Solid Songwriter*. Retrieved from Animated Views: https://animatedviews.com/2009/richard-m-sherman-on-bedknobs-and-broomsticks-a-solid-songwriter/.

Pak, K. 2015. *To Infinity and Beyond!: The Story of Pixar Animation Studios*. San Francisco, CA: Chronicle Books.

Peachment, C. 2008. *The Great Mouse Detective*. Retrieved from Peachment, Chris (2008). "The Great Mouse Detective (aka Basil the Great Mouse Detective)". In Pym, John (ed.). Time Out Film Guide 2009 (17th ed.). Time Out Group Ltd. p. 426.

Placido, D. D. 2018. *Disney's Live-Action Upgrades Are Not Upgrades*. Retrieved from Forbes: https://www.forbes.com/sites/danidiplacido/2018/11/23/disneys-live-action-remakes-are-not-upgrades/#2fad103b5dd5.

Polkinghorne, Donald. 1988. *Narrative Knowing and the Human Sciences*. Albany, N.Y.: State University of New York Press.

Price, D.A. 2009. *The Pixar Touch*. New York: Vintage.

Rideout, Victoria J., Elizabeth A. Vandewater, and Ellen A. Wartella. 2003. *Zero to Six: Electronic Media in the Lives of Infants, Toddlers and Preschoolers*. Menlo Park, CA: The Henry J. Kaiser Family Foundation.

Robertson, B. 1994. Disney let's CAPS out of the bag. *Computer Graphics World* 17 (7).

Rotten Tomatoes. 2016. *Rescuers Down Under Reviews*. Rotten Tomatoes. https://www.rottentomatoes.com/m/rescuers_down_under/.

Rubin, Ellen G.K. 2005. "Pop-up and Movable Books: In the Context of History." *Ideas in Motion* Exhibit, SUNY-New Platz, NY.

Saber. 2019. *What the HELL is Animalympics? (Furry Olympics)*. Retrieved from You Tube Channel Saberspark: https://www.youtube.com/watch?v=u6bDffuQHU4.

Sammond, Nicholas. 2005. *Babes in Tomorrowland: Walt Disney and the Making of the American Child*. Durham: Duke University Press.

Sampson, W. 2010. *So Dear to My Heart: The Secrets Behind the Film*. Retrieved from Mouse Planet: https://www.mouseplanet.com/9333/So_Dear_to_My_Heart_The_Secrets_Behind_the_Film.

Scheuer, P. K. 1948. Disney's 'Melody Time' diverting show. *The Los Angeles Times*.

Seymour, M. 2012. *Alvy Ray Smith: RGBA, the birth of compositing & the founding of Pixar*. Retrieved from fxguide.com: https://www.fxguide.com/fxfeatured/alvy-ray-smith-rgba-the-birth-of-compositing-the-founding-of-pixar/.

Sito, T. 2015. *Moving Innovation: A History of Computer Animation*. Boston: The MIT Press.

Smith, M. 2017. *TRON, A look back at a cult classic*. Retrieved from pressreader.com: https://www.pressreader.com/australia/total-film/20170602/281943132829840.

Smoodin, Eric, ed. 1994. *Disney Discourse: Producing the Magic Kingdom*. London: Routledge.

Snider, B. 1995. The *Toy Story* Story. *Wired* 3 (12).

Snow, R. 2019. *Disney's Land, Walt Disney and the Invention of the Amusement Park*. New York: Simon And Schuster.

Steinmetz, J. 1986. Great Mouse Detective: Vintage Disney, Updated. *Chicago Tribune*.

Surrell, Jason. 2014. *Screenplay by Disney*. New York: Disney Editions.

Taylor, R. 2017. *LOOKER—Computer Topographic Scan (1981)*. Retrieved from Youtube.com: https://www.youtube.com/watch?v=q_wK74Ejnqc.

Telotte, J. 2008. *The Mouse Machine, Disney and Technology*. Chicago: University of Illinois Press.

Thomas, B. 1958. *Walt Disney, the Art of Animation, The Story of the Disney Studio Contribution to a New Art*. New York, NY: Simon and Scuster.

———. 1976. *Walt Disney, An American Original*. New York, NY: Simon and Schuster.

Thomas, Emory. 1998. *Disney Online Ride Worth the Price*. ZDNet US. https://www.zdnet.com/article/Disney-online-ride-worth-the-price/.

Thomas, Frank, and Ollie Johnston. 1995. *The Illusion of Life: Disney Animation*. New York: Disney Editions.

Tieman, Robert. 2007. *The Mickey Mouse Treasures*. New York: Disney Editions.

Times, T. N. 1930. *Times Machine*. Retrieved from The New York Times: https://timesmachine.nytimes.com/timesmachine/1930/11/16/118393856.html?pageNumber=149.

Walt Disney Productions. 1984. *Walt Disney's Donald Duck, 50 Years of Happy Frustration*. Tucson: HP Books.

Watts, S. 1997. *The Magic Kingdom, Walt Disney and the American Way of Life*. Columbia, MO: University of Missouri Press.

Werner, Jane. 1955. *Walt Disney's Vanishing Prairie: a True-Life Adventure*. New York: Simon and Shuster.

Welk, B. 2018. *"Who Framed Roger Rabbit" Creators on How They Broke All the Rules*. Retrieved from The Wrap: https://www.thewrap.com/why-who-framed-roger-rabbit-broke-all-rules-30th-anniversary/.

Whalen, A. 2019. *The Illusion and Emotion behind 'Toy Story 4'*. Retrieved from newsweek.com: https://www.newsweek.com/toy-story-4-animation-bts-behind-scene-1447615.

Williams, Pat. 2004. *How to Be Like Walt: Capturing the Disney Magic Every Day of Your Life*. Deerfield Beach: Health Communications.

Wills, J. 2019. *Bambi*. Retrieved from National Film Preservation Board: http://www.loc.gov/static/programs/national-film-preservation-board/documents/bambi.pdf.

Wong, K. 2017. *How "Who Framed Roger Rabbit" Pulled Off Its Incredible Visual Feats*. Retrieved from Vice.com: https://www.vice.com/en_us/article/78qawg/how-who-framed-roger-rabbit-pulled-off-its-incredible-visual-feats.

Zohn, P. 2010. *Vanity Fair*. Retrieved from Coloring the Kingdom: https://www.vanityfair.com/culture/2010/03/disney-animation-girls-201003.

Zorthian, J. 2015. *How Toy Story Changed Movie HIstory*. Retrieved from Time.com: https://time.com/4118006/20-years-toy-story-pixar/.

# Websites

3D-Blox. http://www.javaonthebrain.com/java/3dblox/.

The Adventures of Mickey Mouse 1931. http://kayaozkaracalar3.blogspot.com/2008/12/adventures-of-mickey-mouse-1931.html, https://disney.fandom.com/wiki/The_Adventures_of_Mickey_Mouse.

The Allegro Movable Book Collection. http://allegrobookcollection.typepad.com/allegrobookcollection/about.html.

The Animation Empire: The History of Animation 11—Walt Disney: Newman's Laugh-o-grams 1921. http://theanimationempire.blogspot.com/2008/03/history-of-animation-11-walt-disney.html.

The Animation Empire: The Complete History and Videos of Walt Disney's Animated Shorts: Part 1 1922–1924. http://theanimationempire.blogspot.com/2008/11/complete-history-of-walt-disneys.html.

Big Bad Wolf's Hut. http://kayaozkaracalar2.blogspot.com/.

Biographie de Walt Disney. http://mapage.noos.fr/dtpdossiers/biographie.htm.

Castle Infinity. https://www.gamesindustry.biz/articles/2017-05-12-a-limited-history-of-castle-infinity.

Chronology of the Walt Disney Company. http://kpolsson.com/disnehis/.

Club Penguin Wiki. http://clubpenguin.wikia.com/wiki/Club_Penguin.

Comics. https://d23.com/first-mickey-mouse-comic-strip/?int_cmp=d23_parksblog_firstmickey-mousecomicstrip_20150113.

Comics Read Free. https://comiconlinefree.com/comic/disney-comics-and-stories.

The Construction of Disneyland. https://www.designingdisney.com/parks/disneyland-resort/construction-disneyland/.

Deja View. http://andreasdeja.blogspot.com/.

Dinner Time by Paul Terry and John Foster | Cartoon Brew: Leading the Animation Conversation. https://www.cartoonbrew.com/brewtv/cartoon-brew-tv-3-dinner-time-by-paul-terry-and-john-foster-7499.html.

Disney Comics and Story Books. http://kayaozkaracalar3.blogspot.com/Disney Golden Age of Cartoons https://tvtropes.org/pmwiki/pmwiki.php/UsefulNotes/TheGoldenAgeOfAnimation.

Disney Dreamer—Walt Disney Quotes. http://www.disneydreamer.com/walt/quotes.htm.

Disney Fairies. https://disney.fandom.com/wiki/Disney_Fairies.

Disney Online's Mike Goslin Talks Pirates. https://www.gamasutra.com/view/news/107296/QA_Disney_Onlines_Goslin_Talks_Pirates_Online.php.

Disney XD—Games, Videos, Television Shows. http://disneyxd.disney.in/.

Disneyland Brochure. https://themousemuseum.com/2017/07/16/your-guide-to-disneyland-bank-of-america-brochure-map-195/.

The Disneylandia Story Part Two (Wade's Wayback Machine) by Wade Sampson. http://www.mouseplanet.com/9371/The_Disneylandia_Story_Part_Two.

Disney's Growing Social Media Efforts | The Disney Blog. http://thedisneyblog.com/2008/04/08/disneys-social-media-efforts/.

Disney's HooZoo. https://nafsk.se/pipermail/dcml/1993-February/000236.html.

Disney's 'Prep & Landing' Transmedia Strategy—Derek E. Baird: Barking Robot. http://www.debaird.net/blendededunet/2009/12/stream-disney-abc-tv-prep-landing-online-for-free.html.

Disney Family Museum. https://www.waltdisney.org.

Disney History, 2719 HYPERION: Walt Disney's Los Angeles 1923–1931: Pedaling Past History. http://2719hyperion.blogspot.com/2015/06/walt-disneys-los-angeles-1923-1931.html.

Disneyland '55. http://andeverythingelsetoo.blogspot.com/2010/07/disneyland-55.html.

Flipbooks. http://www.flipbook.info/typology.php.

The History of Club Penguin. https://clubpenguin.fandom.com/wiki/Club_Penguin.

The History of Zork. http://www.gamasutra.com/view/feature/1499/the_history_of_zork.php?print=1.

Gertie the Dinosaur. https://publicdomainreview.org/collection/gertie-the-dinosaur-1914.

King's Quest 1 Game—Download and Play Free Version. http://www.download-free-games.com/freeware_games/kings_quest1.htm#pp-review-box.

Koko the Clown Flip Book. http://journeytojohnsbrain.blogspot.com/2009/02/koko-clown-flip-book.html.

LARRY'S TOON INSTITUTE—Overlapping Action. http://www.awn.com/tooninstitute/lesson-plan/overlapping.htm.

Laugh-O-Grams Fairy Tales Lost tales. https://www.cartoonbrew.com/classic/lost-disney-laugh-o-grams-at-moma-29630.html.

The Legendary Laugh-O-Grams: Fairy Tales by Walt Disney • Animated Views. http://animated-views.com/2007/the-legendary-laugh-o-grams-fairy-tales-by-walt-disney/.

Lotte Reiniger. http://www.awn.com/mag/issue1.3/articles/moritz1.3.html.

Max Fleischer Series—Bray Animation Project. http://brayanimation.weebly.com/max-fleischer-series.html.

Mickey Mouse Comic Universe—Television Tropes & Idioms. http://tvtropes.org/pmwiki/pmwiki.php/Characters/MickeyMouseComicUniverse.

Mickey Mouse Club—Saturday January 11, 1930. https://discuss.micechat.com/forum/lounges/micechat-main-lounge/9646-mickey-mouse-club-saturday-january-11-1930#post497468.

Mickey Mouse Club Downtown Tucsonan: May 2005 Issue. http://azarchivesonline.org/xtf/view?docId=ead/uoa/UAMS560.xml.

Mickey Mouse in Death Valley. http://www.oocities.org/soho/easel/4942/30-06-03f.htm.

The Mickey Mouse Waddle Book, RareLibrary.com. http://library.missouri.edu/specialcollections/bookcol/digital/waddle-inside/.

Mickey Mouse Magazine. http://filmic-light.blogspot.com/2011/02/mickey-mouse-magazine-1938-valentines.html.

Mickey Mouse Handkerchief 1930. https://gainsboroughretreats.briefyourmarket.com/Newsletters/A-Gift-From-Gainsborough-Retreats/Were-these-gifts-on-your-list-.aspx.

MUD1. http://en.academic.ru/dic.nsf/enwiki/4151152.

Multiplane Camera 2—One1more2time3's Weblog. http://one1more2time3.wordpress.com/2010/02/12/multiplane-camera-2/.

Newman Laugh-O-Grams—Disney Wiki. http://disney.wikia.com/wiki/Newman_Laugh-O-Grams.

Oswald Image, The Evening Class, Sunday, July 12. http://theeveningclass.blogspot.com/2009/07/sfsff09michael-hawley-previews-line-up.html.

Pantages Big Orange Landmarks: No. 193—Pantages Theatre. http://bigorangelandmarks. blogspot.com/2008/10/no-193-pantages-theatre.html.

Pop Goes The Page: Movable and Mechanical Books from the Brenda Forman Collection. https:// explore.lib.virginia.edu/exhibits/show/popgoesthepage.

The Pop History Dig—Disney. http://www.pophistorydig.com/?tag=snow-white-and-the-seven-dwarfs.

Posts from the Pirates Of The Caribbean Online Category at Massively. http://massively.joystiq. com/category/pirates-of-the-caribbean-online/page/3/.

Somewhere In Dreamland: The Max Fleischer Color Classics. http://www.dvdverdict.com/ reviews/somewhereindreamland.php.

Traditional Principles of Animation. Overlapping Action. http://en.wikibooks.org/wiki/ Traditional_Principles_of_Animation/Overlapping_action.

Pixar—Ratatouille—The Characters. http://www.pixar.com/featurefilms/rat/popc6.html.

The Pop History Dig - Disney Dollars. http://www.pophistorydig.com/?tag=silly-symphonies.

Remembering UB IWERKS. http://www.crazycollege.org/IwerksFilmFax.htm.

SamLand's Disney Adventures: What Is A Disneyland? Part 5. http://samlanddisney.blogspot. com/2011/05/what-is-disneyland-part-5.html.

Streetswing's Dancer History Archives—Fanchon and Marco Wolff—Main Page. http://www. streetswing.com/histmai2/d2fanch1.htm.

TellzAll. http://www.ohiokids.org/tellzall/2004/october.shtml.

TweenParent.com: Disney XD Launched to Tween Boys. http://www.tweenparent.com/articles/ view/127.

The Uncensored Mouse. http://jimhillmedia.com/alumni1/b/jim_korkis/archive/2003/09/10/1097. aspx.

Vintage Disney Collectibles: Kay Kamen—Playthings Magazine. http://vintagedisneymemora-bilia.blogspot.com/2008/05/kay-kamen-photo.html.

Vintage Disney Collectibles: Walt Disney—the first Academy Awards. http://vintagedisneymemo-rabilia.blogspot.com/2008/02/walt-disney-first-academy-awards.html.

Walt Disney. http://pictureland.info/have-some-fun/walt-disney.

Walt Disney and More. http://disneyandmore.blogspot.com/2009/12/walt-disneys-birthday-cele-bration.html.

Walt Disney, Wish Upon a Star. http://jimhillmedia.com/editor_in_chief1/b/jim_hill/ archive/2008/02/07/the-story-that-walt-didn-t-want-you-to-hear.aspx.

The Walt Disney Company—Kids' Privacy Policy. http://corporate.disney.go.com/corporate/kids. html.

Walt Disney Treasures: Mickey Mouse! Here In Duckburg. http://texcap.wordpress. com/2008/07/28/walt-disney-treasures-mickey-mouse/.

History of BigLittle Books. http://www.biglittlebooks.com/historyofBLBs.html.

UNT Libraries: Pop-up and Movable Books: A Tour Through Their History, S. Louis Giraud. http://www.library.unt.edu/rarebooks/exhibits/popup2/giraud.htm.

Vintage Disney Collectibles: Mickey Mouse Book—Bibo & Lang—1930. http://vintagedis-neymemorabilia.blogspot.com/2007/12/mickey-mouse-book.html.

Vintage Disneyland Tickets: Disneyland—1955 Bank of America. http://vintagedisneylandtickets. blogspot.com/2008/05/disneyland-1955-bank-of-america.html.

Vintage Disneyland Tickets: Disneyland—1956 Bank of America. http://vintagedisneylandtickets. blogspot.com/2009/05/disneyland-1956-bank-of-america.html.

# Online Disney Shorts

Alice and the Dog Catcher (1924). https://www.youtube.com/watch?v=7d3aBMFEOns
Alice and the Jailbird (1925). https://www.youtube.com/watch?v=h_ocb5eQQyY
Alice and the Three Bears (1924). https://www.youtube.com/watch?v=tag2zSRC37A
Alice the Toreador (1925). https://www.youtube.com/watch?v=ECRXqxEKLjw
Alice's Day at Sea (1924). https://www.youtube.com/watch?v=659v5kGpmM4&t=8s
Alice's Egg Plant (1925). https://www.youtube.com/watch?v=vCUQRhcGLxU
Alice in Cartoonland Promo. https://www.youtube.com/watch?v=nkabTAHLdRk
Alice's Spooky Adventure (1924). https://www.youtube.com/watch?v=laho5lV6FSQ
Alice's Wonderland (1923). https://www.youtube.com/watch?v=tIFEIVkYSnw&t=87s
Babes in the Woods (1932). https://www.youtube.com/watch?v=FuB3Mp02mFw
The Barn Dance (1929). https://www.youtube.com/watch?v=zuvfZ-DwYio
The Barnyard Broadcast (1931).
    https://www.youtube.com/results?search_query=the+barnyard+broadcast+1931
Flowers and Trees (1932). https://www.youtube.com/watch?v=rH-OTZm0Xtk
The Gallopin Gaucho (1928). https://www.youtube.com/watch?v=DnjSVSykNsA
The Goddess of Spring (1934). https://www.youtube.com/watch?v=37o11Qclgx4
Karnival Kid (1929). https://www.youtube.com/watch?v=i8ud8eXUYW4
Laugh O Grams — Cinderella (1922). http://www.youtube.com/watch?v=VLZagf7FfuA.
Laugh-O-Grams Films — Little Red Riding Hood (1922).
    http://www.youtube.com/ watch?v=Hz31ZQOASno.
Laugh-O-Grams Films — Four Musicians of Bremen (1922).
    https://www.youtube.com/watch?v=1_3sI9WW6_A
Mickey's Mechanical Man (1933). https://www.youtube.com/watch?v=o1JNNcSkKkI
Mickey Mouse — On Ice (1935). https://www.youtube.com/watch?v=iNc5ISkvpIg
Mickey Mouse — On Ice (1935) [Pencil Test]. https://www.youtube.com/watch?v=TibZyONsiNs
Mickey Mouse, The Mad Doctor (1933). https://www.youtube.com/watch?v=LPW70q4w5pw
Midnight In A Toy Shop (1930). https://www.youtube.com/watch?v=WIIfB5SuTZI
Newman Laugh-O-Grams (1921). https://www.youtube.com/watch?v=51CRL1EtMN4&t=10s
The Old Mill (1937). http://www.youtube.com/watch?v=MYEmL0d0lZE.
Oswald the Lucky Rabbit, Oh What a Knight (1928).
    https://www.youtube.com/watch?v=zums-cxust0&t=2s
Plane Crazy (1928). https://www.youtube.com/watch?v=kCZPzHg0h80
Skeleton Dance (1929). https://www.youtube.com/watch?v=vOGhAV-84iI&t=66s
Snow White—Far into the Forest (1937).
    https://www.youtube.com/watch?v=Z4zQ1txgD94&t=12s
Steamboat Willie (1928). https://www.youtube.com/watch?v=BBgghnQF6E4&t=315s
Three Little Pigs (1933). https://www.youtube.com/watch?v=RQ-66ZfXOnE
Three Orphan Kittens (1935). https://www.youtube.com/watch?v=wo8hbZkscGw&t=4s
When The Cats Away (1929). https://www.youtube.com/watch?v=aldMRcWAYok&t=5s
The Wise Little Hen (1934). https://www.youtube.com/results?search_query=the+barnyard+bro
    adcast+1931

# Index

---

The original version of this chapter was revised. The correction to this chapter is available at https://doi.org/10.1007/978-3-030-42738-2_18

Printed in the United States
by Baker & Taylor Publisher Services